TRANSCENDENCE AND MATURE THOUGHT IN ADULTHOOD

D1714932

TRANSCENDENCE AND MATURE THOUGHT IN ADULTHOOD

The Further Reaches of Adult Development

Edited by
Melvin E. Miller
Susanne R. Cook-Greuter

Rowman & Littlefield Publishers, Inc.

ROWMAN & LITTLEFIELD PUBLISHERS, INC.

Published in the United States of America
by Rowman & Littlefield Publishers, Inc.
4720 Boston Way, Lanham, Maryland 20706

3 Henrietta Street, London WC2E 8LU, England

British Cataloging in Publication Information Available

Library of Congress Cataloging-in-Publication Data

Transcendence and mature thought in adulthood : the further
reaches of adult development / edited by Melvin E. Miller,
Susanne R. Cook-Greuter.
p.   cm.
Chiefly papers presented at the Adult Development Symposia,
1989 to 1991, organized by the Society for Research in Adult
Development.
Includes bibliographical references and indexes.
1. Maturation (Psychology)—Congresses.   2. Adulthood—
Psychological aspects—Congresses.   3. Transpersonal
psychology—Congresses.   I. Miller, Melvin E.   II. Cook-
Greuter, Susanne R.   III. Adult Development Symposia
(1989–1991)
BF710.T73   1994   155.2'5—dc20   93–48364 CIP

ISBN 0–8476–7918–7 (cloth : alk. paper)
ISBN 0–8476–7919–5 (pbk. : alk. paper)

Printed in the United States of America

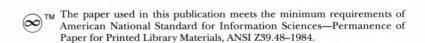

To unity and diversity

Contents

Figures and Tables

FIGURES

TABLES

Preface

In this era many people have begun to ponder the inadequacy of purely technological solutions to human problems. A sense of futility has overcome some in the face of a seemingly growing tide of global strife and human suffering. This book is intended to be a welcome contrast to the prevailing uncertainty. It is a resource for those looking for evidence of new possibilities of understanding and hope. It highlights positive adult development beyond the conventional wisdom of our time, even beyond self-actualization towards self-transcendence and transpersonal consciousness.

The current volume grew out of papers presented at the Adult Development Symposia (1989 to 1991), organized by the Society for Research in Adult Development. Two additional chapters were invited.

This book is written by experts in the fields of both postconventional and transpersonal psychology. It is an optimistic book that outlines ways and possibilities for humanity to evolve towards more balanced and integrated ways of being.

It is the first book that consciously tries to bridge the currently separate fields of traditional Western and Eastern theories of human development. It shows that the paths leading to self-actualization as made popular by Maslow may also lead to some initial form of Being Cognition or transcendent awareness. Likewise, it presents growth-oriented theories of human development that offer a comprehensive view of our potential as participants in an integrated, unified field of consciousness.

In contrast to much of Western developmental theory which focuses upon separate domains (cognitive, affective, behavioral), our theories posit the increasing interconnection and integration of these different dimensions of human nature, and thus implicitly advocate a more interdisciplinary, holistic approach to research in the field.

This volume, therefore, should be of interest not only to researchers and academic psychologists, students in human development, clinicians and educators, but to everybody fascinated by the mystery of adult growth. It is meant to be inclusive. Since the theories presented here reach into the metaphysical and spiritual realm of human existence, they may also appeal to those drawn to philosophy and religion. In short, it is a book with a wide and timely appeal.

We hope that its contents will interest, stir, and engage the reader to grapple with the perennial questions of who we are as individuals and where we are headed as an evolving species. In the spirit of continued dialogue and learning, we welcome your thoughts, comments, and reactions.

Montpelier, Vermont   *Melvin E. Miller*
September 1993   *Susanne R. Cook-Greuter*

Acknowledgments

We wish to tell our spouses and children how grateful we are that they allowed us the time and space to bring this project to fruition. They had to put up with our many absences and tolerate our shifting moods throughout the different phases of the editing process. Thanks go to Rebecca Power for her persistent and diligent proofreading. Special thanks go to Loren Miller, who not only hosted our editing parties in Montpelier, but who also selflessly gave us her expertise in proofreading, indexing, typesetting, and in creating the many tables.

From Postconventional Development To Transcendence: Visions and Theories

Melvin E. Miller
Norwich University

Susanne R. Cook-Greuter
Harvard University

Out of a desire to know more about who we can be as individuals and where we are headed as a species, we ask in this volume what constitutes optimal growth in adulthood. What do mature adults think and feel? How do they reason, act, and respond? What ideas move them and what moral and ethical concerns do they contemplate? What are the processes and approaches which take people to higher levels of being?

Throughout history, exceptional individuals have used alternatives to the more established approaches to understanding the meaning of human existence. They have thus created novel possibilities and broader horizons for those around them to contemplate. We believe that we must study such extraordinary human beings, both past and present, for several reasons: First, we wish to understand and describe the nature and potential of individual human lives more comprehensively. But we also, and more poignantly, must ask ourselves what their lives might tell us about the future of humankind as a whole. As meaning makers in these divisive times, we hope to demonstrate the existence of an inclusive, unifying, evolutionary trend in the species, and then trace its gradual unfolding.

Why should we be concerned about human development beyond the accepted norms? Our society is clearly built upon conventional, rational premises. Western cultures, by and large, want their youth to develop into independent, abstract thinkers, and to experience a way of looking at the world known since Piaget (1972) as formal operations. This way of thinking is variously referred to by other developmental psychologists as conscientious (Loevinger, 1976), institutional (Kegan, 1982), and procedural (Belenky et al., 1986)—terms which reflect the socially embedded nature of this stance. It is implied that only if young people become capable of this kind of reasoning can they participate as full members in society's affairs and institutions and carry on its legacy. To be considered members, they are expected to be able to anticipate and plan for the future, to understand cause and effect, to base their judgments on evidence and facts, to be capable of considering another's point of view, and to be objective. They must also believe that problems can be solved through the proper scientific approaches and methods. Having these abilities and views promises one entry into the full range of adult roles, responsibilities, and rights. Nevertheless, as Kegan (1994) argues in *In Over Our Heads*, many members of society do not develop these more objective, "mature" attitudes and ways of reasoning (cf. Capon & Kuhn, 1979). They therefore experience manifold difficulties with surviving in a society which implicitly requires these skills.

While those below the formal operations level are "in over their heads," those *at* the formal operations stage are basically "up to their chins" and coping within this narrow, rationalistic Western mindset. What we need is a new vision and a more comprehensive, integrative perspective at both the individual and collective levels. Unless we have an expanded notion of the possibilities of human reasoning and meaning making, we are unlikely to develop beyond the status quo, beyond what we deem possible or even "normal" for human growth. We should keep in mind that how we conceptualize what is possible enhances *and* limits our individual and cultural development.

It is within this context that we believe we must study individuals who have moved beyond formal operations into other modes of meaning making that include the transpersonal and metaphysical. The effort to study these people and the forces, ideas, and circumstances that have spurred them forward on their journeys has both theoretical and practical value. Our research offers a new vision of human development, one that moves into the spiritual realm beyond commonly shared notions of what is real and beyond cognition based too narrowly on logic. Perhaps the study of these exceptional individuals will also help to reanimate psychology, bring back the "psyche" or "spirit" to it.

This is a timely book in the sense that there is a degree of urgency exhibited in the effort to make such expanded notions of development more widespread—as humankind strives to enhance its own collective development and evolution. Many individuals and organizations are already beginning to move in this direction. Even the federal government has added to this momentum as it has established an Office of Alternative Medicine within the National Institutes of Health (Angier, 1993). This office was formed with the express purpose of exploring and supporting research on various alternative approaches to mental well-being and health. Not surprisingly, these alternatives are already being used by approximately one-third of the population according to a recent survey conducted by the *New England Journal of Medicine* (Toufexis, 1993). Meditation, Vedic and Oriental medicine, biofeedback, and homeopathic treatments are among the many nonconventional, more holistic paths to wellness being investigated by this new office. This volume, then, joins the spirit of the times. Much of conventional psychology is embedded in a narrowly mechanistic, rational view of human nature. To be viable as a discipline, it must be receptive to the zeitgeist and explore all arenas of human experience.

This book is comprised of a collection of original articles written by contemporary scholars who are attempting to address such issues. It outlines possibilities of cognitive development beyond the norms and conventions of mainstream Western society. It presents and explores ancient Eastern paths towards growth which beckon towards transcendent stages of self-development and deeper personality growth than may be possible via the models of Western psychology.

The articles in this volume are based on rigorous and systematic research and theorizing. The authors draw upon systems of knowledge and heuristic models found in traditional Western psychology and philosophy, as well as upon the Eastern meditative and contemplative disciplines. One of our goals in writing this book is to make both approaches more meaningful to our readers, another is to bridge the gap between the two traditions. By including articles on empirical research related to Eastern and meditative approaches, we hope to illustrate the merits of such modes of thought and avenues of research to readers raised in the traditional Western milieu of psychology. In a sense, we hope to enter into a dialogue with you in a familiar language about theoretical concepts that you may consider fairly esoteric. By comparing and contrasting different models within the same text, we hope to bring them into a more accessible and immediate context. As we do this, we consciously remind ourselves that our theories originate from and must be relevant to real human beings.

By mature modes of thought, we mean those that are at least formal operational (in a Piagetian sense), and especially those which are postformal or postconventional and beyond. By transcendence, we are speaking of deeper reaches of consciousness that exist beyond the verbal or symbolic domain, and sometimes beyond thought altogether. Transcendent experiences culminate in the conscious apperception of an underlying unity of life. Such awareness transcends all dualism including prevalent dichotomies in the Western psychological repertoire such as mind and body, subject and object, knower and known. It has been said that people reaching these highest stages exist in the everyday world but are often not part of it. Perhaps for this reason enlightened individuals are misunderstood by those who have not had similar experiences. Nonetheless, we find that they are often very active agents of both social and personal change. These non-ordinary ways of being are described consistently as more adequate and fulfilling than earlier ones by those who practice them as well as by those who observe them.

Mature thought, as we conceive of it, can be considered an important way station generally preceding transcendent consciousness. Few mature thinkers, however, develop transcendent awareness; in fact, most do not. A fully developed, separate, stable self-sense seems to be a regularly observed, and a possibly necessary, precursor to later ego-transcendence. Spiritual or transcendent experiences as momentary states—those states classified by Maslow as peak-experiences—however, are possible at any stage of development long before attainment of enlightenment. They also are reported more frequently as individuals develop beyond the conventional ways of seeing the world.

Mapping the Territory of Postconventional and Transcendental Growth

From the above, you can see that the authors of this book resist the notion of formal operations being the final stage of cognitive development. Moreover, we challenge the popular theory that people reach the apex of their cognitive development by their early twenties and equilibrate or atrophy thereafter. Nonetheless, experience shows that most adults do not develop beyond the conventional realm. Though several current developmental psychologists (e.g., Loevinger, 1976; Kegan, 1982) have identified the self-realized/integrated stage as cognitively and affectively more developed, this book even challenges the postulate that this further differentiation represents the limits of human growth and understanding.

We believe this position will become clearer as you move through the various chapters ahead. In order to guide you through the upcoming adventure, a map of the most commonly used terms in the realm of human development and consciousness theory is provided below.

A complete explanation of all the terms and concepts in Table I.1 is not possible here, but many will be covered in considerable detail in subsequent chapters. For now, we will explain the general trends involved and the relationships existing among the various terms. Overall, we divided human development into four tiers: preconventional, conventional, postconventional, and transcendent. Thus, this table depicts the pattern of growth for most individuals from birth to adulthood as well as the experiences of adults who function at the top two tiers. Estimates derived from research conducted over the past decade indicate that the top two tiers combined include about 10% of all adults (Cook-Greuter, 1990).

At the bottom of the table we find the earliest phases of human development. This tier has been called by various labels such as *preconventional* and *prerational:* it includes both the sensorimotor period (0–2 years) and the entire preoperational period (2–7 years). The world of infants at the sensori-motor stage is action-oriented, animated by impulses and desire. Only at the end of this period do symbolic representations and language emerge. At the preoperational level, which begins at about the third year, we find that children have acquired some basic concepts and symbols, but they are not well organized or systematic. Although children naturally evolve out of this orientation, we note that about 10% of adults operate from this preconventional tier.

We find the majority of individuals in Western societies are at the second or conventional tier of development. We estimate that approximately 80% of adults are found here. This tier has been called *conventional* by Kohlberg (1969) due to the social conventions, norms, and roles adults at this tier tend to embody, and because of its prevalence. The Piagetian stages of concrete, abstract, and formal operations are included herein. People at this tier tend to view reality in an *abstract-linear* manner. Individuals at the formal operational stage in particular see reality as made up of separate, clearly identifiable parts that can be analyzed (Koplowitz, 1984); they also believe they can understand and logically deduce the underlying laws of reality and nature. Conventional adults feel in charge of themselves and often view their lives as tasks to be judiciously and effectively managed. Adults at this stage may unduly favor their intellectual acuity and rationality. Formal operations is the stage most often cited by conventional psychology as the highest, most desirable cognitive achievement that can be attained.

The third tier is best depicted as *postconventional* and *postformal*—labels or terms that illustrate both the individual's attitude or orientation to society's conventions, as well as the degree to which one's cognitive development has moved beyond the "restrictions" of conventional thought and formal operations. Mental operations themselves are seen as interdependent variables in a larger system of meaning making which also includes affective and visceral input. At the highest representational stage, paradigmatic operations, we find that whole families of systems can be coordinated (Commons & Richards, 1984), and that the function of the symbolic codifications themselves can become transparent. Alexander et al., 1990; Fischer et al., 1990; Pascual-Leone, 1984; and Cook-Greuter, 1990 have elaborated upon various dimensions of this third tier. Postconventional individuals have greater access to feelings, affective states, and intuition.

Table I.1

Correspondence of Some Commonly Used Terms to Describe the Four Tiers of Development from Infancy to Higher Stages of Consciousness

View of Reality*	Representation	Four Tiers of Development	Cognitive Dimension	Ego Stages#	Levels of Mind ☼
Unitary (Unified)	Postsymbolic Post-representational	**Transcendent** Transpersonal Metaphysical	Direct, nonsymbolically mediated apperception; metacognitive	>6	Higher Self
				6	
	Representational	**Postconventional Postformal**	Paradigmatic§ operations	5/6	ego
	Symbolic		Metasystematic operations	5	feeling-intuition
Systems		Advanced development of affect and ego	Systematic operations	4/5	

Koplowitz (1984) *		Cook-Greuter (1990) #	Commons and Richards (1984) §	Alexander ✿	
Abstract-Linear	Representational Symbolic	**Conventional**	Formal operations	4	intellect
		Adult capacities for feeling and reason	Abstract operations	3/4	
			Concrete operations	3	mind
Prerational	Early representations	**Preconventional**	Primary actions		
			Preoperational Nominal actions	2	desire
	Prerepresentational Presymbolic		Sensory and motor actions	1	action and senses

*   Koplowitz (1984)

§   Commons and Richards (1984) system describes stages in the representational realm

\#   Cook-Greuter (1990) based on Loevinger (1976)

✿   Alexander based on Maharishi Mahesh Yogi (1972)

They can look at ambiguities and conflicts as inevitable in both the intra- and interpersonal realms, and in and among systems of thought. They experience themselves as "autonomous" with respect to society's expectations and conventions. Estimates suggest that about 9% of adults are found here.

The fourth tier is most appropriately called the *transcendent* or *postrepresentational*, because at this level ordinary reasoning (mentation) and symbolic representations can be transcended. The branch of psychology which deals exclusively with this tier calls itself *transpersonal*. Reality, for those at the transcendent tier, is directly experienced without filters and representational mediators. Life is felt in its cohesive, fluid, incommensurable immediacy. Furthermore, one's innermost, infinite self is recognized and fully known. The individual self is no longer seen as a separate entity, but as an unbounded part of a dynamic web—a universal, all-permeating consciousness. Often this metaphysical awareness is associated with the experience of the Absolute or God. The perceptions and sense of self of those experiencing transcendence are no longer embedded in or restricted to the individual ego.

The last two tiers are the ones explored in this volume. They illustrate more advanced, comprehensive, and differentiated ways of thinking and experiencing that exist beyond conventional views of reality. Though the contributors to this volume may not concur on the paths and end points to mature thought and transcendence, we generally agree on the direction of development. Below we will acquaint you with some theoretical issues with which we wrestle.

Contrasting Perspectives to Understanding Postconventional and Transcendental Growth

One of the intractable problems in trying to talk about these nonordinary modes of experience is the lack of a vocabulary adequately reflecting the gestalt nature and nonlinearity of the concepts used. Seen from a universal perspective, there is only an indivisible reality, an interconnected web of phenomena. Prior to language, there is no higher and lower, no earlier and no later, no good and no evil. With language we give special weight to some aspects of the phenomenal flow, but not to others. We analyze, cut apart, compare, categorize, evaluate experience, and thus build our human world of verbal constructs. Experience in the human realm is mediated and shared through language. But words are never neutral: they have been abstracted, made special by our attention. To most people, "higher" means "better": a higher salary, higher achievement, higher development. The journey of development, however, is more adequately described as a journey inward to deeper and more subtle levels of perception. It leads to a progressively more direct experience of the nonverbal, nonrepresentational realm of being. The belief in the "reality" of words is a powerful, all-pervasive illusion. Even though we are conscious of this dilemma, we are caught between its horns. We say higher when we could say or should say deeper or closer to unfiltered, unified reality. As writers in a field where the ineffable is the rule, we struggle to become as clear as possible within the wonderful and frustrating medium of verbal communication.

These problems with communication notwithstanding, we advocate a vastly expanded view of development. We agree that the traditional, rational, Western perception of reality—language-based as it is—permits us to at least trace the topography of these more subtle cognitive and experiential realms. We also believe that valuable personal and societal gain could result from encouraging all people to be open to more mature and integrated forms of development regardless of their background, orientation, and perspective.

On the other hand, we do not claim that all paths leading to higher stages of development discussed in this volume are identical or equally effective. Nor would we dream that we could do justice to the manifold paths towards self-realization that have been taken by humanity. What can be said is that many of the paths studied here lead in a similar direction—to both greater differentiation and integration (see Table I.1 above and Figure I.1 below).

As you, the reader, shall see, many of the milestones and experiences described on the paths to maturity and transcendence are quite similar. Whether they lead to one ultimate, direct experience of the underlying territory which is posited as the endpoint of all development is still being debated. That there are differences lies again, in part, in the very nature of symbolic representations. The segmentation of the underlying reality into the concepts of a language initially depends on the emphasis or point of reference of the culture in question. In the case of partially uncharted territory, such as the one explored in this volume, the maps also reflect the theoreticians' training, focus, and own area of expertise. Thus from a semantic point of view, such differences in mapping out the paths and critical markers are unavoidable.

We have argued back and forth about several other points as well. For instance, most of us have wrestled with the notion of invariant hierarchical sequences of development in our own work and in the writings of others. Must the stages be encountered in a strict order? Can any stages be skipped? Do higher stages build upon the resolution of the previous ones? What happens if the tasks of an earlier stage are not completely resolved? A uniform perspective on these issues is not offered here.

Different authors also disagree about how the stage sequences align with each other. For instance, Cook-Greuter believes that the highest stage identifiable within her system is a universal one which is not yet fully transcendent or equivalent to cosmic consciousness. This is so because the stages which can be measured with the Washington University Sentence Completion Test are by their very nature tied to the representational realm. Torbert (see Chapter 7), on the other hand, aligns his Magician stage with both Cook-Greuter's universal stage and with the cosmic consciousness stage of the Vedic paradigm as indicated in Table 7.1. Such discrepancies do not go unnoticed; eventually clarifying them is part of working in this discipline.

We would also like to emphasize that we do not imply a strictly linear progression of movement through stages. Though we do describe sequences of stages that are progressively more subtle, more structurally complex and integrated, people do not completely function from one single stage at any given point in their lives. While most people tend to operate from a perspective that explains the world best or most comprehensively to themselves, they also often experience earlier modes of responding to life and may temporarily function from as-yet-unstabilized emergent perspectives.

Alexander et al. (1990) and Cook-Greuter (1990) point out that the transitions from stage to stage are not of equal significance. The transitions within the representational domain—between early representations and the highest postformal stage—are smaller and more continuous than the shift from presymbolic to early representations and from the representational to the postsymbolic realm. These latter shifts constitute quantum leaps in the development of consciousness. Wilber et al. (1986), on the other hand, describes the sequence through the stages as more continuous based on regular structural differentiations, while Commons defines his stage sequence following rigorous laws established in the logico-mathematical domain (Commons & Richards, 1984).

The proponents of different paths to more mature development also debate whether development can be stabilized or permanently equilibrated at these higher stages. Moreover, they disagree as to whether the highest stages entail their own stage-specific problems and dilemmas, and whether there is less and less suffering the deeper one progresses.

Alexander and Langer (1990) engage in a systematic investigation of some of the finer points of the existing theoretical debates around such issues in the introduction to their volume on *Higher Stages of Human Development*. Much of the disagreement and discussion is also aptly articulated by Funk in Chapter 1, where he suggests that the disagreements are often (and sometimes merely) the result of differently placed emphases and orientations.

An interesting contrast in approaches to higher consciousness or enlightenment is revealed in the differences that exist between Buddhism and the Vedic path. Both approaches have received increasing attention in the contemporary literature over the past few years. The Vedic approach, on the one hand, is more teleological as it is directed towards experiencing the ultimate unity of life. It depicts development towards that unity through a sequence of clearly differentiated stages. The Buddhist approach, on the other hand, seeks a heightened awareness of existence that is generally not as concerned about "higher" stages *per se*. It is directed towards demasking the false self and breaking down the habitual modes of perception, eliminating illusions and distortions in thinking. The Vedic approach, by contrast, emphasizes transcending thought altogether—allowing the higher, universal self to emerge. Buddhism focuses on problems in daily living by cutting through the fetters of representational thought. It promises alleviation of human suffering and thus seems to have an immediate appeal. This emphasis on the illusory aspects of our interpretations of reality may account, in part, for the growing interest in Buddhism shown by psychotherapists and transpersonal clinicians. On the other hand, applications of the Vedic path and TM technology have also gained mainstream recognition especially in government and business settings. The integration of thought and action, and insight into the laws of nature made possible through the practice of TM have helped many to act with greater insight and more love. Four chapters in this book are written from the Vedic perspective while one includes Buddhist precepts. We hope that the inclusion of both perspectives will encourage more dialogue between these historically and uniquely Eastern paths to human development.

One can address the issue of mapping the entire spectrum of human development from many contrasting perspectives. One end of the spectrum offers theory-driven or "top-down" approaches. The authors writing from this perspective, and the experts and teachers whom they cite, posit end points, top rungs, or destinations to the journey of development. They do this on the basis of "expert knowledge" which they have attained, often through direct experience or spiritual training and/or through investigation of teachings and classic texts, and in discussions with those who have experientially and intellectually investigated these states. The Alexander et al. and Nuernberger chapters may best represent this approach. They posit theories of development (or the outline of spiritual paths) and then seek to support their veracity through either empirical research or experiential studies. At the other end are researchers (e.g., Cook-Greuter, Miller, and Vasudev) who follow more of a "bottom up" or data-driven orientation. In this method, empirical studies are conducted, findings are analyzed, and theories or constructs are developed to explain the findings. For example, Cook-Greuter (Chapter 5) analyzed thousands of responses to sentence completion stems. A refined theory of higher ego stages was then constructed based on evidence from these completions.

Similarities in both the milestones passed along the way and in the "endpoints" of mature development are noted between the top-down and the

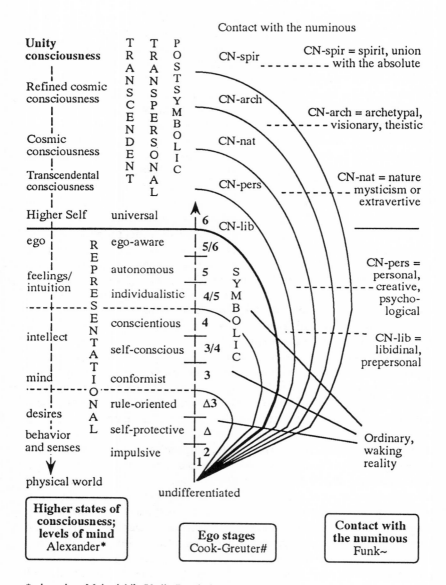

Figure I.1. Higher States of Consciousness, Levels of Mind,
Ego Development, and Contact with the Numinous

bottom-up approaches as illustrated in both Table I.1 and Figure I.1. Despite these similarities, the bottom-up approaches investigated here did not reveal the fine nuances in stage and substage distinctions at the highest levels such as those found in the ancient Eastern theories of human development. Miller's interview results only hinted at the existence of the post-autonomous and transcendent. Cook-Greuter's research, on the other hand, enabled her to propose one transcendent ego stage; but, given the data-based methodology, did not permit a clear or subtle definition of development beyond the representational realm such as that which exists for Buddhism (Wilber et al., 1986) and the Vedic theory of human development. Alexander et al., in their chapter, outline three clearly differentiated, higher stages or levels in the transcendental realm of consciousness.

In attempting an explanation of these differences, we find that the more strict empirical or bottom-up approach is sensitive to the subject pools drawn from and more limited by the assessment tools used. Clearly the representational aspects of the ego as a separate construct end when ego-transcendence begins. Thus ego development theory, as formulated by Loevinger (1976) and expanded by Cook-Greuter (1990), posits its own theoretical limit. It cannot shed as much light on the innermost reaches of human development. We might consider this phenomenon as evidence of one advantage of the theory-driven schemes. It may also be considered as a confirmation of the need for us to pay attention to the visions of exemplars and teachers as they create some of the preliminary maps of the transcendental territory—and a reason for us to see both them and their theories as subjects for our research. On the other hand, we need the empirical and hypothetico-deductive approaches for balance. The empirically driven and theory-driven approaches need each other to create a dynamic system of mutual checks and balances.

Figure I.1 also illuminates the issue of conceptualization of the internal psychological structure of the subjects or initiates at each stage or tier. Although some authors may prefer to speak of levels of mind (Alexander), or ego stages (Cook-Greuter), or contact with the numinous (Funk), it should nevertheless be noted that remarkably similar developmental milestones are identified within these different foci. If we think of these milestones in terms of structural changes in the dynamic interaction between inner and outer reality, how can we make sense of and articulate the concomitant structure of the ego or psyche at each stage? Does stage change mean a fundamental change in structure? What are the mechanisms or events giving rise to such changes? Alexander et al. (Chapter 2), for example, contend that the practice of Transcendental Meditation facilitates stage change across all four tiers. The process of regularly transcending to deeper, intrinsic levels of mind and experiencing unity consciousness—in combination with the gradual removal of accumulated stress in the nervous system—can lead to permanent, positive change. Torbert (Chapter 7), on the other hand, suggests that postformal development is effectively cultivated through a process of "action inquiry" based on complex organizational tasks in tandem with a rigorous practice of refining self-exploration and self-awareness. Miller (Chapter 6) finds that a desire or motivation to continually change and develop seems to be a critical factor contributing to the development of mature thought in his subjects.

Although theoretical differences among the experts are acknowledged, most articles in this volume focus on the human journey, the yearning or striving for further, continued development throughout adulthood. We recognize in our subjects and in ourselves a desire to remove imbalances in our lives, and to seek more understanding and integration. Our subjects express an urge to move beyond the conventional ideas of the separate self—even beyond self-actualization—towards self-transcendence and deeper wisdom. So, what are the motivators and forces that encourage certain individuals to seek these more integrated and transcendent realms of being? You, the reader, will find a variety of responses to these and other questions in the forthcoming chapters. As you anticipate your passage through them, we hope you will be able to appreciate the variety of developmental approaches noted herewith, while at the same time realizing that the overall orientation of these articles is actually similar as they challenge existing theories in developmental psychology in particular—and in modern psychology in general.

Overview of the Chapters

We would recommend reading the chapters in this book in order. The terrain ahead is rich and varied. We have attempted to arrange the progression of chapters in a manner that will facilitate navigation. However, some readers may prefer to focus first on topics that particularly interest them. The chapters have been grouped according to four major topics: a theoretical overview, theory-based frameworks of development, data-based models, and ethical and moral development. A brief discussion of each of the chapters in their respective groupings follows.

Section I is *A Theoretical Overview of the Field*. Funk offers a critical comparison of several major transpersonal theories in his chapter entitled *Unanimity and Disagreement among Transpersonal Psychologists*. He points out some of the striking similarities evident in contemporary transpersonal theories. He notes a uniformity of opinion about the existence of hierarchically ordered series, or levels, of consciousness among transpersonal theorists. Most of the chapters in this book seem to support this perspective. On the other hand, transpersonal theorists also disagree on pivotal points. For example, they dispute theoretical notions such as the "deconstruction of the ego" and the idea of "self-remembering." Must the usual and familiar structure of the ego be "deconstructed" or lost as a matter of course, if one aspires towards transpersonal levels of development? Funk addresses these, and other equally controversial questions, in a provocative effort at integration and synthesis. He completes his chapter by outlining a three-factor model of consciousness that differentiates "ego as representation," "ego as process," and "contact with the numinous." The model allows for new distinctions among ordinary, psychopathological, and transpersonal states.

The chapters comprising Part II have been grouped under the heading *Theory-Based Frameworks of Mature Development and Transcendence*. All three chapters in this section have been influenced by the ancient Vedic tradition of India—as has Druker's (Chapter 8) in the moral development section. All of these authors highlight the potential of this tradition to enrich contemporary psychology's understanding of the further reaches of human development, although they each interpret the Vedic tradition differently. Of the Vedic approaches mentioned here, the Vedic Science as presented in Transcendental Meditation has received the greatest degree of empirical scrutiny.

In Chapter 2, Alexander, Heaton, and Chandler argue the efficacy of this Vedic psychological path to higher stages of development. They contend that a transpersonal "unity consciousness" is the highest stage obtained through the Vedic discipline of Transcendental Meditation (as illuminated by Maharishi over the past 35 years). Alexander et al. discuss the importance of both training and having a guide to reach these higher levels, and offer research evidence to support their claims. The research measures used include those discussed by Cook-Greuter in Chapter 5. Maharishi's Vedic Science introduces a theoretical model of the development of consciousness that subsumes ordinary stages of consciousness as described by contemporary psychology in a more comprehensive system.

In Chapter 3, Thomas offers a new transpersonal theory of consciousness, one which conflicts with currently accepted theory. He contrasts Kohlberg's approach to developmental stages and structures (along with those of other mainstream developmental theorists) with that espoused by Wilber—as extrapolated from Vedic theory. He suggests that Wilber's developmental theory is more effective in designating and describing stages beyond the rational level. However, he finds it necessary to modify Wilber's abstract theory in order to accommodate the data from his research with mature individuals. Finally, he challenges mainstream psychology as he wonders why there is such difficulty in accepting the developmental theories of transpersonal psychology in general, and transcendent stages in particular. What is this resistance to novel paradigms and higher stages about, he asks.

In Chapter 4, Nuernberger discusses the structures of the mind and the mind's various resources from the perspective of the nondualistic theory of the Advaita Vedanta. He compares his approach to those found in more traditional Western psychologies, and argues that the Vedic approach is more complete or whole than Western ones. He also presents us with a list of ontological assumptions about mind which are subscribed to by this orientation, and outlines their relationship to the mind's resources. He insists that personal experience and practice are the only means by which such a view of reality can be verified and validated.

Part III, *Theories of Mature Development Based on Empirical Research*, is a set of three chapters which draws upon the findings of fairly traditional research approaches to describe the cognitive and emotional attributes of those reaching the more mature stages of adult development.

In Chapter 5, Cook-Greuter draws upon her analysis of numerous responses from the Washington University Sentence Completion Test (WUSCT) given by a diverse sample of adult subjects. She found 0.8% of them to be rare, postautonomous responses. These responses suggest that many subjects at the upper level of postformal development begin to investigate the mechanisms of their own meaning making and often spontaneously experience the transpersonal domain (see Table I-1 and Figure I-1). Cook-Greuter is critical of the inability of Loevinger's WUSCT scoring system to accommodate such responses. Based on her data, she developed an original schema for scoring and labeling two postautonomous stages: 1) a construct-aware stage and 2) a universal, ego-transcendent stage. She illuminates the view of reality inherent in Loevinger's autonomous and integrated ego stages and then discusses how the continued journey through the symbolic realm of cognition can evolve into self-transcendence.

Miller, in Chapter 6, presents the results of a longitudinal study on world views, ego development, and epistemological changes in adults. He describes a world view as a set of ideas that people hold or champion. These sets of ideas serve as a lens through which experiences are filtered, as they function in a manner similar to Kuhn's (1973) paradigms discussed by Thomas in Chapter 3. Miller organized subjects' responses to a lengthy World View Interview (Miller, 1982; Miller & West, 1993) according to the themes and contents that emerged. A ten-year follow-up study suggested that certain world views were more conducive than others to ego development and epistemological changes as measured by the WUSCT and the Rokeach and Perry scales. The follow-up study also revealed that developmental growth did not occur as readily as anticipated. The more notable changes were found in those who were open to new experience (less dogmatic/less cognitively rigid), and in those who had initially evidenced higher levels of ego development. The percentage of rare responses was similar to that observed by Cook-Greuter.

In Chapter 7, Torbert presents the results of a research project he directed that attempted to "cultivate" or promote postformal development in graduate business students. The method used is "action inquiry"—an *in vivo* approach which presents actual problems/tasks to participants and, simultaneously, involves the continuous monitoring and refinement of one's awareness and behavior. Torbert contends that such an approach is often preferable to one that teaches some predetermined and more formally defined path. He contrasts his method with the TM technique discussed by Alexander et al. in Chapter 2. Torbert cites research data indicating that his method has successfully moved several of his subjects into postformal stages of development.

The fourth section includes a set of chapters which address important issues in *Postconventional Ethical and Moral Development*. These chapters make a very appropriate conclusion to this volume, especially as they speak to one of our basic questions: does the attainment of the highest stages of development make a real difference in people's experience? How do developmentally mature people solve moral and ethical problems, and how do they behave when facing the challenges of contemporary living? Vasudev and Druker persuasively address these issues while, at the same time, they offer thoughtful critiques of popular contemporary theories of moral development.

In Chapter 8, Druker criticizes Kohlberg's scheme of moral development for not being open to a more transcendent, nonegoic perspective. He contends that even at the highest stages of Kohlberg's theory, the perspective remains that of the individual ego. He asserts the need, from a Vedic perspective, for a cosmic, unified orientation. Druker feels that the inability of Kohlberg's theory to make room for the ontological orientation expressed in the Vedic philosophy is a serious flaw. Vasudev, in contrast, seems to be most critical of the absence of a connectedness with all life forms in Kohlberg's scheme. Druker shares this concern as he reflects on the Gilligan (1982) critique of Kohlberg. Druker then presents the Vedic Science theory of moral development as explicated by Maharishi—an approach emphasizing the importance of responsiveness, relatedness, and care. Druker integrates these principles with universal ones based on a natural law perspective.

Vasudev, in Chapter 9, presents evidence that challenges Kohlberg's description of postconventional morality and its reliance on a Western, restricted view of reason. In her study, she interviewed a number of mature adults from India using Kohlberg's methodology as she explored indigenous values in moral reasoning. Although Vasudev found some support for Kohlberg's model among Indian subjects (especially at moral stages 1 through 4), she argues that his approach is too driven by a qualified form of rationality which precludes a comprehensive respect for all life forms.

It is noted that his model cannot accommodate a concern for *Ahimsa*—the focus on nonviolence and the sanctity of all life embraced by her subjects.

Postscript

As editors of this volume we faced the trials and challenges of orchestrating a difficult project such as this—a project which integrates such an array of developmental paths and theories. To accomplish our goal we had to stretch ourselves in many ways, not least of which was to push the limits of our own tolerance and understanding. We trust that the reader will venture with us on this collective journey, and challenge us with questions and comments that will keep this vital dialogue alive.

Acknowledgments

We would like to thank Dina DuBois, Alan N. West, and Charles N. Alexander for their invaluable comments and suggestions on earlier versions of this chapter.

References

Alexander, C. N.; Druker, S. M. & Langer, E. J. (1990). Introduction: Major issues in the exploration of adult growth. In C. N. Alexander & E. J. Langer (Eds.), *Higher stages of human development* (pp. 3–34). New York: Oxford University Press.

Angier, N. (1993). Where the unorthodox get a hearing at NIH: Head of new office tries to add rigor to alternative medicine. *The New York Times*, 16 March 1993, p. B5.

Belenky, M. F.; Clinchy, B. M.; Goldberger, N. R. & Tarule, J. M. (1986). *Women's ways of knowing: The development of self, voice and mind*. New York: Basic Books.

Capon, N. & Kuhn, P. (1979). Logical reasoning in the supermarket: Adult females' use of proportional reasoning strategy in an everyday context. *Developmental Psychology* 15: 450–452.

Commons, M. L. & Richards, F. A. (1984). A general model of stage theory. In M. L. Commons; F. A. Richards & C. Armon (Eds.), *Beyond formal operations: Late adolescent and adult cognitive development* (pp. 120–140). New York: Praeger.

Cook-Greuter, S. (1990). Maps for living: Ego development stages from symbiosis to conscious universal embeddedness. In M. Commons, T. Grotzer & J. Sinnott (Eds.), *Adult development, models and methods in the study of adolescent and adult thought*, 2 (pp. 79–104). New York: Praeger.

Fischer, K. W.; Kenny, S. L. & Pipp, S. L. (1990). How cognitive processes and environmental conditions organize discontinuities in the development of abstractions. In C. N. Alexander & E. J. Langer (Eds.), *Higher stages of human development* (pp. 162–187). New York: Oxford University Press.

Gilligan, C. (1982). *In a different voice*. Cambridge, MA: Harvard University Press.

Gowan, J. C. (1977). Creative inspiration in composers. *Journal of Creative Behavior* 11 (4): 249–255.

Kegan, R. (1982). *The evolving self*. Cambridge, MA: Harvard University Press.

Kegan, R. (1994). *In over our heads: The mental demands of modern life*. Cambridge, MA: Harvard University Press.

Kohlberg, L. (1969). Stage and sequence: The cognitive developmental approach to socialization. In D. A. Goslin (Ed.), *Handbook of socialization theory and research*. New York: Rand McNally.

Koplowitz, H. (1984). A projection beyond Piaget's formal operations stage: A general system stage and a unitary stage. In M. L. Commons; F. A. Richards & C. Armon (Eds.), *Beyond formal operations: Late adolescent and adult cognitive development* (pp. 272–295). New York: Praeger.

Kuhn, T. S. (1973). *The structure of scientific revolutions*. Chicago: University of Chicago Press.

Loevinger, J. (1976). *Ego development: Conceptions and theories*. San Francisco: Jossey-Bass.

Maharishi Mahesh Yogi (1972). *The science of creative intelligence*. Fairfield, IA: Maharishi International University Press.

Miller, M. E. (1982). World view and ego development in adulthood. *Dissertation Abstracts International* 42: 3459–3460.

Miller, M. E. & West, A. N. (1993). Influences of world view on personality, epistemology, and choice of profession. In J. Demick & P. Miller (Eds.), *Development in the workplace* (pp. 3–19). Hillsdale, NJ: Lawrence Erlbaum Associates, Publishers.

Pascual-Leone, J. (1984). Attention, dialectic, and mental effort: Toward an organismic theory of life stages. In M. L. Commons; F. A. Richards & C. Armon (Eds.), *Beyond formal operations: Late adolescent and adult cognitive development*. (pp. 182–215). New York: Praeger.

Piaget, J. (1972). Intellectual evolution from adolescence to adulthood. *Human Development* 15: 1–12.

Toufexis, A. (1993). Dr. Jacobs' alternative mission. *Time*, 1 March 1993, p. 43.

Wilber, K.; Engler, J. & Brown, D. P. (1986). *Transformations in consciousness: Conventional and contemplative perspectives on development*. Boston: Shambhala, New Science Library.

PART I

A Theoretical Overview of the Field

CHAPTER ONE

Unanimity and Disagreement
Among Transpersonal Psychologists

Joel Funk
Plymouth State College

There is a widespread notion among transpersonal psychologists that all schools of transpersonal psychology and philosophy, all forms of mysticism, all religions, and all esoteric traditions, if one were only to penetrate to a deep enough level, are essentially delivering the same message. This is made explicit in the titles of Schuon's (1984) *The Transcendent Unity of Religions* and Huxley's (1944) *The Perennial Philosophy*, and in the writings of such perennialists as philosophers Huston Smith (1976) and Walter Stace (1960), and psychologists Frances Vaughan (1989) and Ken Wilber (1977, 1980, 1983).

Is this unanimity veridical or just appearance? To be sure, there *does* seem to be substantial agreement on a number of themes among students of transpersonal and mystical experience. For example, most transpersonal psychologists would accept as tenable the majority of the following metaphysical and psychological assumptions, which to a large extent set them apart from other psychologists and philosophers (Huxley, 1944; Shapiro, 1989; Vaughan, 1989; Marcoulesco, 1987):

1. There exists an Absolute (however defined) which transcends time, space, "thing-ness," and all forms of dualism, ultimately transcending any conceptualization whatsoever.

1-a. The Absolute is mysterious and inexplicable by ordinary rational means (*mysterium tremendum et fascinans*).

1-b. Paradox, therefore, is the inevitable means of describing or symbolizing the ineffable; the mystic uses symbols, images, and poetic metaphors to convey the meaning and form of transpersonal experience to the extent that this is possible.

1-c. On a somewhat intermediate level, there exist higher (Platonic/Pythagorean) forms or archetypes, which inform the material world we live in; these archetypes can be intuited in some transpersonal states.

2. Self-transcendence is not only a possibility but a desideratum, i.e., the individual ego is not the terminus of development.

2-a. There is posited a hierarchy of levels of consciousness, culminating in a stage in which union with the Absolute has been fully realized. Thereafter ensues a sense of Ultimate Belonging, since the Absolute is our true "Self."

2-b. Intermediate levels of consciousness (parapsychological, visionary) are generally held to exist, but are typically to be avoided as a subtle distraction from the true goal of mystical union.

2-c. Union with the Absolute is described as sublimely blissful, beyond the understanding of the lower mental and emotional faculties, as well as beyond time and space.

2-d. The enlightened individual is a wholly dispassionate (detached) and compassionate being, free of cravings and desires; in a word, the enlightened individual can be called "selfless."

3. Mysticism is the "art of arts," demanding not merely intellectual assent, but dedication of one's entire being. Although the Absolute draws the mystic towards union (through "grace"), generally arduous efforts, such as meditation, prayer, ritual, and related practices, are also required.[1]

Corresponding ethical, axiological, and pragmatic directives derive from these assumptions. For example, in the moral sphere, moderation, selfless love, compassion, charity, and service are emphasized in most transpersonal traditions (Huxley, 1944; Firman & Vargiu, 1977).

Corollary epistemological claims derived from the transpersonal view are:

1. That mystical experiences are cross-culturally identical or very nearly so.

2. That mystics can "Transcend their own conceptual framework, as well as conditioned modes of knowing and being in general" (Rothberg, 1989, p. 5). The mystical experience is typically described as "unconditioned."

An existentialist, by way of contrast, would undoubtedly reject many of these assumptions, e.g., the existence of the Absolute and the importance of self-transcendence. Instead, self-determined choice in the face of an indifferent or hostile universe might be held to characterize the human condition.

Indeed, the majority of Western psychologists, even many of those concerned with adult development, tend to ignore or even denigrate the transpersonal view, although the situation has changed somewhat in the past decade (Commons, et al., 1984; Commons, et al., 1989). Compare, for example, the current mainstream approaches to creativity (Sternberg, 1988) with those proposed by transpersonalists like Harman and Rheingold (1984), Gowan (1975, 1977), and Funk (1989).[2]

Areas of Disagreement

In point of fact, however, there have been some major disagreements among transpersonal psychologists. While some of these are of relatively recent vintage, many are enduring dilemmas of theology, philosophy, or comparative religion, which have been recirculating through this newly emergent field (Faivre, 1987; Marcoulesco, 1987; Dupre, 1987). For the most part, these areas of dispute have not received sufficient attention. Thus, the first purpose of this essay is to delineate a few of the more problematic areas of controversy. The second is to propose a highly schematic model of consciousness in the hope of clarifying the nature of some of these debates.

Below is a consideration of several disputed issues:

1. A number of postmodern thinkers (Katz, 1978; Gimello, 1983) have argued that the notion of some perennial cross-cultural transpersonal experience is invalid. Katz and his colleagues argue that since all experience is mediated or filtered by culture, language, tradition, and psychosocial "myths" (Keen, 1983), there can be no unmediated mystical experience. There is not and could not be a common core to transpersonal experience:

> Buddhist mystical experiences . . . are in no sense the same as the Christian mystic's experience of the Trinity . . . or the Godhead; nor the same as the Jewish mystic's experience of *En-sof;* nor even the same as the Vedantist's experience of the identity of *atman* and *brahman*. (Gimello, 1983, p. 63)

It is widely accepted by social scientists that our everyday "reality" is socially constructed (Berger & Luckmann, 1967). The question for transpersonal psychology is whether, on the developmental ascent through the "thickets" of culture there is some sort of "timberline" above which culture has no, or at least no relevant, influence.

A pivotal study by Brown (1986) may shed light on this issue. Brown intensively examined the stages along three Eastern meditative paths and concluded that the Buddhist and Hindu (Yogic) traditions, although positing essentially an identical sequence of steps in the deconstruction of the structures of ordinary consciousness during meditation, *actually experience the stages differently*, the Hindu tradition emphasizing continuity, the Buddhists discontinuity.[3] Thus Brown reaches a conclusion:

> Nearly the opposite of that of the stereotyped notion of the perennial philosophy according to which many spiritual paths are said to lead to the

same end. . . . [W]e have to conclude . . . : *there is only one path, but it has several outcomes*. There are several kinds of enlightenment, although all free awareness from psychological structure and alleviate suffering. . . . While all . . . the kinds of enlightenment are valid, each represents a different point of view. (pp. 266–7)

Thus even the highest, nondualistic stages of enlightenment may be influenced by implicit cultural themata.[4] Pragmatically, however, the differences do not seem nearly as crucial as Katz (1978) and the relativists would have it. Rothberg (1989), in a cogent philosophical refutation of the extreme relativist position, makes slight concessions to the relativists but concludes:

[Brown] holds that there is in all three traditions an initial "enlightenment" experience, understood as a transcendence of all constructed states of consciousness. . . . Paradoxically, each path of deconstruction or deconditioning is itself constructed or conditioned in a certain way. . . . [It is] thus correct to suggest that the experiences of mystics are almost always in part constructed or mediated, but . . . there are experiences in which all or certain forms of construction and mediation are not present. (p. 13)

The relativist/perennialist controversy has endured for millennia and is far from resolved, but the postmodern stance of extreme relativism seems increasingly inadequate in the light of the findings of transpersonal psychology.

There are other accounts of differences among transpersonalists. Shapiro (1989) has analyzed the implicit and explicit assumptions held by transpersonal scholars and demonstrated that there exist at least five important areas of divergence of belief. These focus on:

• the nature of reality (benign or not),
• the role of evil (existence addressed or not),
• the orientation to the spiritual (theistic or nontheistic),
• the significance of human will (effort or grace), and
• the choice of spiritual path (universal or particular).

Using Shapiro's dimensions, one could theoretically articulate up to 32 distinct transpersonal philosophies!

2. Even among the perennialists, however, there is general acknowledgment that not all transpersonal states are equal. On a somewhat obvious level, Stace (1960) distinguishes extravertive from introvertive mysticism. The former, lower state of consciousness remains in contact with the environment; the latter, higher state transcends it (Gowan, 1975). Going farther, Wilber (1983) has distinguished four levels of mysticism: the *panenhenic* (nature mysticism; extravertive sense of all-in-Oneness), the *theistic* (visionary approach to Absolute), the *monistic* (experience of union

with and as the Absolute), and the *nondualistic* (union of the Absolute with the relative). These differ, though, only in distance traveled along essentially the same transcendental path. Wilber's transpersonal stages are usually, but not necessarily, experienced in sequence: A mystic can experience theistic states without necessarily passing through the panenhenic stage, for example (Wilber, 1983).

Farther still, Gowan (1975), summarizing the results of previous research with a special reliance on classic Buddhist cartographies, has distinguished a continuum of over a dozen transpersonal states. His finely tuned distinctions include, for example, sensing the presence of the Absolute, hearing the Absolute, seeing the Absolute, "touching" the Absolute, penetrating the Absolute, merging with the Absolute, and so on. Brown (1986) offers a somewhat comparable 18-step model of the stages of Buddhist and Yogic meditation.

The appropriate placement of any particular transpersonal state is, however, subject to debate. Gowan (1975), for example, notes some minor disagreement over whether nature mysticism should be considered as a truly ecstatic (nonordinary) state of consciousness. More crucially, there has recently been a flurry of articles on the appropriate interpretation of shamanic and near-death experiences (NDE's), which Ring (1989), among others, sees as formally identical. Wilber (1981, 1983) and Vaughan (1989) view shamanism and even theistic visionary states as transpersonal but as *lesser* than true, nondual mystical experience, in that visionary states remain subtly dualistic. That is, the self remains somewhat apart from the Absolute. Furthermore, experiences imbued with some sort of "sensory" content, however transcendent, are nevertheless treated as inferior to those states of "pure consciousness" which transcend such content. Similarly, Walsh (1989a, b), by careful phenomenological analysis, has discriminated between the shamanic and other altered or mystical states of consciousness.

Gowan (1975), however, while acknowledging the presence of the "numinous" in shamanism, feels that shamanic trance is largely *prepersonal*—"parataxic" in his terminology—in that ego, memory, and volition are largely deficient or even absent. Peters (1989) and Walsh (1989a, b), notwithstanding, provide solid evidence that volition is indeed (often) present in shamanic soul traveling and healing. Peters, in fact, holds the position, contrary to most others, that at some level, "The different spiritual methods represent different practices to achieve the same state of unity consciousness" (p. 130). Peters is aware of the apparent differences between Eastern mysticism and shamanism, but feels that the similarities (identities?) are compelling. For example, both Vipassana meditation masters and Apache shamans produce the same "integrative" teaching style on Rorschach protocols (Peters, 1989). Generally, those transpersonalists with anthropological or parapsychological leanings have a more favorable interpretation of shamanism and related states, while those aligned with meditative traditions and the purification of consciousness are more critical.

3. A third major issue is one which, although well known to students of comparative religion (Faivre, 1987), does not appear to have surfaced in the recent literature of transpersonal psychology. This is the contrast between *mysticism* and *esotericism*. The latter term might best be understood initially by way of some illustrations. The Gurdjieff method (Ouspensky, 1949), for instance, appears to be rather different in purpose from the meditative or contemplative traditions, be they Hindu, Buddhist, or Christian. Concepts like "self-remembering" and establishing a "permanent 'I'" at the very least *sound* quite different from self-transcendence and the Buddhist *sunyata* (void), an experience of emptiness meant to "crush the belief in concrete existence" (Guenther, cited in Epstein, 1989, p. 64). Some of the apparent contradiction may be due to linguistic confusion, occasioned by imprecise use of terms like "ego" and "self," but actual differences may indeed remain. Wilson (1986) concluded his critique of the Gurdjieff system by stating that it is "[n]ot a way of meditation, or of mysticism, or of physical self-discipline. This is primarily a way of knowledge, a way that depends on knowing *certain definite things*" (p. 47).

Similarly, Rudolph Steiner parted company from Eastern mysticism. He labeled his school Anthroposophy, in contrast to Eastern influenced Theosophy, to emphasize that, "Whereas formerly the divine wisdom was imparted by the divine world itself to man, now man himself by divine grace, must transmute his earth-born thinking to the higher level of divine wisdom, by the true understanding of himself" (Shepherd, 1954, p. 73). McDermott (1989), a student of Anthroposophy, makes the radical claim that mysticism is only the *penultimate* state of development, whereas "higher cognition" is the ultimate state. Taking an evolutionary approach, McDermott argues that mysticism was more appropriate to an earlier historical era, when the (Western) egoic mode of consciousness was less developed.

Esotericism, then, refers to a special interior or intuitive knowledge of hidden relationships between humanity, the cosmos, and the Absolute. Esotericism sounds quite similar to mysticism, but Faivre (1987) sees the latter as more "feminine," involving renunciation and absorption into a larger unity. Esotericism, in contrast, is

> more "masculine," more solar, cultivates detachment and is more attentive to structures. In his own journey, the mystic discovers the same intermediate entities. . . . But while the [esotericist] views such entities [McDermott's higher cognitions] as a source of enlightening . . . knowledge, the mystic limits their numbers as much as he can and aspires to pass beyond them and be united directly with his God. (p. 158)

If, as Wilber (1981), Gebser (1986), and other historians of consciousness have testified, humanity has indeed evolved fairly recently—since roughly 500 B.C. in the West—to a "solar" egoic stage of awareness, then the more active, intellectual transpersonalism of Gurdjieff, Steiner, and even Jung (1964) might well be considered an equally or more appropriate path for our own age. Perennialists would undoubtedly disagree and so the mysticism-esotericism issue remains another source of contention.

4. In a chapter dedicated to emphasizing the distinctions between his own model of transpersonal development and Wilber's, Washburn (1988) discusses a number of points of controversy. One revolves around the contrast between Wilber's linear model of growth and Washburn's more spiral model. Washburn claims that in the process of ascending to transpersonal stages, one has to first descend to work through repressed prepersonal material, a process he terms "regression in the service of transcendence." Interestingly, Fowler's (1981) analysis of faith development follows an analogous spiralling path, in which earlier issues need to be reassimilated as one approaches a new stage.

Another source of contention is whether the prepersonal and transpersonal realms are similar or not. Wilber (1980) argues that the similarities are merely superficial (both are nonpersonal and nonrational in nature), but formally the two realms are different, even antithetical. Washburn (1988), on the other hand, maintains that the similarities are not merely accidental; prepersonal and transpersonal are both aspects of what he terms the *Dynamic Ground*.

Perhaps the major point of opposition, though, is over the question of the ultimate ontological significance of the "self." Does the self continue to exist in states of transpersonal integration or is it ultimately seen as illusory? Wilber, aligned with the Eastern traditions, treats the ego as illusory, a transition structure based on a false identification. In contrast, Washburn, like Jung (1964), posits two "selves," a lower one (the mundane ego), and a higher Self, which, in ideal development, eventually assumes dominance over the ego. Neither self, however, is dispensed with. Instead, according to Washburn (1988), "[v]iewing the egoic self as a real but pseudo-independent self, prescribes a transcendence that would reunite and 'alchemically' bond the egoic self with its missing superior half" (p. 39). The choice, then, is between two selves or none.[5]

To a great extent, this last controversy overlaps the mysticism-esotericism debate mentioned above. Note the reference to the esoteric tradition of alchemy! Like the esotericists and unlike the mystics, Washburn wishes to transform and realign but not dispense with the self.

5. Campbell's (1976) phenomenology of the higher stages of consciousness, derived from the Vedic tradition via Maharishi Mahesh Yogi (see also Alexander, Chapter 2 this volume) seems rather different from

Wilber's (1980), the former system apparently omitting or de-emphasizing
the visionary/theistic level, emphasizing "pure consciousness"—probably
Wilber's monistic level—from the outset.

6. The precise relationship between personal self-actualization and
transpersonal self-transcendence has also been at issue. Those holding a
roughly linear model of development, like Maslow (1970) and Wilber
(1980), view self-transcendence as more or less a natural outgrowth of
self-actualization. Russell's (1986) topography, in contrast, conceptualizes
self-actualization and self-transcendence as essentially distinct, even
orthogonally related phenomena. One can grow personally (via psychotherapy) by making unconscious material conscious; or one can develop
transpersonally (by meditation) by accessing higher states of consciousness.
The two paths *may* be mutually facilitative, but remain separate
nevertheless.

The proponents of psychosynthesis (Firman & Vargiu, 1977) promote
"self-realization," which entails *both* actualization and transcendence,
visualized as orthogonal to each other, in a subtle balance. Keen's (1983)
highest developmental stage, the "lover," is similarly dialectically poised
between the personal and the transpersonal.

A Three-Factor Model of Consciousness

Below, an admittedly sketchy and rather speculative "model" is
proposed, which, because it is multifactorial, might shed some light on the
problems presented above. It is an attempt to formulate a notational system,
a sort of shorthand, capable of encoding the diversity of schools, languages,
and traditions. The various components of the model are not new; all have
been derived or adapted from previous transpersonal writers, most notably
Gowan (1975), Washburn (1988), M. Epstein (1988), and Wilber (1980,
1986a, b). They have not, however, heretofore been synthesized into a
single framework. Before presenting the model, though, it behooves the
author to explain why existing models, despite their brilliance and
comprehensiveness, have proven problematic.

The difficulty with linear, unidimensional models like Wilber's (1980)
has just been discussed (see also Washburn, 1988). Gowan (1975) has
proposed a two-factor model: the essential element in all nonordinary
experience he calls, following theologian Rudolf Otto, *contact with the
numinous*. The other factor is the level of ego development. Gowan's
scheme entails essentially three basic levels of ego functioning, with
numerous subdivisions. These three levels he calls, borrowing again from
Harry Stack Sullivan, prototaxic, parataxic, and syntaxic: non-egoic/
body-oriented, quasi-egoic/iconic, and egoic/symbolic respectively.
Gowan's finely tuned cartography of the syntaxic (transpersonal) stages has

already been noted. It is not clear, however, whether all the variability of these higher states is due entirely to changes in ego functioning, or whether there is such a thing as variability in the depth of penetration into the numinous. It appears as though only one factor varies, which again limits the model.[6]

Washburn's (1988) model is also bifactorial or bipolar, but here both ego and numinous, or in his terminology, the Dynamic Ground, are variable. The ego levels correspond crudely to the levels demarcated by Cook-Greuter (1990; this volume) and others,[7] but the Ground is also divided into prepersonal (libido, instinct), personal (psychic energy), and transpersonal (Spirit) manifestations. The Ground for Washburn functions as a "nonspecific amplifier" (p. 111) that energizes all psychic systems, but which is not itself "reducible to or exclusively expressive of any particular system or systems" (p. 111). With his bipolar model, Washburn claims to have dealt with developmental issues, such as the death/rebirth process in midlife, in a more subtle way than Wilber, as noted above.[8]

The notion of contact with the Dynamic Ground (or numinous) is a prerequisite for any transpersonal model, but terms like "ego" are too oversimplified and/or confused as ordinarily presented. Precisely what is transcended in ego-transcendence? How does "ego loss" in schizophrenia differ, if at all, from "ego loss" in mysticism? It proved more productive to divide the ego's functions into two "systems," or groups of functions, thus yielding a three-factor theory. Each of these three factors can in turn be divided into at least two or more subfactors, in effect yielding a complex multifactorial schema. However, it is unlikely that these factors are causally independent. Some of the interrelationships between factors are sketched below.[9]

M. Epstein (1988), synthesizing findings from psychoanalysis and object-relations theory, differentiates two principal components of the ego system. This distinction became necessary to resolve some of the confusion engendered when Western transpersonalists tried to comprehend Eastern concepts like "egolessness."

> The tendency of contemporary theorists has been to propose developmental schema in which meditation systems develop "beyond the ego". . . , yet this approach has ignored aspects of the ego which are not abandoned and which are, in fact, developed through meditation practice itself. (M. Epstein, 1988, p. 61)

The two major components of the ego are the *functional*—concerned with reality testing, mediation between inner and outer, and synthesis or integration, and the *representational*—concerned with the formation of self and object representations, and also the source of the sense of "I" that is normally felt. These two components, in a somewhat adapted form, will here be called *ego as process (EPro)* and *ego as representation-individualization (ERep)*, respectively. It is important to note that the functions of EPro refer only to dynamic capabilities possessed by the ego, but without any notion of I-hood, or a separate self-sense implied. This parallels Wilber's (1986a) distinction between basic structures, devoid of "self," and transitional, phase-specific stages of the self per se. ERep, in contrast, refers to the ego's relatively solidified sense of itself as a separate self/agent, and to its reflected image of itself.

These two subfunctions of the ERep require further elaboration. A century ago, William James (1890/1950) divided these two aspects of the self into the "I" and the "me" and that distinction will be employed here. As De Martino (1963) has so carefully observed:

> Human existence is . . . ego-conscious existence. . . . Ego-consciousness means an ego aware or conscious of itself. Awareness of itself is expressed as affirmation of itself, the "I." . . . Affirmation of itself also entails, however, a bifurcation of itself. . . . As affirmer it performs the act of affirming itself. As affirmed it is an existential fact presented to itself. . . . The ego as subject-affirmer is not chronologically prior to itself as object-affirmed. Nor does its individuation precede its bifurcation. . . . This is the initial situation of man . . . , which may be characterized as contingent or conditioned subjectivity. (pp. 142–3)

The fundamental sense of being a separate self, possessing continuity, distinctness, and agency, De Martino's affirming-subject, James's "I," will be referred to as *ERep-I*. One's reflected image of one's physical, behavioral, interpersonal, and psychological functioning, the affirmed object, James's "me," will be referred to as *ERep-M*. Contrary to the popularly held notion, "the 'I' is not identical with the ego, but is more precisely a component" (M. Epstein 1988, p. 64). Although Epstein (1988) includes the defensive function of the ego, so diligently elaborated by the Freuds and their followers (Freud, 1936/1966), within the functional rubric (i.e., EPro), here the defenses will be subsumed under ERep-M, because it is largely this image that is being defended.[10] Wilber (1986a) also locates the defenses in the self (representational) system.

Along with a sense of I and an image of me, people also have a corresponding sense and image of others and of the world, the "objects" of object-relations theory. In De Martino's (1963) words, "Affirmation of itself involves the individuation of itself, the ego . . . discriminated from that which is not itself— . . . 'not-I'" (p. 143). Generally, in this paper, the focus will be on changes *within* the person, the inevitable corresponding changes in relation to world and objects remaining implicit.

M. Epstein (1988) explicitly states that in the course of Vipassana meditation, and presumably other forms of transpersonal development, it is the *representational* component of the ego (ERep) that is deconstructed, while the *functional* component, particularly the synthesizing capability (an aspect of EPro), is actually *strengthened*. Meditation does not lead "beyond ego" (such that the faculties of EPro are somehow eliminated), but rather effects change within the ego (discussed more fully below).

In M. Epstein's (1988) usage, the functional component of the ego refers primarily to short-term dynamic processes. At the risk of theoretical fuzziness, EPro will be broadened to include long-term stages of ego development as well (Cook-Greuter, 1990), since most theories of adult development adopt a stage orientation (Commons et al., 1984). A structure such as a developmental stage will therefore be interpreted as process or function slowed down and generalized.[11]

EPro can also be subdivided. It seems fruitful to differentiate first-level ego processes per se, the sorts of capabilities and awarenesses described on the process level by M. Epstein (1988), and structurally by Cook-Greuter (1990), from *meta-awareness* of one's thought processes, such as occur in Vipassana (insight) meditation. The insight meditator "witnesses" the very structures—thoughts, images, feelings, perceptions, fantasies—through which one normally constructs the world (Kornfield, 1989).

> Insight practices operate within the ego system itself. Attending to both the subjective intimation of the experiencing I *and* to the abstract cognitions that form it on a conceptual level, insight practices seek to uncover the elementary particles of the "I" experience. (M. Epstein, 1988, p. 65)

Cook-Greuter (1990) maintains that at postformal levels, past stage 4 and especially at stage 5/6 in her scheme, the person spontaneously begins to see through cultural norms, linguistic conditioning, and related structures, but that this awareness is not identical to what occurs in meditation. Rational, mediated "thinking about" one's self and culture is a different process from intuitive, unmediated awareness of the "elementary particles of the 'I' experience." Therefore, the model treats these processes as distinct: EPro will be used for regular ego processes and stages, and *EPro*, for the special case of trained meta-awareness of one's own ego processes. One caveat: *EPro* probably will emerge to some extent, indeed may be somewhat constitutive of Cook-Greuter's stage 6, the universal stage.[12]

In fact, the universal stage presents something of an anomaly, in that by this level of development, the egoic posture has to some extent been surrendered. Paradoxically, the more developed the ego, the greater the likelihood of the person adopting a universal perspective and experiencing a sense of interconnectedness. A number of transegoic capacities begin to emerge at stage 6, variously called intuition, prajna, insight, unitary concepts, illumination, etc. (Wilber, 1980). In effect, the boundary between ego and the numinous has become porous (Wilber, 1977).[13]

Combining Washburn (1988) and Gowan (1975), contact with the numinous or Dynamic Ground (hereafter *CN*) can be subdivided into, minimally, five levels:

- CN-lib—the libidinal (or lower), instinctual, prepersonal aspect of the Ground;
- CN-pers—the psychological or personal aspect, manifested, for example, in "charismatic" individuals (Washburn) or in creative activity (Gowan);
- CN-nat—the extraverted (nature-oriented) transpersonal aspect;
- CN-arch—the archetypal, visionary transpersonal aspect; and
- CN-spir—the spiritual, (monistic, nondualistic) transpersonal aspect.

Finer subdivisions of the transpersonal are of course possible (Gowan, 1975, Wilber, 1980), but three levels seems a reasonable compromise between the competing demands of precision and parsimony. The degree of intensity of CN is also assumed to vary.

Finally, it seems essential to divide contact with the numinous not only into developmental levels, but, following Grof (1980), into aspects of the numinous that seem located in ordinary reality, and those—henceforth called CN* to indicate their unusual nature—located in some apparently "non-ordinary" reality, as are many near-death experiences (NDE's) (Ring, 1984) and shamanic experience (Peters, 1989; Walsh 1989a, b).[14]

Interactions of the Three Factors

The various factors delineated are undoubtedly not independent. As illustrated in Figure 1.1, they typically interact in specifiable ways, notably:

a. Typically, as ERep decreases and/or EPro increases, CN also spontaneously increases. That is, the numinous is presumed to be ever-present but veiled by the defenses and distortions of ERep and/or undetected by inadequately developed EPro. Sufficiently high ego development (Maslow, 1971; Cook-Greuter, 1990) in and of itself often leads to greater CN. ERep is posited by many traditions, especially Buddhism, to be ultimately illusory—no matter how congruent in Rogers's (1961) sense—so that ERep diminishes as CN increases. As EPro evolves through *EPro*, ERep decreases and may vanish entirely as a factor in the enlightened state.[15]

b. ERep-M and EPro tend to have a seesaw effect. Many traditions argue that we have overinvested in self-image, i.e., ERep-M, at the expense of EPro, and that meditation, therapy, self-remembering, etc., can serve to redress this imbalance. As defenses yield, one becomes more "realistic,"

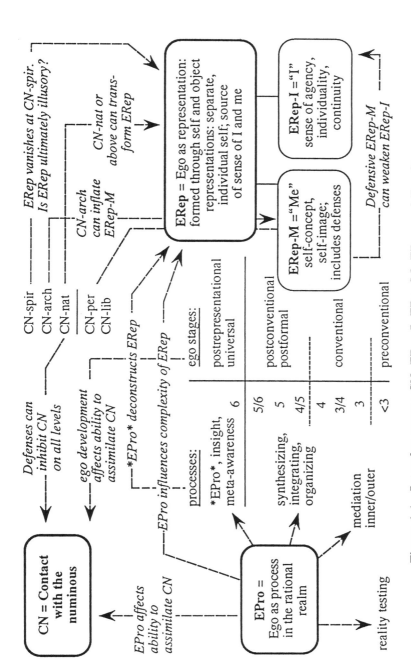

Figure 1.1. Interplay among CN, ERep-I, ERep-M, EPro, and Ego Stage

i.e., ego as process (EPro) actually begins to improve. As noted above, M. Epstein (1988) is careful to point out that what is transcended in ego-transcendence is ERep, not EPro.

Beyond a certain point, ERep-M and ERep-I also tend to have a seesaw effect. Overinvestment in ERep-M can begin to weaken one's actual sense of individuality and agency (ERep-I). This can be seen clearly in some of the personality disorders (schizoid, narcissistic) discussed below.

Sometimes ERep and EPro can both be fairly strong, which leads to the sort of paradox Barron (1969) observed when studying very creative people, namely, the simultaneous coexistence of competence and ego-strength (EPro) alongside neurotic and even psychotic tendencies (ERep; the model assumes that such defenses are part of a highly developed ERep-M system).

c. ERep-M, especially the defenses, can repress CN. The psychoanalysts (Freud, 1936/1966) discovered this when exploring the lower level (CN-lib), Reich (1976; Baker, 1980) extended this principle to the middle level of ordinary personality functioning (CN-pers) with his notions of character rigidity and contactlessness, and Jung (1964) and Maslow (1971) found the same process at work on the higher (CN-nat, -arch, -spir) levels. Maslow called the repression of one's higher nature the Jonah complex, Wilber (1980), "repression of the emergent unconscious." ERep-M can also usurp the energy and power of the numinous for its own ignoble ends, a phenomenon Jung (Rosenthal, 1987) named ego inflation (discussed below).

d. ERep-M, especially the defenses, can also inhibit development of EPro (see b above). In other words, a strongly defended, fearful representational ego may not allow higher levels of consciousness/cognition to emerge. The paranoid is extremely unlikely to reach postformal stages.

e. EPro, in turn, will influence the complexity of ERep, especially ERep-M, as well as affect one's appreciation of CN. Obviously, one's self-concept depends on one's overall cognitive capacity (Harter, 1983). As for CN, Wilber (1983), for one, has described what happens when an adult "fixated" at a prepersonal level ("mythical") undergoes a transpersonal experience; typically it only reinforces this undeveloped mode of reality apperception. CN is assimilated into a network of prerational ideation. (But see g below.)

f. As Armstrong's (1985) study of transpersonal experiences in childhood makes clear, even those at low levels of EPro can sometimes experience the higher levels of CN in a profound way. The transpersonal aspect of the numinous can theoretically be experienced from any ego state, although, as we have seen, certain conditions (very advanced EPro/*EPro*) are more conducive. Childhood, though, typically has the advantage of a rather undeveloped ERep-M (see c above).

g. CN can greatly affect ERep and probably EPro as well. Maslow wrote of neuroses that cleared up after a single profound peak experience (CN-nat, -arch, -spir), and studies of near-death experience (presumably CN-arch) indicate vast changes in personality, values, and world view in the majority of experiencers (Ring, 1984).

Given this preliminary treatment of the three (or more) factors, the model can now be used to examine the different stages, states, paths, and therapies specified by various personal and transpersonal writers and schools.

Applications of the Three-Factor Model

1. Normal States

The discussion below and Tables 1.1 through 1.3 depict the main features and directions of various states of development and paths of change. The author's familiarity with many of these states and paths is second hand, so the tables and their elaboration must remain tentative.

What would "normality" consist of in this model? ERep-M manifests rather prominently, providing fertile ground for much "standard" psychology. In the reasonably "healthy" person this self-concept is positive—probably, as Lewinsohn et al. (1980) have observed, somewhat illusorily so—and reasonably congruent with who one is organismically in Rogerian terminology (Rogers, 1961). ERep-I is, at least in the West over the past several centuries, sharply articulated, possessed of a strong sense of agency, uniqueness, and continuity (Keen, 1983; Wilber, 1981). EPro will vary, most normal people in industrialized countries reaching abstract or formal operations (Cook-Greuter's stages 3/4 and 4), with a much smaller percentage entering the postformal realms (4/5 or 5, and very rarely 5/6 or 6). *EPro* is likely to be weak, however, except in those who have undergone certain types of therapy, who meditate, or who have on their own reached stage 6. CN is limited to CN-lib/pers and in any event is typically fairly minimal in the majority. Washburn (1988) explains how and why the average person inevitably represses the Dynamic Ground from early childhood onward. In normalcy, the numinous is typically approached sporadically, if at all, through sex, nature, certain types of music (Funk, 1989), childbirth, falling in love, creative activity, and moments of great accomplishment (Maslow, 1971). Note the somewhat "extraverted" flavor of these peak experiences (CN-nat at best). In sum, as Tart (1987) and Ouspensky (1949) among many others have noted, the combination of strongly filtered experience (due to ERep), moderate EPro, and weakly cultivated *EPro* and CN produce a "normal" state more accurately viewed as "waking sleep" or cultural hypnosis. Only in fleeting peak moments is the person truly "awake" (Tart, 1987).

Table 1.1

Application of the Three-Factor Model to Normal and Pathological States

State	ERep-M	ERep-I	EPro	CN
Normalcy	prominent, mildly positive and congruent, but "normally" illusory	moderately strong	stage: mostly 4 or lower, rarely higher; processes: adequate	minimal, limited to CN-lib and CN-pers
Nonpeaking self-actualizer	more positive and congruent	strong, active	stage: 5 or 5/6; processes: awareness of cultural and linguistic conditioning, beginning *EPro*?	strong, but limited to CN-lib and CN-pers
Neurosis	very prominent, defensive; overly negative or idealized; incongruent	weak	variable; if high may be creative	repressed on all levels
Schizoid	dominates entire life; fantasy; highly incongruent	very tenuous	may be high, but more typically reality testing, etc., weakened	extremely repressed; sense of unrealness or "shut-upness"
Schizophrenia	confused, fragmented; very negative or grandiose	extremely weak or absent; "ego loss"	more intact in paranoids, but generally processes regress	debatable: CN-lib likely; sometimes CN-arch may occur

The highest stage of personal development, but which lacks the transpersonal dimension, would be what Maslow called the nonpeaking self-actualizer, or in Cook-Greuter's (1990) system stage 5 (or 5/6). These stages are postformal, but not yet unitary. From descriptions by Maslow (1970) and others, EPro will be higher than normal, some incipient sense of *EPro* might be dawning, and ERep-M will be highly congruent and positive. Although CN-nat, CN-arch, CN-spir are minimal or absent in the nonpeaker, CN-lib/pers may be strongly present, serving as an "energizing" background in daily activity (Washburn, 1988).

2. Pathological States

Neurosis is simply a more problematic version of normality (Becker, 1973). ERep-M is strongly present, but is either overly negative and/or incongruent, or overly idealized (Horney, 1950). As Keen (1983) noted, "The neurotic has a godlike, idealized image of the self and a wormlike, degraded image of the self, but very little sense of real limits, abilities, or power" (p. 225). ERep-I is most likely somewhat weaker (i.e., less solid, more anxiety-ridden) than in normality, in that the sense of agency (in obsessions) or continuity (in dissociative disorders) is more tenuous. EPro is highly variable; if high, the person may be fairly creative, despite neurotic motivation (Barron, 1969; Storr, 1972). More usually EPro will be low to moderate. CN, even CN-lib, will probably be weaker due to the greater defensiveness and rigidity present.

The schizoid personality (Laing, 1965) can be viewed as transitional between neurosis and psychosis. In this disorder investment in ERep-M is extremely high; in a sense, the schizoid lives almost entirely in a symbolic world, but one which does not correspond well to the conventional one (Becker, 1973). Defenses such as fantasy, withdrawal, idealization, and splitting predominate in the schizoid and related personality disorders (e.g., borderline, narcissistic). ERep-I is highly tenuous; as Laing (1965) has noted, the schizoid's outward behavior reflects a conforming "false self," while the hidden, protected "true self" rarely engages others or the world. EPro, in some cases, may be high—Storr (1972) cites Einstein as an example—but is probably as often low to moderate. Despite the schizoid's claims, true self-insight (either stage 5/6 EPro or stage 6 *EPro*) is not likely. Extreme defensiveness is prone to inhibit development of ego as process. CN is probably at its absolute lowest in the schizoid, who typically feels trapped in a condition of "shut-upness" (Kierkegaard's phrase, cited in Laing, 1965) and drained of "realness." Even the normal's sense of libidinal embodiment (CN-lib), which gives a certain degree of zest and energy to everyday living, is highly attenuated if not absent in the disembodied schizoid disorder.

If the schizoid position cannot be maintained, the next "logical step" is schizophrenia (Laing, 1965). The schizophrenic's ERep-M is often highly negative and/or confused, although magical, delusional attempts at restitution (grandiosity) are fairly common. ERep-I is at its absolute lowest; the schizophrenics (or severe depressives) not uncommonly claim they have died. EPro may not change at first, especially in paranoid schizophrenics, although prolonged schizophrenia tends to be regressive.[16] The loss of the abstract attitude noted by Goldstein (1964) and the lack of logical ability to organize parts into whole systems (Angyal, 1964) can be cited as examples.

One of the most controversial issues surrounding schizophrenia is whether CN exists, and if so, of what order. The conventional view is that either CN does not occur, or that perhaps aspects of CN-lib, grossly misinterpreted, may be experienced. On the other hand, transpersonalists like Laing (1979), Lukoff (1985), Perry (1974), and Van Dusen (1979), based on clinical studies of archetypal and related experience in psychosis, maintain that in some cases CN-nat/arch does indeed occur, although often muddled with ego fragments (ERep-M/I).

3. Transpersonal States

In extraverted or nature mysticism, the lowest transpersonal stage (Wilber, 1983), ERep-M/I remains, although attention is focused outward away from the self. In fact, one nature mystic described this experience as that of "having no head" (Harding, 1963). That is, one's sense of separateness and self-consciousness is quite minimized, ERep-M perhaps even temporarily suspended. However, ERep-I does not entirely disappear in these beginning transpersonal stages. Wilber (1977) illustrates this by diagramming the boundary between organism and environment with a dashed rather than a solid line. EPro remains as developed as before and will probably be enhanced (*EPro*), at least transiently. Someone embedded at stages 5 or 5/6 might permanently advance to stage 6 after such an experience. CN is now tangibly present, but at the low end of the transpersonal spectrum, CN-nat (Gowan, 1975). Since ERep is still present, the experience is usually not of all-consuming intensity either. Again, this may vary; in the case of Walt Whitman, quite powerful CN-nat, or even CN-arch/spir was, perhaps, an ingredient in his nature mysticism and poetry (Bucke, 1901/1969).

Visionary, archetypal, shamanic, and near-death states still retain vestiges of subtle dualism. ERep-M and ERep-I remain, although ERep-M may now seem superfluous and the boundaries of ERep-I may become highly permeable and fluid. One is still an individual, but *who* one is has altered (Tart, 1975). The fate of EPro is less definite. Certain functions, useful in ordinary experience, may be temporarily lost or suspended; others

Table 1.2

Application of the Three-Factor Model to Transpersonal States

State	ERep-M	ERep-I	EPro	CN
Peak experience (Extraverted mysticism)	weak, may be temporarily suspended	dimly present	probably enhanced, possibly to *EPro*; possible advancement to state 6	CN-nat usually, but may involve higher levels of CN
Visionary experience	superfluous, if present at all	permeable, fluid, but still subtly present	some lower functions may be temporarily suspended; *EPro*; higher processes, unitary concepts, etc.	CN-arch, often intense; possibly permanent CN as a result; CN* explorations often claimed
Inflation	similar to visionary experience except that CN-arch is usurped by ERep-M			
Theistic mysticism	similar to visionary experience except CN more likely to be at upper regions of CN-arch or beginnings of CN-spir; insight may occur spontaneously			
Enlightenment	nonexistent, or seen as illusory; both ERep-M and ERep-I deconstructed		*EPro* at its most advanced; strong synthesizing capacity	CN-spir; CN* unclear—more likely in esoteric than in meditative traditions
Salvation	remains; being member of spiritual elite part of self-concept; projection used as defense	unchanged	stage: typically not high, 4 or lower; processes: rigid, dualistic, absolutistic	may occur; if present, usually CN-lib, alone or mixed with higher levels; meaning of CN distorted

may be enhanced (Tart, 1975). On the other hand, during an NDE, EPro may be temporarily enhanced to *EPro* as a result of the sudden, intense CN-arch. Furthermore, the long-term aftereffects of an NDE on a previously "normal" person can be dramatic, with modifications in ERep-M, ERep-I, and probably EPro. Permanently enhanced CN may even result (Ring, 1984).

Kornfield (1989) describes what can happen if CN is contaminated by ERep-M. The resulting usurpation of the powers of the numinous by the ego is called "inflation" by Jungians (Rosenthal, 1987) or "corruptions of insight" in Buddhism (Kornfield, 1989). In a sense, inflation may be seen as a pathological variant of the visionary states described above.[17] Because of the risk of inflation by the still (if subtly) present ERep, virtually all traditions caution students to avoid attachment to visions, insights, psychic powers, and so forth. Instead, they are encouraged to press on with meditation until ERep has decreased in potency.

Theistic mysticism presents a pattern similar to that of the visionary, except that ERep becomes increasingly weaker as one becomes more and more unified with the Absolute (Wilber, 1980), EPro progressively more likely to advance to *EPro* (Stage 6), and CN more likely to be at the higher levels of CN-arch or even the lower levels of CN-spir (Gowan, 1975). *EPro* may occur spontaneously, as one's separate self (ERep) is seen as increasingly unimportant and illusory. Autonomy yields to "theonomy" (Keen, 1983).

Finally, complete nondual enlightenment would look as follows: ERep-M would either no longer exist, or, if that is not possible, would be seen (via *EPro*) as so illusory that it no longer held any potency. One would no longer be "attached" to the ego and its cravings, in Buddhist terminology (Kornfield, 1989). ERep-I, the sense of oneself as separate, would have been deconstructed along with other unnecessary concepts about one's socially constructed "reality" (Brown, 1986).[18] The Buddhist axioms of *anatta* and *anicca* (impermanence of self and external objects, respectively) speak definitively to this point.

Although the representative component of the ego has been eliminated or at least drastically reduced, the necessary egoic functions are still operative (Epstein, 1988). In fact, EPro is presumably at its maximum (*EPro*):

> Advanced stages of insight meditation involve profound experiences of dissolution and fragmentation, yet the practitioner . . . is able to withstand these psychic pressures. It is the ego, primarily through its synthetic function, that permits integration of the experience of disintegration. In true egolessness, there could be only disintegration, and such a state would manifest as psychosis. (Epstein, 1988, p. 67)

With ERep eliminated, the person is integrated with the numinous or Absolute (CN-spir).[19] The issue of CN* is less than clear. CN* seems to be ignored or deemed irrelevant in the quest for enlightenment, being more emphasized in esoteric traditions (Faivre, 1987). If CN* and ensuing "higher cognition" (McDermott, 1989) are absent in mystical but not in esoteric states, McDermott's previously noted contention that "mysticism should be seen as the penultimate rather than the ultimate . . . attainment" (p. 33) seems plausible. The esoteric path is described below.

Finally, for purposes of comparison, the "salvation" offered by many elitist cults or "dualistic" (Anthony & Ecker, 1987) in-groups is most decidedly not enlightenment. ERep-M remains as prominent as ever, only the illusory belief that one is now a member of a spiritual elite has become a major component of one's self-concept. The defense of projection is frequently favored. ERep-I remains as it was. EPro has not advanced and is typically not high. Rigid, dualistic thinking is incompatible with postformal levels. Indeed, flexible, relativistic thinking is characteristic of postformal thought and experience (Cook-Greuter, 1990; Commons et al., 1984). CN may or may not occur. What is problematic is that even if some measure of CN has been experienced—and most likely it is CN-lib or a conflated mixture of CN-lib and CN-pers, with a tinge of the transpersonal—the less than ideal ego functioning is likely to distort the meaning of the experience. Anthony et al. (1987) have amply documented the catastrophes that have often followed in the wake of what they call dualistic/charismatic groups, e.g., Jonestown.

4. Transpersonal/Meditative Paths

Although thus far the model has been applied assuming essentially static conditions, it can also describe change and development. Historically, there have been numerous transpersonal paths and techniques for attaining transpersonal states, including dozens of varieties of meditation and contemplation (Goleman, 1977), prayer, movement, and related attentional techniques (Ouspensky, 1949). Some of the major categories will be examined briefly in light of the proposed model; for the sake of comparison, a number of (personal level) psychotherapies will be briefly included.

It should be noted that most traditional meditative techniques were not taught in isolation, but as part of an entire cultural/historical tradition (Katz, 1978). Most mystical schools insist on a preparatory phase (a *via purgativa*) in which one's personal life—thoughts, feelings, actions, moral decisions, and daily behaviors—is brought to a point at which the transpersonal training can truly begin. These preparatory techniques, which are maintained during meditative training as well, include the well-known

Table 1.3

Application of the Three-Factor Model to Transpersonal/Spiritual Paths

Path	ERep	EPro	CN
Kaballah	Preliminary requirements (age, marriage, exoteric mastery); *bittul hayesh*, purification prior to exploration of CN (stage of Awe)	Stage 4 minimally; enhanced through prayer, concentration, etc.; induction of *EPro*	CN-arch (stage of Love); later CN-spir (*devekuth*), or cleaving; CN* in some branches?
Vipassana (insight) meditation	Techniques of insight (*EPro*), deconstructs ERep in series of specifiable stages; two stages of preliminary and ascetic practices	Two stages to develop concentration, EPro, then two to develop insight *EPro*	Anaphatic theology says little of CN, except emptiness, Void, etc.; presumably CN-spir occurs as ERep is deconstructed
Concentration techniques: Yoga, Zen	Preliminary practices, moral purification, etc. Typical ERep preoccupations dispelled by concentration on mantra, koan, etc.	EPro enhanced, but insight not developed. Gradual or sudden (*satori*) emergence of *EPro*	CN-spir; CN-arch considered *makyo*, a subtle distraction
Gurdjieff (esoteric) traditions	ERep-M as illusory, but ERep-I remains. It must be transformed, harmonized. Permanent "I" as goal	Self-remembering to establish permanent "I"; disidentification from ERep-M; higher (esoteric) knowledge as goal	CN-lib rechanneled; CN-per/nat/arch enhanced; some traditions explore CN*; CN-spir possibly, but union is not primary goal
Psycho-therapy	Variable, ranging from modifying ERep-M alone, to integrating ERep with CN-lib/per, to reorganizing ERep around a higher Self (a positive symbol of CN-arch?)	Enhanced by techniques ranging from free association to body/mind integration to active imagination to disidentification to cognitive restructuring, etc. *EPro* unlikely	CN-lib derepressed; CN-per derepressed; in Jungian and other therapies, CN-arch becomes guiding focus; balance of personal and transpersonal; CN-spir very unlikely

Eightfold Path of Buddhism, the "abstentions and observances" (moral training) of Yoga, and the Kabbalistic requirement that the student, prior to initiation, has reached the age of forty, has met the ordinary challenges of daily life, including marriage, and has achieved mastery over the intellectual (exoteric) aspects of the tradition (P. Epstein, 1988). In terms of the model, one is first expected to "purify" ERep-M and to some extent ERep-I. A fairly high level of EPro (minimally stage 4 if not higher) is a prerequisite, and gaining control of one's instinctual/emotional life (CN-lib) is insisted upon as well.

The Kabbalah then charts three stages of development. Before exploration of the transpersonal (CN-nat, -arch, -spir) was permitted, the student was required to develop a sense of humility or *bittul hayesh* (literally "ego annihilation"). In other words, ERep must first be reduced significantly through various inner and outer practices. This stage is called the stage of Awe (P. Epstein, 1988), since as egotism diminishes, even mildly transpersonal CN (CN-nat?) is likely to evoke awe. Then, "With his soul sufficiently cleansed by the ethical and spiritual practices centered on awe, the mystic . . . is prepared to reflect a vision of the Absolute" (p. 34). This is not yet true union with God, but an intermediate visionary/archetypal stage, the stage of Love (CN-arch).[20] The highest stage of *devekuth,* or "cleaving" to God, undoubtedly involves minimal (or no?) ERep, highly developed *EPro*, and the presence of CN-spir. Some branches of Kabbalism appear to have explored CN* as well.

Vipassana (insight) meditation has been shown (Brown, 1986) to follow a somewhat similar six-stage path: two preliminary stages involving ascetic and preliminary practices, two stages of concentration, and two of insight. This path involves a progressive deconstruction of the components of the static ego, including eventually the sense of "I-ness."[21] More precisely, the model suggests that EPro is strengthened by the meditation, facilitating *EPro*, with *EPro* being cultivated as the means to deconstruct ERep-M and ERep-I. It is crucial to remember that the synthesizing capacity of consciousness (part of EPro) is actually enhanced, as ERep vanishes (M. Epstein, 1988).

Interestingly, CN receives scant direct mention by Buddhist influenced writers like D. Brown (1986) and M. Epstein (1988), although the implicit hypothesis is that, as the veil of ego is dispelled, CN-spir is all that remains. The student is steered away from any aspects of CN-arch that may appear (Wilber, 1980). Unfortunately, the anaphatic or "negative" theology of Buddhism and various other traditions can superficially obscure the numinous aspect for those more familiar with positive (cataphatic) traditions (Dupre, 1987).

Purely concentrative types of meditation focus attention away from its usual fixation on ERep and its objects. ERep presumably diminishes and

EPro is definitely enhanced, although *EPro* is not cultivated. It deserves mention that many writers (Goleman, 1977) consider concentration techniques preliminary to the more advanced methods of insight (*EPro*). The Zen koan is a concentrative technique (De Martino, 1963) that works by presenting the student with a nonlogical problem that demands a solution. Existentially, the koan is an analogue of "the exact frustration and despair known by the ego [ERep] in its natural quest to fulfill itself" (De Martino, 1963, p. 161). As the meditator focuses intently on the nonrational koan (e.g., the sound of one hand clapping), EPro, as process, is enhanced dramatically; attention is shifted away from ERep as the koan consumes all the student's energy. The hope is that there will occur a flip of consciousness (*satori*) to *EPro* and CN-spir, but apparently (Johnston, 1970) this can also lead to "Zen Madness," a little advertised form of psychosis! Other techniques, like Transcendental Meditation, appear to use a synthesis of concentration and insight more or less in tandem (Campbell, 1976; Alexander, Chapter 2 in this volume). The more devotional traditions, such as the mysticism of "love" or "image" (Dupre, 1987) focus on various aspects of CN directly, although EPro is undoubtedly enhanced in the process, and attention and energy are likewise being withdrawn from ERep.

Washburn (1988) believes that prayer is actually a form of meditation and that it can take either concentrative or receptive (insightful) forms. While both Eastern meditation and prayer "access the unconscious in the same way" (p. 145), Washburn feels that the submissive attitude of prayer is better suited to his bipolar model of consciousness:

> If it is true that the ego is inherently related to such a sovereign power [i.e., the Dynamic Ground], then it is fitting that the ego should meditate with an attitude of submission to this higher power—which is simply to say that the ego should meditate in the manner of prayer. (p. 145)

It is difficult to determine decisively, but ERep-I, very transformed via *EPro*, retains its presence in Washburn's final integrated stage, except possibly in rare moments of mystical illumination (CN-spir). Here the ego, paradoxically, is strong enough to surrender to absorption by the Dynamic Ground. Mystical illumination, however, cannot be willed by the ego; it is a "gift of grace" (p. 232).

In contrast to mystical traditions whose ultimate goal, regardless of technique, is complete transcendence of ERep and the nondualistic union of CN-spir, other techniques and therapies have somewhat different ends. In esoteric schools, such as Anthroposophy or the Gurdjieff tradition, in visionary and shamanic paths, ERep is not entirely eliminated. ERep-M may be drastically modified or rendered illusory, but ERep-I seems to remain or even be enhanced in an extraordinary manner. Gurdjieff's self-remembering technique was designed to establish a "permanent I," i.e., one capable of a degree of agency and continuity considerably beyond the normal. CN, especially CN-arch, is frequently cultivated in esoteric traditions, and often exploration of CN* is encouraged as well (Shepherd, 1954; Walsh 1989a, b). As noted above, the purposes of the esoteric traditions are to alter, not eliminate, one's sense of self and to seek knowledge of the higher realms rather than union per se.

Most forms of psychotherapy have less exalted aims. In Coan's (1977) terms, inner harmony and relatedness take precedence over transcendence. Many forms of therapy have the more modest goal of modifying ERep-M, so as to decrease defenses and/or enhance self-esteem and/or achieve congruence of self-concept with organismic processes (CN-lib/pers perhaps). Reichian therapy, in particular, emphasizes integrating the ego with CN-lib/pers, and possibly even CN-nat at peak moments (Baker, 1980). Frequently, although the major focus is on body/emotional awareness, spontaneous changes in ERep will occur. The Reichian literature is replete with reports of dramatically altered sense of self (ERep-I), and with spontaneous changes in, for example, political beliefs (ERep-M) (Baker, 1980). Jungian therapy includes work on all levels of CN except perhaps CN-spir, taking a special interest in CN-arch (Jung, 1964). The desired goal of analytic therapy is the integration of the personality around the archetype of the Self. ERep-I is not eliminated—Jung was adamant about this point (Jung, 1964; Kalff, 1983)—but balanced both internally, e.g., in terms of extraverted and introverted orientations, and more importantly with regard to its subservience to the higher Self archetype. Despite some obvious points of divergence, Jung's view does actually converge with Buddhism:

> Both attempt, each in their own way, to develop the notion of a relative ego, and both move away from a concept that sees it as an isolated, independent entity. . . . The Buddhists prefer a non-affirming negation of those aspects that are wrongly attributed to the mere "I.". . . By contrast Jung's approach concentrates more on the positive aspect of the negation of the ego. . . . Jung puts a positive symbol, namely the self, that emerges when the . . . wrong aspects of the ego have been given up. . . . Such an idea of the union of opposites excludes the notion of independent existence and emphasizes relativity and relationship. (Kalff, 1983, p. 122)

Psychosynthesis (Assagioli, 1965) somewhat similarly aims at a balance of personal and transpersonal integration, the lower self being guided by a gradually manifesting higher Self. The key technique (a form of *EPro*?) involves the process of disidentification from the stereotypical ideas, emotions, and habits that constitute much of the ego (ERep).

Conclusion

Not all of the controversies in transpersonal psychology have been resolved. Indeed, many were not even raised! However, this essay has attempted to accomplish two things: the careful analysis of a number of the more important areas of controversy, and, via the three-factor model, the clarification of precisely how and where different writers and schools disagree. Some claims that sound similar or identical turned out to be not so upon further scrutiny. Likewise, opposing views often turned out to have some underlying areas of convergence. It seems likely that arguments will continue to appear in print, but this is all to the good. While in its infancy transpersonal psychology required the posture of a united front, the field has now matured sufficiently to withstand the exposure of its many internal controversies.

Notes

1. More broadly, Walsh (1980) has summarized the characteristics of the ontology underlying transpersonal psychology and its related disciplines as "dynamic, fluid, impermanent, holistic, interconnected, interdependent, foundationless, self-consistent, empty, paradoxical, probabilistic, infinitely over-determined, and inextricably linked to the consciousness of the observer" (p. 225).

2. Coan (1977) takes a rather different approach altogether, accepting the legitimacy but not the unqualified supremacy of the transpersonal. Arguing for a multidimensional, as opposed to the more typically linear, unidimensional view of evolution and growth, Coan contends that transcendence is only one of many goals and not the sole index of development—relatedness, intrapsychic integration, creativity, and efficiency being other termini. In a sense, most transpersonalists, consciously or not, are endorsing a secularized version of "monotheism" (or at least a mono-teleology), while Coan holds out for a sort of "polytheism."

3. Somewhat along the same lines, philosopher of science Gerald Holton argues that one of Einstein's dominant themata was continuity, which "allowed" him to accept relativity, but not quantum theory, the latter being dependent on the opposing themata of discontinuity (Briggs, 1988).

4. Naranjo (1977) takes a similar view: "This is not to say that the spirituality attained through the pursuit of one path or the other is identical. . . . [W]e must also understand that the experience of the summit will differ in some respects according to the background of different climbers . . . for each has developed peculiar abilities during the long journey and will now receive the new impressions in a mind that has specialized in a certain way" (p. 87).

5. Assagioli (1965) takes a slightly different position, arguing that there are not really two independent selves, merely one Self which manifests differently depending on the level of self-realization. The lower self is thus a "reflection" (p. 20) of the higher.

6. Gowan's (1975) work, available for well over a decade, has been ignored by

most transpersonal psychologists. Originally, the author had intended to use Gowan's model in its entirety as the framework for this essay. Despite Gowan's originality and comprehensiveness, a number of theoretical problems arose which compelled instead a synthesis of several models. In addition to the vagueness about variability noted above, other problems include a likely misinterpretation (underestimation) of the ego level present in shamanism; a confusion over terms like "creativity," which appears at different classificatory levels in his schema; an overemphasis on the symbolic (if, by his own account, higher stages transcend symbolism, might we not need a "metataxic" stage beyond the syntaxic?); and possibly a residual mind-body dualism implicit in his downgrading of the somatic realm. Furthermore, Gowan's use of the "jhanas" to represent the highest stages of consciousness does not jibe with Brown's (1986) and Goleman's (1977) accounts of the stages of meditation, in which the jhanas (products of concentration meditation) are treated as preparatory to stages of insight meditation and not as ultimate.

7. Of the many stage models of development available (Commons et al., 1984), Cook-Greuter's (1990; this volume) will be routinely relied upon here. It is both sensitive to the nuances of ego development and capable of embracing the transpersonal level, at least in a general way. Furthermore, it includes affective as well as cognitive aspects of development.

8. Washburn's concept of the Dynamic Ground bears strong similarities to Assagioli's (1965) view of the unconscious. The latter distinguishes between the lower unconscious (libidinal, dreamlike, etc.), the middle unconscious (elaborations of thought, imagination, etc.), and the higher unconscious or superconscious (philosophical, artistic, ethical, spiritual). He also posits a noumenal Higher Self, which is contacted in transpersonal states. We will attempt to tease out these aspects of Washburn's Ground below.

9. One other multifactorial map that has undoubtedly influenced the model presented here is that of Clark (1983), whose major components include mood and various facets of attention. No attempt is made to integrate the two models, although this may be possible.

10. On a deeper level one also defends one's affirming-subject, ERep-I. In fact, as has been made abundantly clear by various transpersonal writers (Washburn & Stark, 1979), ERep-I is inherently defensive in nature, being essentially a form of self-contraction. In this model, however, the more widely explored defenses of psychoanalysis will be treated as part of the ERep-M system.

11. Koestler (1964) observes: "[Structure and function] are two aspects of a unitary process, not two processes. In fact both terms . . . are abstractions derived from imaginary cross-sections along the spatial or temporal axis of indivisible spatio-temporal events. Structure is a static concept of a process frozen in the specious present" (p. 416).

12. This multipartite division of the ego may help clarify certain linguistic problems. Thus a faulty (incongruent, unrealistic) ERep-M can lead to a state called "egotistical," in which the ego as reflected content is defective (grandiose self-image). Attachment to ERep-I leads to a condition transpersonalists call "ego-identified," in which the ego as one's context of existence is overly narrow or contracted no matter how normal or well adjusted the person is by conventional standards. Undeveloped EPro leads to that quality of cognition Piaget called

"egocentric," which denotes merely the failure of certain processes to develop, but which does not imply anything about the congruence of one's self-concept, etc. Ego as content, context, and process (Vaughan, 1980) and their corresponding problems are often confused. Finally, a deficiency of *EPro* could be termed "uninsightful." Similarly, Gurdjieff (Ouspensky, 1949) differentiated between one's essence (a blend of EPro and other factors not included in the model, such as one's genetic endowment, temperament, etc.), one's personality (ERep-I), and one's false ego (ERep-M). His technique of self-remembering undoubtedly enhanced *EPro*.

13. Keen (1983) aptly describes the integrated state: The moment the self arrives at the vision of unity of the cosmos, the eye (the I) that sees is dissolved into what is seen. At the top of the world we discover that it is an illusion to struggle to some point that is designated as the top of the world (p. 204). Rather, as Cook-Greuter's (1990) multivectored diagram reveals, "There is no single center where God dwells" (Keen, 1983, p. 204).

14. Undoubtedly one of the most difficult parameters of transpersonal psychology for the classically trained Western psychologist is the concept of "non-objective reality" (Grof, 1980), or what is here labeled CN*. Shamanic travels, NDE's, and other visionary states frequently entail, so it is claimed, awareness outside our normal reality framework. Grof cites as examples spiritistic experiences (see Van Dusen, 1979) and encounters with suprahuman entities or deities (e.g., the Being of Light frequently reported as part of the NDE).

15. Goleman (1980) lists the "primary mental factors" that emerge with enlightenment, which include insight, mindfulness, modesty, confidence, non-attachment, impartiality, nonaversion, buoyancy, and efficiency. In extreme form, these qualities are most assuredly not those of the "conditioned" (De Martino, 1963) ego-consciousness (ERep prominent), but reflect "unconditioned" consciousness (ERep transcended).

16. It is precisely the reasonably adequate functioning of EPro that allows the paranoid schizophrenic, as opposed to the disorganized subtype, to maintain a well-organized delusional scheme. To the extent that EPro is weak, disorganization is likely.

17. Wilber (1986b) has thoroughly analyzed some dozen metapathologies that can occur as a result of transpersonal practice and experience. Inflation is offered only as an example. Others include pseudo-nirvana, i.e., mistaking archetypal illumination for final nondual enlightenment, and the "dark night of the soul," a transpersonal depression occasioned by loss of CN after initial contact. Wilber emphasizes that this is distinct from psychotic, borderline, neurotic, and even existential depression.

18. Koplowitz (1984), for example, has shown how the concept of the permanent object, achieved during the sensorimotor period, becomes seen as a construct during the unitary stage of development.

19. There is an elaborate phenomenology of the substages of this process, too long for inclusion here. For example, the eighth of the ten oxherding pictures of Zen (Hixon, 1984) is entitled "Both Ox and Self Forgotten." This is a profound state of emptiness, in which the ego is absorbed into CN-Spir, such that "Here there is no one, not even the sage" (p. 136). There are two succeeding pictures, however, in which this emptiness opens to fullness, eliminating the final duality between the

enlightened state of pure consciousness and mundane life. This last picture is called "Entering the Marketplace with Helping Hands" and depicts a "jolly rustic" (p. 137) who wanders through everyday life, full of love and compassion. From this perspective, everything inner and outer is observed to be a manifestation of CN-spir, even ERep.

20. P. Epstein (1988) describes in some detail many of the varied techniques used, which involve imagery, concentration (*kavanna*), ecstatic song (*niggun*), breathing exercises, etc.

21. Specifically, the sequence of ego deconstruction is as follows: everyday attitude is altered first, followed by thinking, gross perception, sense of self, time/space, and "extraordinary interactions," i.e., subtle CN-arch/spir that still falls short of true enlightenment. (See Brown, 1986.)

References

Angyal, A. (1964). Disturbances of thinking in schizophrenia. In J. Kasanin (Ed.), *Language and thought in schizophrenia* (pp. 115–123). New York: Norton.

Anthony, D. & Ecker, B. (1987). The Anthony typology: A framework for assessing spiritual and consciousness groups. In D. Anthony, B. Ecker & K. Wilber (Eds.), *Spiritual choices* (pp. 35–105). New York: Paragon House.

Anthony, D.; Ecker, B. & Wilber, K. (Eds.) (1987). *Spiritual Choices*. New York: Paragon House.

Armstrong, T. (1985). *The radiant child*. Wheaton, IL: Theosophical Publishing House.

Assagioli, R. (1965). *Psychosynthesis: A manual of principles and techniques*. New York: Hobbs Dorman.

Baker, E. (1980). *Man in the trap*. New York: Collier.

Barron, F. X. (1969). *Creative person and creative process*. New York: Holt, Rinehart & Winston.

Becker, E. (1973). *The denial of death*. New York: Free Press.

Berger, P. & Luckmann, T. (1967). *The social construction of reality*. New York: Anchor Books.

Briggs, J. (1988). *Fire in the crucible: The alchemy of creative genius*. New York: Saint Martin's Press.

Brown, D. P. (1986). The stages of meditation in cross-cultural perspective. In K. Wilber; J. Engler & D. Brown (Eds.) *Transformations of consciousness* (pp. 219–283). Boston: Shambhala.

Bucke, R. M. (1969). *Cosmic consciousness*. New York: E. P. Dutton. Original work published 1901.

Campbell, A. (1976). *TM and the nature of enlightenment*. New York: Harper & Row.

Clark, J. (1983). *A map of mental states*. London: Routledge & Kegan Paul.

Coan, R. W. (1977). *Hero, artist, sage, or saint?* New York: Columbia University Press.

Commons, M. L.; Richards, F. A. & Armon, C. (Eds.) (1984). *Beyond formal operations: Late adolescent and adult cognitive development*. New York: Praeger.

Commons, M. L.; Sinnott, J. D.; Richards, F. A. & Armon, C. (Eds.) (1989). *Adult development: Comparisons and applications of developmental models,* 1. New York: Praeger.

Cook-Greuter, S. R. (1990). Maps for living: Ego development theory from symbiosis to conscious universal embeddedness. In M. L. Commons, C. Armon, L. Kohlberg, F. A. Richards, T. Grotzer & J. D. Sinnott

(Eds.), *Adult development, models and methods in the study of adolescent and adult thought,* 2 (pp. 79–104). New York: Praeger.
De Martino, R. (1963). The human situation and Zen Buddhism. In D. T. Suzuki, E. Fromm & R. De Martino (Eds.), *Zen Buddhism and psychoanalysis* (pp. 142–171). New York: Grove Press.
Dupre, L. (1987). Mysticism. In M. Eliade (Ed.), *The encyclopedia of religion* (vol. 10, pp. 245–261). New York: Macmillan.
Epstein, M. (1988). The deconstruction of the self: Ego and "egolessness" in Buddhist insight meditation. *Journal of Transpersonal Psychology* 20 (1): 61–69.
Epstein, M. (1989). Forms of emptiness: Psychodynamic, meditative, and clinical perspectives. *Journal of Transpersonal Psychology* 21 (1): 61–71.
Epstein, P. (1988). *Kabbalah: The way of the Jewish mystic.* Boston: Shambhala.
Faivre, A. (1987). Esotericism. In M. Eliade (Ed.), *The encyclopedia of religion* (vol. 5, pp. 156–163). New York: Macmillan.
Firman, J. & Vargiu, J. (1977). Dimensions of growth. *Synthesis,* 3–4: 60–120.
Fowler, J. (1981). *Stages of faith.* San Francisco: Harper & Row.
Freud, A. (1966). *The ego and the mechanisms of defense* (rev. ed.). New York: International Universities Press. Original work published 1936.
Funk, J. (1989). Postformal cognitive theory and developmental stages of musical composition. In M. Commons, J. Sinnott, F. Richards & C. Armon (Eds.), *Adult development: Comparisons and applications of developmental models,* 1 (pp. 3–30). New York: Praeger.
Gebser, J. (1986). *The everpresent origin.* Athens, OH: Ohio University Press.
Gimello, R. (1983). Mysticism in its contexts. In S. Katz (Ed.), *Mysticism and religious traditions* (pp. 61–88). New York: Oxford University Press.
Goldstein, K. (1964). Methodological approach to the study of schizophrenic thought disorder. In J. Kasanin (Ed.), *Language and thought in schizophrenia* (pp. 17–39). New York: Norton.
Goleman, D. (1977). *The varieties of the meditative experience.* New York: Harper & Row.
Goleman, D. (1980). Mental health in classical Buddhist psychology. In R. Walsh & F. Vaughan (Eds.), *Beyond ego: Transpersonal dimensions in psychology* (pp. 131–134). Los Angeles: J. P. Tarcher.
Gowan, J. C. (1975). *Trance, art, and creativity.* Buffalo: Creative Education Foundation.
Gowan, J. C. (1977). Creative inspiration in composers. *Journal of Creative Behavior* 11 (4): 249–255.

Grof, S. (1980). Realms of the human unconscious: Observations from LSD research. In R. Walsh & F. Vaughan (Eds.), *Beyond ego: Transpersonal dimensions in psychology* (pp. 87–99). Los Angeles: J. P. Tarcher.

Harding, D. (1963). *On having no head: A contribution to Zen in the West.* New York: Harper & Row.

Harman, W. & Rheingold, H. (1984). *Higher creativity.* Los Angeles: J. P. Tarcher.

Harter, S. (1983). Developmental perspectives on the self-system. In P. H. Mussen (Ed.), *Handbook of child psychology.* New York: Wiley.

Hixon, L. (1984). Ten seasons of enlightenment: Zen oxherding. In J. White (Ed.), *What is enlightenment?* (pp. 130–138). Los Angeles: J. P. Tarcher.

Horney, K. (1950). *Neurosis and human growth.* New York: Norton.

Huxley, A. (1944). *The perennial philosophy.* New York: Harper & Row.

James, W. (1950). *The principles of psychology.* New York: Dover. Original work published 1890.

Johnston, W. (1970). *The still point: Reflections on Zen and Christian mysticism.* New York: Fordham University Press.

Jung, C. G. (1964). *Man and his symbols.* Garden City, NY: Doubleday.

Kalff, M. (1983). The negation of ego in Tibetan Buddhism and Jungian psychology. *Journal of Transpersonal Psychology* 15 (2):, 103–124.

Katz, S. (Ed.) (1978). *Mysticism and philosophical analysis.* New York: Oxford University Press.

Keen, S. (1983). *The passionate life: Stages of loving.* San Francisco: Harper & Row.

Koestler, A. (1964). *The act of creation.* New York: Dell.

Koplowitz, H. (1984). A projection beyond Piaget's formal-operations stage: A general system stage and a unitary stage. In M. Commons, F. Richards & C. Armon (Eds.), *Beyond formal operations: Late adolescent and adult cognitive development* (pp. 272–295). New York: Praeger.

Kornfield, J. (1989). Obstacles and vicissitudes in spiritual practice. In S. Grof & C. Grof (Eds.), *Spiritual emergency: When personal transformation becomes a crisis* (pp. 137–169). Los Angeles: J. P. Tarcher.

Laing, R. D. (1965). *The divided self.* Baltimore: Penguin.

Laing, R. D. (1979). Transcendental experience in relation to religion and psychosis. In J. Fadiman & D. Kewman (Eds.), *Exploring madness: Experience, theory, and research* (2d ed.) (pp. 113–121). Monterey, CA: Brooks/Cole.

Lewinsohn, P.; Mischel, W.; Chaplin, W. & Barton, R. (1980). Social competence and depression: The role of illusory self-perceptions. *Journal of Abnormal Psychology* 89: 203–212.

Lukoff, D. (1985). The myths in mental illness. *Journal of Transpersonal*

Psychology 17 (2): 123–153.

McDermott, R. (1989). From mysticism to modern spiritual cognition. *ReVision* 12 (1): 29–33.

Marcoulesco, I. (1987). Mystical union. In M. Eliade (Ed.), *The encyclopedia of religion* (vol. 10, pp. 239–245). New York: Macmillan.

Maslow, A. H. (1970). *Motivation and personality* (2d ed.). New York: Harper & Row.

Maslow, A. H. (1971). *The farther reaches of human nature*. New York: Viking.

Naranjo, C. (1977). The way up and the way down: On meditation. In J. Staude (Ed.), *Consciousness and creativity* (pp. 85–93). Berkeley, CA: Pan/Proteus.

Ouspensky, P. (1949). *In search of the miraculous*. New York: Harcourt, Brace & World.

Perry, J. (1974). *The far side of madness*. Englewood Cliffs, NJ: Prentice-Hall.

Peters, L. (1989). Shamanism: Phenomenology of a spiritual discipline. *Journal of Transpersonal Psychology* 21 (2): 115–137.

Reich, W. (1976). *Character analysis*. New York: Pocket Books.

Ring, K. (1984). *Heading toward Omega: In search of the meaning of the near-death experience*. New York: William Morrow.

Ring, K. (1989). Near-death and UFO encounters as shamanic initiations: Some conceptual and evolutionary implications. *ReVision* 11 (3): 14–22.

Rogers, C. (1961). *On becoming a person*. Boston: Houghton Mifflin.

Rosenthal, G. (1987). Inflated by the Spirit. In D. Anthony, B. Ecker & K. Wilber (Eds.), *Spiritual choices* (pp. 305–319). New York: Paragon House.

Rothberg, D. (1989). Understanding mysticism: Transpersonal theory and the limits of contemporary epistomological frameworks. *ReVision* 12 (2): 5–21.

Russell, E. (1986). Consciousness and the unconscious: Eastern meditative and Western psychotherapeutic approaches. *Journal of Transpersonal Psychology* 18 (1): 51–72.

Schuon, F. (1984). *The transcendent unity of religions*. Wheaton, IL: Theosophical Publishing House.

Shapiro, D. (1989). Exploring our most deeply held belief about ultimate reality. *ReVision* 12 (1): 15–28.

Shepherd, A. (1954). *Rudolf Steiner: Scientist of the invisible*. Rochester, VT: Inner Traditions International.

Smith, H. (1976). *Forgotten truth: The primordial tradition*. New York: Harper & Row.

Stace, W. (1960). *Mysticism and philosophy*. London: Macmillan.

Sternberg, R. J. (Ed.) (1988). *The nature of creativity*. Cambridge:

Cambridge University Press.

Storr, A. (1972). *The dynamics of creation*. New York: Atheneum.

Tart, C. T. (1975). *States of consciousness*. New York: E. P. Dutton.

Tart, C. T. (1987). *Waking up: Overcoming the obstacles to human potential*. Boston: Shambhala.

Van Dusen, W. (1979). The presence of spirits in madness. In J. Fadiman & D. Kewman (Eds.), *Exploring madness: Experience, theory, and research* (2d ed.) (pp. 134–150). Monterey, CA: Brooks/Cole.

Vaughan, F. (1980). Transpersonal psychotherapy: Context, content, and process. In R. Walsh & F. Vaughan (Eds.), *Beyond ego: Transpersonal dimensions in psychology* (pp. 182–189). Los Angeles: J. P. Tarcher.

Vaughan, F. (1989). Characteristics of mysticism. *ReVision* 12 (2): 23.

Walsh, R. (1980). The possible emergence of cross-disciplinary parallels. In R. Walsh & F. Vaughan (Eds.), *Beyond ego: Transpersonal dimensions in psychology* (pp. 221–228). Los Angeles: J. P. Tarcher.

Walsh, R. (1989a). What is a shaman? Definition, origin and distribution. *Journal of Transpersonal Psychology* 21 (1): 1–11.

Walsh, R. (1989b). Shamanism and early human technology: The technology of transcendence. *ReVision* 12 (1): 34–40.

Washburn, M. (1988). *The ego and the dynamic ground: A transpersonal theory of human development*. Albany, NY: State University of New York Press.

Washburn, M. & Stark, M. (1979). Ego, egocentricity, and self-transcendence: A Western interpretation of Eastern teaching. In J. Welwood (Ed.), *The meeting of the ways: Explorations in East/West psychology* (pp. 74–86). New York: Schocken Books.

Wilber, K. (1977). *The spectrum of consciousness*. Wheaton, IL: Theosophical Publishing House.

Wilber, K. (1980). *The Atman project: A transpersonal view of human development*. Wheaton, IL: Theosophical Publishing House.

Wilber, K. (1981). *Up from Eden*. New York: Doubleday/Anchor.

Wilber, K. (1983). *A sociable God*. New York: McGraw-Hill.

Wilber, K. (1986a). The spectrum of development. In K. Wilber, J. Engler & D. Brown (Eds.), *Transformations of consciousness* (pp. 65–105). Boston: Shambhala.

Wilber, K. (1986b). The spectrum of psychopathology. In K. Wilber, J. Engler & D. Brown (Eds.), *Transformations of consciousness* (pp. 107–126). Boston: Shambhala.

Wilson, C. (1986). *G. I. Gurdjieff: The war against sleep*. Wellingborough, England: Aquarian Press.

PART II

Theory-Based Frameworks of Mature Development and Transcendence

Advanced Human Development in the Vedic Psychology of Maharishi Mahesh Yogi: Theory and Research

Charles N. Alexander, Dennis P. Heaton, and Howard M. Chandler
Maharishi International University

Throughout the history of both Western and Eastern thought, rare individuals have described transcendental experiences as the most meaningful events of their lives, often providing deep insight into fundamental truths. The treasured literature of various traditions records their testimony that such experiences can be the basis of personal fulfillment and societal well-being, e.g., Lao-tzu (Mair, 1990), Patanjali (1978), Plato (1961). The founder of American psychology, William James (1902), wrote a seminal volume which argued that such experiences have adaptive benefit for daily life. Despite the value attributed to these states, mainstream scientific psychology has made little progress in understanding these experiences and how they relate to psychological health and development.

Challenges in Studying Transcendental Experiences

This chapter addresses three reasons why transcendental experiences have been generally left outside the realm of scientific examination. The first challenge is that modern psychology has lacked a sufficiently comprehensive theoretical perspective to meaningfully interpret the nature, sequence, and utility of possible higher states of consciousness. James (1902) initially reported evidence of a "variety" of elevated experiences; but his work did not fully clarify which features were critical and universal, and how these features were organized or functionally fit together to characterize higher stages. Moreover, because the phenomena he investigated tended to be spontaneous and fleeting in nature, he was not yet in a position to understand how transcendental experiences can sequentially unfold over time to form permanent stable stages.

More recently, some Western psychologists have written about a state of transcendental experience beyond the generally understood endpoint of development; but they have tended to collapse into a single stage what may represent several distinctive stages of growth (Cook-Greuter, this volume; Kohlberg & Ryncarz, 1990; Fowler, 1981; Koplowitz, 1984; and Maslow, 1971; for a multistage model see Thomas, this volume).

A second difficulty for scientists has been that transcendental experiences have been found only in exceptional cases. They often occurred at unpredictable times and were momentary (Maslow, 1971). Thus these subjective states typically have not been amenable to scientific study because they could not be reliably reproduced in the laboratory, nor systematically developed in a sufficiently large pool of subjects to allow longitudinal research.

A third challenge to the study of higher states has been that such states are difficult to comprehend by those who have not yet experienced them. Even within the more familiar range of development, subjects at a particular cognitive or moral level cannot comprehend—though they may prefer—a level even one step beyond their own (e.g., Rest, et al., 1969). If they encounter descriptions of levels too far beyond their own, they are likely to dismiss such states as nonrational, uninterpretable, or as essentially "mystical."

The pioneering psychologists whose personal experiences disposed them to recognize the legitimacy of transcendental states have almost uniformly looked to ancient Eastern traditions as valuable sources of theories and techniques to facilitate such experiences (i.e., Fromm, 1960; James, 1902; Jung, 1969; and Maslow, 1971). For example, James (1902, p. 386) pointed particularly to the ancient Indian tradition of yoga as providing practices that cultivate transcendental experience. However, the theory and experience of higher states which Eastern traditions have purportedly provided have generally not been readily accessible. Differences in language and culture have made the literature of these traditions difficult to interpret. More importantly, over time, the techniques to cultivate higher states of consciousness, and hence the knowledge and experience of these states, have become distorted and sometimes entirely lost.

The Vedic tradition of India is regarded as the world's most ancient and extensive continuous account of such elevated experiences (Mair, 1990). Over the last 36 years, Maharishi Mahesh Yogi (1966, 1969, 1986), a contemporary custodian of this tradition, has re-enlivened the theory and techniques of Vedic knowledge and encouraged their investigation via modern scientific methods. We find that Maharishi's revival of this ancient knowledge in the form of his Vedic Psychology (Orme-Johnson, 1988) provides a platform for studying advanced human development which directly addresses the three challenges outlined above. In this chapter, Vedic Psychology always refers to this knowledge as brought to light by Maharishi.

First, Vedic Psychology addresses the need for a theoretical framework identifying the major features, functional organization, and developmental sequence of a series of potentially universally available higher states of consciousness. The applied aspect of Vedic Psychology addresses the second challenge—the need for reliable methods to promote transcendental experiences. Maharishi has now brought out 20 applied approaches for promoting human development (Wallace, 1993), of which the mental approach, comprising the Transcendental Meditation (TM) technique and the TM-Sidhi program (an advanced variant of the TM technique), is primary. Because TM requires no life-style changes and has been learned by more than four million individuals throughout the world, it has been the most widely researched meditation technique. Our own longitudinal study on advanced self-development, reported later in this chapter, was made possible due to the availability of long-term practitioners of this technique.[1]

Vedic Psychology maintains that its theoretical concepts can be subjectively confirmed through the progressive unfolding of one's own personal experience over time. Thus the third challenge—that of recognizing and understanding states of awareness that one has not experienced—can be addressed by utilizing these techniques to confirm the nature of higher states in the laboratory of the researcher's own awareness (see also Nuernberger, Chapter 4). However, until such experiences directly unfold, this third challenge can be partially addressed by means of conceptual bridges between theories about higher states of consciousness and contemporary psychological theories with which researchers may be more familiar. Such conceptual bridges allow investigators to extrapolate from sequences of development which they have already intellectually and experientially traversed to states that may lie beyond their immediate comprehension. A disadvantage of such conceptual bridges is that in presenting new ideas in the language of more conventional psychological models, their original meaning may be distorted or lost.

For this very reason we begin this chapter by presenting Maharishi's Vedic Psychology in its own terms. Then, the second section presents a conceptual model integrating ancient Vedic Psychology with current modern psychology. This model proposes that higher states of consciousness represent the natural continuation and dramatic extension of human development in adulthood. The final section presents striking empirical evidence supporting this theoretical proposition.

Seven States of Consciousness in
Maharishi's Vedic Psychology

The theory of human development in Vedic Psychology delineates seven major states of human consciousness (Maharishi, 1972; Orme-Johnson, 1988). Each state of consciousness is said to have distinct physiological correlates and to give rise to different forms of knowledge. The first three are familiar experiences of every individual and the last four are higher states. The seven states of consciousness (also identified by their Sanskrit names) are 1) sleeping (*shushupti chetna*); 2) dreaming (*swapn chetna*); 3) waking (*jagrat chetna*); 4) transcendental consciousness (*turya chetna*), involving temporary experience of an inner unified unbounded Self that completely transcends the boundaries or divisions between knower, known, and process of knowing; 5) cosmic consciousness (*turyateet chetna*), in which the inner unified Self is maintained along with but separate from the active levels of the mind and the changing reality of outer diversity; 6) refined or glorified cosmic consciousness (*bhagavad chetna*), characterized by refinement of perception and feeling, allowing profound intimacy between Self and environment; and ultimately, 7) unity consciousness (*Brahmi chetna*), involving the complete unification of inner and outer worlds, and with all levels of creation appreciated in terms of the unified Self.

Each of the higher states of consciousness is further described below and illustrated with experiences which were collected for this chapter from advanced TM practitioners who are students at our university (Maharishi International University). To support the theory that these states are universal developmental potentials, descriptions from Western authors are quoted which indicate spontaneous experiences of these states. Having them does not necessarily indicate that each subject is fully established in a higher state. The mind can temporarily access these states before the nervous system is sufficiently refined and flexible to sustain them permanently because the capacity to experience all the higher states is said to be inherent.

Transcendental Consciousness: Unity of Knower, Knowing, and Known

Vedic Psychology compares the mind to an ocean (Maharishi, 1969, pp. 470–471, cf. p. 338). An ocean has localized or bounded waves of activity on the surface, which are the expression of an underlying silent depth. Waking state is the experience of diverse bounded waves of mental activity without realization of the underlying unbounded and unified basis of the mind as transcendental consciousness or silent inner Being.

The characteristic of all experience in the waking state is that the

WAKING CONSCIOUSNESS

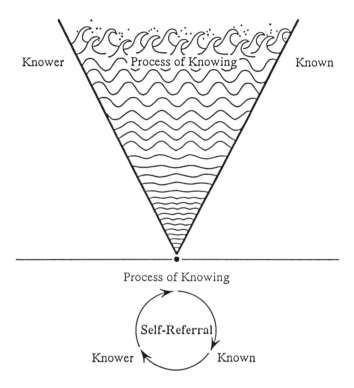

Process of Knowing

Knower   Known

TRANSCENDENTAL CONSCIOUSNESS

Figure 2.1. Knower, Process of Knowing, and Known in the States of Waking Consciousness and Transcendental Consciousness

self, or knower, is experienced as localized in time and space, and separated from the known by active processes of knowing—perceptions, thoughts, and feelings—which filter or qualify one's experience of self and world. This state is represented as the top part of Figure 2.1. A fundamental limitation of the waking state is that the subject of experience is never able to directly know itself; instead, knowledge of the self, like knowledge of any other object, is mediated by these active processes of knowing which are in turn conditioned by all memories. All one actually knows is thoughts, perceptions, and feelings *about* oneself as an object (a process which Maharishi calls "object referral"), but one lacks immediate, direct experience of one's own inner Being as the "I" or subject of experience (a process which Maharishi calls "self-referral").

Maharishi (1966) further explains why awareness of simple Being is unavailable in the ordinary waking state:

> Experience shows that Being is the essential, basic nature of the mind. But since the mind ordinarily remains attuned to the senses, projecting outwards towards the manifested realms of creation, it misses or fails to appreciate its own essential nature, just as the eyes are unable to see themselves. Everything but the eyes themselves can be seen through the eyes. (p. 30)

To experience the mind's underlying unified nature it is necessary to reverse its usual engagement in active thought and projection into the outer world. Just as it is possible for waves to subside, leaving a still and silent ocean, so it is possible for the active, localized, and divided state of waking to settle down so that the underlying silent, unbounded, and unified basis of all mental activity can be directly experienced. On rare occasions this process can occur spontaneously; it can also be systematically produced using the TM technique:

> The Transcendental Meditation technique is an effortless procedure for allowing the excitations of the mind gradually to settle down until the least excited state of mind is reached. This is a state of inner wakefulness with no object or thought or perception, just pure consciousness aware of its own unbounded nature. It is wholeness, aware of itself, devoid of differences, beyond the division of subject and object—transcendental consciousness. (Maharishi, 1976, p. 123)

In the ordinary waking state, mental activity proceeds "horizontally" on the surface of the mind. The TM technique allows awareness to effortlessly settle in a "vertical" direction until the subtlest mental activity separating the subject from the object is transcended, and knower, known, and process of knowing become unified in one silent wholeness of awareness (see bottom of Figure 2.1). Maharishi (1969) describes this undivided wholeness of awareness as the absolute (unmanifest, unconditioned, and universal) Self in order to distinguish it from the relative (manifest, limited, and individual) self:

> Self has two connotations: lower self and higher Self. The lower self is that aspect of the personality which deals only with the relative aspect of existence. It comprises the mind that thinks, the intellect that decides, the ego that experiences. . . . The higher Self is that aspect of the personality which never changes, absolute Being, which is the very basis of the entire field of relativity, including the lower self. (p. 339)

The rediscovery of the silent Self is said to be blissful and fulfilling: "This is the glory of the nature of the Self. Having come back home, the traveller finds peace. . . . This state of self-sufficiency leaves one steadfast in oneself, fulfilled in eternal contentment" (Maharishi, 1969, p. 424).

The Mandukya Upanishad describes transcendental consciousness as *turiya*, meaning the fourth, in contrast to the three ordinary states of waking, dreaming, and deep sleep:

The first . . . whose sphere is the waking state, whose consciousness relates to things external . . . and who enjoys gross things. . . . The second . . . whose sphere is the dream state, whose consciousness is internal . . . and who enjoys subtle objects. That state [the third] is deep sleep where the sleeper does not desire any enjoyable thing and does not see any dream. . . . They consider the fourth to be that which is not conscious of the internal world [dreams], nor conscious of the external world [waking] . . . nor unconsciousness [sleep]; which is . . . unthinkable, indescribable . . . in which all phenomena cease; and which is unchanging, auspicious and non-dual. That is the Self, and that is to be known. (Gambhirananda, 1977, pp. 182–190, 205–206)

Just as waking, dreaming, and sleeping have their own psychophysiological correlates, research on the experience of transcendental consciousness during TM indicates it is a distinctive state of "restful alertness" that can be distinguished from the aroused alertness characteristic of waking and the more inert states of dreaming and deep sleep (for reviews see Wallace, 1993; Alexander, et al., 1987). Respiration rate, skin conductance level, and blood lactate are significantly lower during TM than during simply relaxing with eyes closed—indicating deep rest (Dillbeck & Orme-Johnson, 1987). Also in cross-sectional and longitudinal random-assignment experiments, an increase in frontal alpha EEG coherence was observed during TM compared to resting controls—indicating increased alertness (Gaylord, et al., 1989). Research specifically on experiences of transcendental consciousness during TM—signalled by subsequent button-press—correlated highly with both virtual respiratory suspension (indicating deep rest) and elevated alpha EEG coherence (e.g., Farrow & Hebert, 1982). Higher alpha EEG coherence is correlated with improved postmeditation behavior on measures of fluid intelligence, principled moral reasoning, concept formation, and creativity (suggesting enhanced alterness: Orme-Johnson & Haynes, 1981).

In the following account, a TM practitioner describes her experience of transcendental consciousness during meditation:

As my mind settles down to deeper and subtler levels of awareness, mental activity fades away leaving an infinitely expanded inner space filled with complete silence and peace. Faint thoughts may come and go but they cannot touch this silent unbounded field of Being; at this time I know that this is my true Self, who I really am, beyond all confines of time and space.

There are striking similarities between the preceding description and those reported by others at different times and places throughout Western history. One example is British social philosopher Edward Carpenter's (1921) vivid account of spontaneously transcending the thinking process of the "local self" to identify fully with the "deeper Self" within:

> The Man at last lets Thought go. . . . He leans back in silence on that inner being, and bars off for a time every thought, every movement of the mind, every impulse to action, or whatever in the faintest degree may stand between him and That; and so there comes to him a sense of absolute repose, a consciousness of immense and universal power, such as completely transforms the world for him. This true Ego—this Self above and beyond the separate Me—to know it one must, as I say, become identified with it; and that is ultimately the only way of knowing it. (pp. 228-230)

This quote from Carpenter, like the above passage taken from the Upanishads, highlights the transcendental nature of pure consciousness as beyond the grasp of the ordinary mind, and makes clear the importance of *experiencing* it by being one with it (rather than just intellectually conceiving of it).

Cosmic Consciousness: Witnessing Activity from the Silent Self

According to Vedic Psychology the fifth state of consciousness (cosmic consciousness) is gained when the fourth state (transcendental consciousness) is maintained as a continuous nonchanging level of awareness along with the changing experiences of waking, dreaming, and sleeping. Initially, transcendental consciousness is not sustained outside of meditation because the nervous system, restricted by accumulated stress, lacks the flexibility and refinement of functioning to maintain inner silence while engaged in dynamic activity. Deep rest is described as the most natural antidote to stress (Maharishi, 1972). Over time, repeated experience of the profound restfully alert state of transcendental consciousness is said to dissolve all deeply rooted stress and cultivate the style of nervous system functioning necessary to sustain experience of silent inner Being along with outward dynamic activity.

Maharishi also emphasizes the role of engaging in dynamic activity after TM practice for stabilizing cosmic consciousness. He likens alternating transcending during TM and activity during the day to the dyeing and fading of a cloth. First the cloth is dipped in dye, then the colored cloth is exposed to the sun and allowed to fade; the repetition of this dyeing and fading eventually leads to color that cannot fade (1969, pp. 312-313). In a similar way, repeated experience of transcendental consciousness followed by dynamic activity cultivates the nervous system to sustain transcendental consciousness: "When the mind becomes infused with Being, then no thought, word or act can take the mind out of Being. This is the state of cosmic consciousness" (Maharishi, 1969, p. 291).

Maharishi (1969, p. 339) describes cosmic consciousness as a state in which "the Self has separated itself completely from the field of activity" and stands as a peaceful inner observer or "silent witness" (1969, p. 98) to daily life. According to the Bhagavad-Gita, an individual in this state experiences an unshakable inner contentment and independence which is "beyond the pairs of opposites [e.g., pleasure or pain], free from envy, balanced in success and failure" (Maharishi, 1969, chapter 4, verse 20, p. 287, brackets added). In this unrestricted state of contentment the individual no longer acts out of want or narrow self-interest; instead, actions are now said to be naturally motivated by the need of time and to take place in a highly efficient and effortless manner (Maharishi, 1969, p. 151). A TM practitioner describes experiences indicative of cosmic consciousness:

> The inner silence and stability of this state is not overshadowed by anything. All experiences are registered only on the surface of the mind. Inside I dwell in the eternal, in the Self, remaining a witness to everything that is going on. It's an experience of permanent fulfillment, contentment and bliss. In this state I continue to act in the world, only instead of being guided by personal desires, I feel I am guided by the needs of nature. When one is fulfilling the needs of nature, all the details and requirements of individual existence are naturally taken care of.

Although rare, experiences indicating growth of cosmic consciousness have been reported throughout Western history. The early twentieth-century phenomenologist Edmund Husserl appears at times to have experienced pure consciousness as a "transcendental spectator" or witness to the ordinary activity of the individual ego:

> I reach the ultimate experiential and cognitive perspective thinkable. In it I become the disinterested spectator of my natural and worldly ego and its life. . . . The transcendental spectator . . . watches himself, and sees himself also as the previously world immersed ego. (Husserl, 1970, p. 15)

Husserl's description of the transcendental spectator watching his ordinary ego is similar to Carpenter's earlier description of this "true Ego" as being "above and beyond the separate me." Both accounts explicitly identify this experience as a most developed state in which the Self, pure consciousness, witnesses the ordinary functioning of the individual ego.

The fifth state of consciousness is also predicted to have unique physiological correlates:

In the state of cosmic consciousness two different levels of organization of the nervous system function simultaneously while maintaining their separate identities. By virtue of this anatomical separation of function, it becomes possible for transcendental consciousness to coexist with the waking state of consciousness and with the dreaming and sleeping states of consciousness. (Maharishi, 1969, p. 314)

Physiological indicators of increased ability to maintain the restful alertness of transcendental consciousness outside of meditation include: significantly lower resting baselines of spontaneous galvanic skin response, respiration rate, heart rate, and plasma lactate (Dillbeck & Orme-Johnson, 1987), and enhanced autonomic stability during mental tasks or in responses to stressors (Alexander, et al., in press; Orme-Johnson, 1973).

The most unambiguous indicator of cosmic consciousness is the ability to maintain silent inner wakefulness even during the inertia of deep sleep. Both surveys and longitudinal studies indicate that frequency of experiences of witnessing sleep increases with length of time practicing TM, and that these experiences are positively correlated with measures of self-actualization, creativity, fluid intelligence, and choice reaction time (e.g., Cranson, 1989; Orme-Johnson & Haynes, 1981). The following physiological research provides preliminary evidence of the coexistence of two opposite styles of activity in the nervous system during the witnessing of sleep. Advanced meditators who report witnessing during deep sleep show a distinct EEG pattern of theta and alpha spindles superimposed upon slow delta waves (usually characteristic of deep sleep) similar to those seen during transcendental consciousness in Transcendental Meditation. Fast Fourier transform analysis, comparing the sleep of these subjects to new meditators, found similar levels of EEG delta activity (indicating deep sleep). However, there was significantly greater EEG power in the alpha and theta ranges in the witnessing subjects. These results are interpreted as evidence of the growing capacity to maintain inner awareness during sleep (Mason, et al., 1990).

Refined Cosmic Consciousness: The Subtlest Value of Perception

In cosmic consciousness the differentiated Self appears as completely separate from everyone and everything else. The inner contentment and full Self-knowledge said to be available in this state provide the natural basis for gaining greater appreciation and knowledge of others (Maharishi, 1966, p. 217). In the growth of the sixth state of consciousness, perception and feeling become highly refined, allowing profound intimacy with the environment, naturally culminating in complete unification of Self and world in unity consciousness.

Refined or glorified cosmic consciousness is promoted by engaging in activities that cultivate the most refined feelings of service, reverence, and love (Maharishi, 1969, p. 315; 1972, p. 23:7). Maharishi (1972) explains that development of this state unfolds the ability to perceive increasingly refined levels of manifest creation until the subtlest level of creation is appreciated:

> When only the surface value of perception is open to our awareness, then the boundaries of the object are rigid and well-defined—the only qualities that are perceived are those which distinguish the object from the rest of the environment. However, when the unbounded awareness becomes established on the level of the conscious mind . . . then the perception naturally begins to appreciate deeper values of the object, until perception is so refined that the finest relative [aspect of the object] is capable of being spontaneously perceived on the gross, surface level. (23:6-7)

In cosmic consciousness the material world may still be viewed as essentially lifeless and inert. As one gains greater intimacy with creation, one begins to appreciate directly that "each layer of existence has its own nature, its own laws, or we could say, its own level of intelligence" (Maharishi, 1972, p. 23:6), and that the intelligence of the finest relative level, which is responsible for mediating the expression of all the more manifest levels of natural law, is almost infinite (Maharishi, 1969, p. 206). When perception becomes so refined that it is able to perceive the mechanics of creation at this finest level, there is a spontaneous upsurge of love and devotion for the harmony and grandeur of nature. Then only the slightest separation remains between the unboundedness of the Self and the boundaries of the objects known. This state of glorified cosmic consciousness is also called "God consciousness" because at this level the individual is filled with appreciation for both creation and its creator (however this may be conceived).

An advanced TM practitioner describes growth of refined cosmic consciousness in terms of refinement of perception and feeling:

> My perception of the environment has changed. I started to see and appreciate in all objects and events the subtlest fibers of creation which are vibrant with radiant light. It is very beautiful and brings me great bliss and joy. My attention has naturally turned to the author of this glorious creation, and I have begun to recognize the creator in everything. As I see the divine in everyone, all people have become very dear to me, and all interactions are filled with love and sweetness.

The twentieth-century English poet, Kathleen Raine (1975) describes a singular moment in which she also experienced refined perception of objects. She identifies a finer level of existence or "living" common to all forms:

There was also a hyacinth growing in an amethyst glass; I was sitting alone.
. . . All was stilled. I was looking at the hyacinth, and . . . I dared scarcely
to breathe, held in a kind of fine attention in which I could sense the very flow
of life in the cells. I was not perceiving the flower but living it. I was aware
of the life of the plant as a slow flow or circulation of a vital current of liquid
light of the utmost purity . . . of a spiritual not a material order . . . or of a
matter itself perceived as spirit . . . and as such inspired a sense of
immaculate holiness. Living form—that is how I can best name the essence or
soul of the plant. . . . Either everything is, in this sense, living, or nothing is.
(p. 119)

Unity Consciousness: Everything in Terms of the Self

In refined cosmic consciousness the finest relative level of objects of
perception is appreciated, but it is witnessed by the Self as different from
its own value. Thus, for growth of complete unification between Self and
environment, one last step of integration is required. The gap at the junction
point between the inner unbounded Self and objective expressions is bridged
in unity consciousness, when the object of perception is fully appreciated
in terms of the unbounded Self. In the state of unity consciousness, "the
Self, which held its identity as separate from all activity in the state of
cosmic consciousness, finds everything in itself" (Maharishi, 1969, p. 307).
Maharishi describes this highest state of consciousness as follows:

This seventh state of consciousness could very well be called the unified state
of consciousness because in that state, the ultimate value of the object, infinite
and unmanifest, is made lively when the conscious mind, being lively in the
unbounded value of awareness, falls on the object. The object is cognized in
terms of the pure subjective value of unbounded, unmanifest awareness. . . .
In this unified state of consciousness, the experiencer and the object of
experience have both been brought to the same level of infinite value and this
encompasses the entire phenomenon of perception and action as well. The gulf
between the knower and the object of his knowing has been bridged. . . . In
this state, the full value of knowledge has been gained, and we can finally
speak of complete knowledge. (1972, p. 23:9)

Even within unity consciousness, Maharishi's Vedic Psychology
describes phases of evolution. In the initial phase of unity consciousness,
only the primary object of perception is experienced in terms of the Self.
Gradually, secondary and tertiary objects of perception are appreciated in
terms of the Self, until eventually all of creation is realized to be nothing
other than the Self interacting with itself. This fully ripened state of unity
consciousness is called Brahman consciousness, which refers to the ultimate
wholeness or oneness of life (Maharishi, 1986). As expressed in the
Bhagavad-Gita, at this highest level, one "sees the Self in all beings, and

all beings in the Self" (Maharishi, 1969, chapter 6, verse 29, p. 441).

In the following report a TM meditator describes rising unity consciousness:

> In this state I experience my Self as observer, observed, and process of observation at the same time: there is only my Self relating to Itself. I see my Self in every object. The whole universe is experienced as just a vibration or fluctuation of my own consciousness. There is nowhere to go, nothing to look for, everything is inside. In activity, instead of being a channel of nature, I am nature itself, flowing within my Self, doing what is appropriate at each moment to maintain the balance of the universe.

Passages suggesting growth of unity consciousness can be found in historical writings. The nineteenth-century French novelist Gustave Flaubert apparently, on several occasions, had glimpses of unity consciousness in which the gap between knower and objects known was closed:

> It is true, often I have felt that something bigger than myself was fusing with my being. . . . It was like an immense harmony engulfing your soul with marvelous palpitations, and you felt in its plenitude an inexpressible comprehension of the unrevealed wholeness of things; the interval between you and the object, like an abyss closing, grew narrower and narrower, until the difference vanished, because you both were bathed in infinity; you penetrated each other equally, and a subtle current passed from you into matter while the life of the elements slowly pervaded you, rising like a sap; one degree more, and you would become nature, or nature becomes you. . . . Immortality, boundlessness, infinity, I have all that, I am that! (cited in Jephcott, 1972, p. 31)

A Conceptual Model Connecting Maharishi's Vedic Psychology and Contemporary Developmental Psychology

Thus far the nature and sequence of higher states of consciousness have been described solely in the language of Vedic Psychology. However, the question naturally arises, what is the relationship of these states to sequences of development described by contemporary psychology? Else-where we have related higher states of consciousness to various theories describing different dimensions of psychological development—including cognitive development (Alexander et al'., 1990); ego developemt or self-development (Alexander, 1982; Chandler, 1991); and self-actualization theory (Alexander, et al., 1991).

In this section we will draw connections to structural-developmental theories of cognitive and self-development. However, this is not to imply that higher states of consciousness are primarily cognitive in nature or that they unfold through the exact same structural-developmental dynamics conceived by such theorists as Piaget, Kohlberg, or Loevinger. In fact, the higher states of consciousness as described by Vedic Psychology involve not only cognitive development, but development of self, affect, perception, ethics, action, and most fundamentally a unified field of consciousness underlying all these dimensions of life. (Druker's chapter in this volume complements ours by covering ethical and affective aspects of higher states of consciousness in Vedic Psychology.)

Are the higher states described by Vedic Psychology particular to the ancient East and therefore of no practical relevance to the contemporary West? The conceptual model to be presented makes the claim that these higher states are neither Eastern nor Western, ancient nor modern, but instead represent a natural continuation and dramatic extension of human development as typically conceived in contemporary psychology. These states are described as "higher" in the language of Vedic Psychology; the current section will suggest why they may be also considered "higher" (or more developed) according to criteria devised by contemporary psychology.

Table 2.1 presents a conceptual model linking theories from Vedic Psychology to contemporary developmental psychology. The chart is divided into three bordered boxes to help distinguish:

   1) the terms and concepts of Vedic Psychology;
   2) the authors' proposed model to connect developmental psychology to Vedic Psychology and to expand the range of contemporary psychology; and
   3) theories of cognitive and ego development in contemporary psychology.

The central column of this figure ties together the familiar periods of development with the higher states of consciousness in terms of three major tiers of development: prerepresentation, representation, and postrepresentation (see also Alexander et al., 1990). During the prerepresentational period, especially during the first several months of life, a sensorimotor or action mode of knowing appears to be dominant. Following this, the child begins to develop symbolic or representational capacities which reorganize all experience. After reviewing the growing body of research in cognitive development, Flavell (1985, pp. 82–85) concluded that the single clear stagelike transition in childhood development takes place with the onset of symbolic or representation competencies. He suggests that subsequent symbolic development from early childhood through adolescence is more gradual and less qualitatively distinct. "Postformal" modes of knowing as typically conceived (Commons, et al., 1984) appear to involve increasingly abstract symbolic skills that complete the representational tier rather than involve momentous change on the order of the shift from action to thought in early childhood.

Table 2.1
**A Conceptual Model Connecting Vedic Psychology
and Contemporary Developmental Psychology**

MAHARISHI'S VEDIC PSYCHOLOGY Levels of the Mind	CONNECTING MODEL Developmental Tiers (Alexander et al., 1990)	DEVELOPMENTAL PSYCHOLOGY	
		Cognitive Development (Piaget, 1969)	Self-development (Loevinger, 1976)
senses ▶	Prerepresentation (sensorimotor mode of knowing)	▶ sensorimotor	Presocial *(undifferentiated individual self)*
desire ▶		preoperational ▶ *object permanence*	Impulsive
mind ▶		concrete operations ▶ *conservation of quantity*	Conformist *(conventional psychosocial self)*
	Representation (symbolic mode of knowing)		·····Self-aware····
intellect ▶		formal operations ▶ *conservation of motion*	Conscientious
			········ Individualistic ·······
feeling ▶		▶	Autonomous
ego ▶		postformal operations	▶ Integrated *(differentiated individual self)*
Higher States of Consciousness		**Proposed Milestones of Extended Development**	
transcendental consciousness (Self)			
cosmic consciousness ▶	Postrepresentation (self-referral mode of knowing)	▶ *permanence of subject (Self)*	*differentiation of universal Self*
refined cosmic consciousness ▶		*conservation of* ▶ *finest level of all objects*	*profound intimacy between Self and environment*
unity consciousness ▶		*conservation of* ▶ *underlying unity across all its manifestations*	*complete unification between Self and environment*

In contrast, the proposed developmental advance to postrepresentation appears to be at least as momentous as that from prerepresentation to representation, as described by Flavell. A primary constraint of the symbolic mode of knowing is that it does not permit direct self-knowledge (e.g., Russell, 1977). What distinguishes the postrepresentational tier is the experience of a new "self-referral" mode of knowing that allows consciousness to know itself directly as Being without conceptual mediation. Just as thought goes beyond the restrictions of gross sensorimotor activity and at the same time enables sensorimotor functioning to become automatic, this next major tier of development transcends from representational thought to a completely unrestricted level of silent pure consciousness and at the same time enables representational functioning to become effortless and highly effective.

The most fundamental cultural support for cognitive growth from the sensorimotor to the representational tier is informal and formal language learning and symbol use (Bruner, 1972). We propose that meditation— specifically the Transcendental Meditation technique—is as fundamental a technology for promoting development beyond the representational tier as language/symbol-use is for facilitating growth beyond the sensorimotor tier. Whereas language acquisition frees attention from the control of immediate sensory stimuli, a practice that facilitates transcending of representational thought frees attention from the habitual domination of symbolic representation.

Levels of the Mind and Development within Waking State

Maharishi's goal has been to reintroduce the knowledge and experience of higher states of consciousness; he has not primarily focused on describing possible subperiods of development within waking consciousness. Nevertheless, he has identified fundamental levels of the mind that function in both waking state (albeit in a less developed form) and the higher states of consciousness (Maharishi, 1969; Orme-Johnson, 1988).

The levels of mind are ordered from more concrete to more abstract functions: they include the senses, desire, mind, intellect, feeling, and ego. The senses of perception and organs of action (such as the mouth and hands) serve as the link between the individual mind and the environment. Desire motivates the flow of attention and connects the mind with the environment through the senses. The mind engages in thought and memory; it considers possibilities and relationships among mental contents. (In addition to indicating a specific mental level, mind is sometimes also used to refer to all the levels taken together.) The intellect functions to discriminate and make decisions regarding these contents of the mind. Delicate feelings and intuition connect the intellect to the ego and inform or guide the decision-making process. The ego is the active experiencer in individual life that synthesizes information gained through the other levels of mind.

As psychologists familiar with both Vedic and Western Psychology, we have constructed a model which proposes specific parallels between the degree of development of the levels of mind (left side of Table 2.1) and corresponding subperiods of development within the waking state as described in cognitive and self-development theories (right side of Table 2.1). The parallels proposed between cognitive development and ego development are based on Loevinger (1976). Maharishi (1978) has described a relationship between perception through deeper levels of the mind and more advanced ways of knowing which we believe to be consistent with this approach.

We propose that the functioning of conscious awareness through each progressively deeper intrinsic level of the mind may provide the corresponding foundation for each sequentially higher expression of cognitive and personality growth observed by developmental psychologists. Although the ultimate status of the knower or "I" is always pure consciousness (Maharishi, 1969), in the waking state of consciousness, awareness becomes localized or conditioned by the active processes of mind and corresponding structures of the nervous system. We suggest that the deepest level of mind through which awareness predominantly functions would determine an individual's current developmental subperiod in waking stage because the capacities available at this level would shape the individual's understanding of self and world in a fundamental way. As deeper levels of the mind open to conscious awareness, previously dominant ways of knowing would remain active, but would become subordinated to the next more abstract and comprehensive way of knowing. Although all levels of mind contribute to every thought and action, the subtlest levels functioning below the current threshold of conscious awareness would be less available for utilization and control.

Specific parallels are as follows. In the early months of life, when the mind and corresponding structures of the nervous system are least developed, we suggest that the awareness of the knower is primarily conditioned by and identified with (i.e., is unable to clearly differentiate from) the most concrete sensory and action level of functioning. (See also Figure I.1.) This style of functioning would underlie the sensorimotor period in cognitive development or presocial period of ego development. As the next deeper level of mind develops, the "I" becomes identified with or preoccupied by immediate desires. This corresponds to the preoperational period of simple representation, egocentrism, impulsive behavior, and preconventional morality. The comparative and relational activities of the thinking mind dominate during the next period, characterized by concrete operational thought, conventional morality, and a conforming self. The discriminative and reflective activities of the intellect permit more abstract and deductive thought during the formal operational period. At this stage one conscientiously adheres to a consistent intellectual construction of the world and oneself. Research has found that this level constitutes a functional threshold beyond which few individuals in this society, or any society, continue to develop.[2]

Based on this model, the unfolding of delicate feelings and intuition and the synthesizing capacity of the individual ego result in the period of "postformal" cognition believed to be characterized by greater integration of affect and cognition and increased creativity (Gilligan, et al., 1990). Actualization of these subtlest intrinsic levels of the individual mind would also correspond to development of Loevinger's autonomous and integrated ego stages, postconventional moral reasoning, and Maslow's (1971) self-actualization, which are achieved by approximately 1% of the population (Cook-Greuter chapter, this volume). According to Vedic Psychology, the natural basis for higher states of consciousness is provided when awareness transcends primary identification with any of the active levels of mind and becomes permanently established in transcendental consciousness at the source of thought.

Why would realization of even postconventional levels of growth (prior to higher states of consciousness) be so rarely achieved? Formal education focuses almost entirely on enhancing symbolic skills (reading, writing, and mathematics) to promote intellectual development within the representational domain. Students and adults are continuously involved in active mental processes (conditioned by previous internalized information) that mask the more delicate intrinsic functioning of feeling and individual ego. Moreover, accumulation of stress actions tends to hinder awareness from spontaneously settling to such deeper mental levels. According to Maharishi (1969, p. 422), experience of the "pure individuality of the 'I'" is only available when awareness is stationed at the subtlest possible level of mind immediately prior to the experience of complete transcendence. Thus a method for cultivating systematic transcendence and alleviating stress may be highly useful for experiencing the delicate intrinsic functioning of feelings and ego, as well as for ultimately nourishing them from their basis in Being.

Thus, our model suggests that in the process of gaining higher states of consciousness, the individual will unfold the developmental potentials associated with each deeper level of mind. However, this growth may not be as strictly linear, or lockstep, as it appears in Table 2.1. We do not mean to imply that experiences of transcendental consciousness and glimpses of higher states of consciousness are not possible before achievement of certain corresponding subperiods of development as conceived in contemporary psychology. According to Vedic Psychology, because all the fundamental structures or levels of mind are inherent, they can thus be experienced whenever awareness settles down to a sufficient degree. Research and experience have shown that during TM, pure consciousness (and consequent benefits) can sometimes be experienced rather quickly, irrespective of the initial developmental level of the practitioner.[3]

Meeting Criteria of Advanced Development

In the context of our connecting model, we will now consider whether higher states of consciousness, as conceived in Vedic Psychology, meet eight criteria for major qualitative advances proposed in developmental psychology.

1. *Momentous advance should be characterized by the development of entirely new modes of knowing (Flavell, 1985).* This criterion from developmental psychology parallels a similar principle of Vedic Psychology that knowledge is different in different states of consciousness (Maharishi, 1972, p. 9:3). The self-referral mode of transcendental consciousness, which forms the basis of higher states of consciousness, is clearly distinct from the mode of representational thought.

2. *This new mode should allow solution of problems inherent in the prior level of development (Kohlberg, 1969; Piaget, 1970).* Stabilization of transcendental consciousness in cosmic consciousness solves a fundamental problem of the representational tier—that the "I" of awareness cannot be directly known. A further problem of representational modes of knowing is that equilibration is never fully achieved—knowledge of objects can only be successively approximated through interaction with the outside world. Vedic Psychology describes that in unity consciousness the dynamics of natural law are uncovered within the structure of pure consciousness (Maharishi, 1986). In this state the Self is realized as identical with the universe, sharing the same inherent dynamic structure; no equilibration or adjustment is required when pure consciousness apprehends itself in this self-referral mode of knowing.

3. *In accordance with the orthogenetic principle (Werner, 1957; cf. Piaget, 1970), qualitative advances should involve increasing differentiation and hierarchical integration of cognitive structures.* In cosmic consciousness the Self is said to become fully differentiated from and hierarchically integrated with the activities of thinking, feeling, and even with the individual ego. Representational thought processes are not abandoned but now function as a subsystem within, rather than as the executor of, mental life. This process of differentiation and integration culminates in unity consciousness in which all the diversity of creation is found to be integrated on the level of the unity of the Self.

4. *Qualitative cognitive advances should be characterized by more "veridical," invariant knowledge of objective reality (Piaget, 1970).* Milestones of cognitive development in the representational tier (as described by Piaget and others) included appreciation of the permanence of objects (preoperational period); conservation of quantity (concrete operations); conservation of motion (formal operations). Further developmental milestones in the postrepresentational tier appear to include

appreciation of the permanence of the subject (the unchanging Self in cosmic consciousness); perception of the invariance (conservation) of the finest level of all objects (refined cosmic consciousness); and conservation of the underlying unity of existence across all of its subjective and objective manifestations (unity consciousness).

5. *Fundamental advances should involve major neurophysiological reorganization and maturation (Bower, 1987).* Research so far has examined major neurophysiological changes associated with the experience of transcendental consciousness and the stabilization of transcendental consciousness throughout daily life in cosmic consciousness.

6. *Advanced development should be associated with a range of changes indicating increasingly adaptive and effective thought and behavior and greater personal well-being (Maslow, 1971).* Anecdotal reports and correlative studies of spontaneous experiences of higher states (in non-TM subjects) indicate enhancement of living, as seen in increased creativity and self-actualization (Alexander & Boyer, 1989). Longitudinal studies on systematic transcendence through TM indicate these and other signs of enhanced effectiveness, including improved health, productivity, and satisfaction (see review by Alexander, 1993, and the research section below).

7. *In accordance with the principle of universality of stage (Kohlberg, 1969; Piaget, 1970), momentous advances and their functional benefits should be available across cultural, ethnic, and historical conditions.* This is suggested by anecdotal reports extolling higher state experiences across a wide range of cultural and historical conditions (e.g., Smith, 1976). Moreover, systematic transcendence through TM has been shown to produce consistent functional improvements in such diverse groups as inner-city youth, corporate executives, institutionalized elderly, prisoners, and drug abusers (see review, Alexander et al., 1991).

8. *Finally, in accordance with the principle of invariance of sequence (Kohlberg, 1969; Piaget, 1970), if higher states of consciousness represent the natural continuation of human development beyond rare postconventional levels of self-development, then subjects should routinely achieve these postconventional levels in the process of realizing higher states of consciousness.* Research supporting this hypothesis is presented in the next section.

Research on Advanced Self-development and the Transcendental Meditation and TM-Sidhi Program

The model we have presented depicts higher states of consciousness as natural extensions of the developmental continuum which has been mapped by contemporary psychology. We argue that developmental advances take place through the shifting of attention to deeper intrinsic levels of the mind and through the release of stress which blocks the expression of these inherent potentials. Vedic Psychology (Maharishi, 1972, lesson 13) describes TM as a technique which simultaneously promotes transcending and spontaneous purification of stress in the nervous system. It thus predicts that the practice of TM will promote advances throughout development. We therefore expect (in accordance with criterion eight, above) that post-conventional stages of self-development would become a commonplace achievement en route to fully realizing the universal Self in higher states of consciousness. In prior research relating practice of the TM technique to developmental advances, Alexander (1982) found that prison inmates with 20 months' TM experience scored a full step higher cross-sectionally on Loevinger's scale of self-development (Self-Aware vs. Conformist) than did nonmeditating inmates interested in learning TM or in other treatment programs. After 17 months, this initial TM group increased another step (to the Conscientious level), and a new group that learned TM after pretesting likewise increased one full step. Demographically similar controls wait-listed to learn TM and volunteers participating in other rehabilitation programs showed no longitudinal increases. Longitudinal studies have also reported accelerated development on Piagetian and information processing tasks among young children practicing a children's version of TM (Alexander et al., 1990).

Related research findings have indicated that the TM technique promotes changes in characteristics associated with postconventional stages of development (i.e., beyond the Conscientious level): including growth of self-actualization (Alexander, et al., 1991), field independence (Pelletier, 1974), advanced moral development (Nidich, et al., 1983), fluid intelligence (Cranson et. al., 1991), and creative thinking (Travis, 1979).

Longitudinal Ego Development through the TM Program

A ten-year longitudinal study of self-development (Chandler, 1991; Chandler, et al., in preparation) directly investigated the prediction that systematic transcendence through the TM program promotes postconventional stages of self-development in early adulthood. Loevinger's Sentence Completion Test (SCT: Loevinger, 1979), a projective test which is relatively nonfakable, was chosen for its construct validity and reliability as a measure of holistic self-development, inclusive of cognitive, affective, moral, and social growth (Loevinger, 1976; Loevinger et al., 1985).

Prior research suggests that significant change to postconventional stages in adult subjects is highly unlikely. Based on available longitudinal studies, Loevinger et al. (1985, p. 960) concluded: "If the foregoing studies justify a single general conclusion, it is that whatever the SCT measures is

relatively stable in adult life, approximately after high-school graduation."
Also in over 40 prior studies reporting the distribution of subjects across
developmental stages, only a few percent are found beyond the Conscientious stage.

Experimental subjects were drawn from Maharishi International
University (MIU) in Fairfield, Iowa, an arts and sciences university which
is accredited through the Ph.D. level, where TM is included as part of the
educational program. The control groups were from a leading midwestern
liberal arts university (LibArt), a major northeastern technical university
(Tech), and Utah State University at Logan (Utah). Subjects in all groups
were posttested on the SCT 10 to 12 years following their pretesting as
undergraduate students. The posttest samples from each college were
matched for age and sex and had been pretested within a few years of each
other.

Statistically controlling for initial differences between groups, the TM
sample increased significantly in self-development by .91 steps compared
to the control groups, $t(131) = 5.3, p < .000001$. The MIU and LibArt
groups had relatively high scores at pretest (Conscientious level). Previous
longitudinal studies had found that the scores of initially high-scoring
subjects do not increase and may decline (Loevinger et al., 1985).
Consistent with such findings, LibArt actually decreased significantly
compared to its pretest level, $t(33) = -3.1, p = .004$; in contrast, MIU
significantly increased, $t(33) = 3.4, p = .001$.

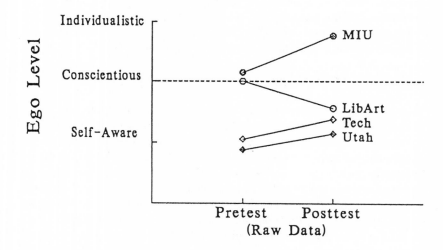

Figure 2.2. Mean Pretest and Mean Posttest Ego Development Scores
for Four Groups of University Alumni Showing Change over Ten Years

Figure 2.2 shows clearly that the mean score for the MIU alumni rose above the Conscientious threshold which has been observed in previous samples and in the control groups. At posttest, 53% of the MIU alumni scored above the Conscientious level; and 38% achieved fully postconventional Autonomous or Integrated levels (up from 9% at pretest), compared to 1% of control samples at both pretest and posttest. The proportion of MIU subjects achieving fully postconventional development is the highest observed among over 40 published studies. The highest previous proportion was 10% among Harvard alumni in their fifties. MIU subjects also increased in principled moral reasoning as measured by the Defining Issues Test (Rest, 1986) from a mean of 50.9% to 58.0%, $t(33)$ = 3.4, p = .001, one-tailed). At the same time, MIU subjects increased significantly in positive affect in interpersonal situations, as measured by the projective Thematic Apperception Test, from a mean of 3.4 to 5.12, $t(25)$ = 2.5, p = .01, one-tailed, where the cumulative adult norm is 3.5 (McAdams, 1984). These results support the hypothesis that the practice of the Transcendental Meditation technique over time promotes advanced self-development.

An alternative explanation might be proposed that MIU subjects would have grown to postconventional levels regardless of their TM practice. However, no other sample from self-selected social and/or academic communities encouraging personal growth has shown either similar longitudinal growth or remotely comparable levels of postconventional functioning (Haan & Stroud, 1973; Snarey & Blasi, 1980; Torbert, this volume; White, 1985). In fact, Rosen and Nordquist (1980) found no postconventional SCT scores among a group of self-selected yoga practitioners who were demographically similar to our MIU sample and who were long-term residents of a community where "the most important beliefs and values concern self-realization as the ultimate goal of human aspiration" (p. 1153). Moreover, Alexander's (1982) finding that meditating prisoners advanced one full step in self-development over a period of a year and a half indicates that TM is sufficient to promote self-development even in a population highly recalcitrant to change.

Our research on self-development did not test the comparative effectiveness of TM to other mental techniques. However, a comprehensive statistical meta-analysis of advanced self-development as measured by standardized questionnaires (complementary to Loevinger's projective measure) found that the longitudinal impact of TM on self-actualization was substantially larger than that produced by other relaxation and meditation techniques (Alexander, et al., 1991: based on 42 independent outcomes). Other meta-analyses on reduced trait anxiety (Eppley, et al., 1989: 146 independent outcomes), and drug rehabilitation (Alexander, et al., 1993) also found that TM's effect was significantly larger than that of other relaxation or meditation techniques taken together. This differential effect may be due to the effortlessness of TM practice compared to other techniques (see footnote 1). From the perspective of Vedic Psychology (Maharishi, 1972, p. 18:8) any individual effort hinders the experience of transcending and diminishes the realization of natural and balanced personal development.

Postconventional Self-development in Advanced TM Subjects

MIU subjects' self-development stages may actually have been underestimated in this research because the SCT appears to be less sensitive to detecting higher stages (Sutton & Swensen, 1983). Subjects capable of conceptually complex (i.e., higher-stage) responses often do not approach the test in an ego-syntonic way which reflects their true ego stage. Instead they give shorter, simpler responses that save time and mental energy but result in the appearance of a lower stage. To investigate whether advanced TM subjects may actually score at even higher levels of self-development than were estimated by the standard SCT for MIU alumni, we administered a modified version of the standard 18-item "short" form SCT (Loevinger, 1985) to a select group of 45 male, long-term practitioners of the Transcendental Meditation and TM-Sidhi program. The modified format increased space for responses (6 items per page instead of 18) and had instructions that encouraged subjects to "give the reader an idea of who you are and of what your inner experience is." Protocols were blind-scored by the same rater who scored our university samples. Under these modified conditions, 87% of the sample scored above the Conscientious level, with 22% Individualistic, 36% Autonomous, and 29% Integrated. By comparison, Torbert (this volume, using the standard format) reported that only 14% in two studies of senior managers and executives scored above the Conscientious stage. When debriefed about the research design, our expert rater expressed confidence that the modified format provided an accurate assessment of subjects' true stages. In another study where formats encouraging longer responses were scored for self-development, Sutton and Swensen (1983) similarly found that "[for high ego level subjects] the raters . . . consider the higher scores of the [alternative formats] to be more valid ego level estimates than the [standard] SCT scores" (p. 472). However, when these other samples were tested under modified formats and/or instructions, some similar to our own (Jurich & Holt, 1987; Sutton & Swensen, 1983), the highest group mean (for a select sample of retired university professors) was still one and a half levels below these TM subjects.

Some subjects who score at the highest level measured by the SCT might be at even more advanced stages of development than the instrument could measure. To examine how higher scores on the SCT are related to development of higher states of consciousness, our subjects were interviewed about their subjective experiences. We found that subjects who scored as postconventional on the SCT also tended to report more frequent experiences of pure consciousness coexisting with waking, dreaming, and sleeping. Indeed, many reported that these experiences had developmentally matured to a point where witnessing was quite stabilized. One man gave this report:

> The silence and peace of Being used to be pretty much confined to meditation. But it's more and more dominant now [outside TM]. It's just the silence of inner wakefulness. So alive and real. That Silence just witnesses the drama of life that my individuality acts in. And because I identify most deeply with the Silence [Self], I don't tend to get caught-up in the drama like I used to. So even while my individual ego is involved and dynamic and having ideas and making decisions, the sense of being transcendent to all that lets the whole thing become a sort of spontaneous flow. . . . There's so much happiness and contentment inside that I'm at ease and comfortable with whoever or whatever's outside.

This account illustrates the growth of characteristics of cosmic consciousness. For this man, witnessing from the silent Self is a nonrepresentational experience ("It's not that I think about it or make some mood") which allows truly nonattached, objective cognition ("I don't get caught up in the drama"). This subject's report is also consistent with Vedic Psychology's description of cosmic consciousness as a state in which outer joys and sorrows never overshadow the inner "bliss" of Being.

Similar characteristics of transition to cosmic consciousness were even evident in some responses to items on the SCT. Another subject gave the following response to the sentence stem "When I am criticized," which was scored at the Integrated stage:

> I use the criticism for what is useful in it, ignoring the rest. I also may find myself getting "caught" by the criticism—little ego threatened; in that case I usually recover evenness quickly by letting my attention be with the silence that is Me; on this level criticism is irrelevant because it was of my little self that, after all, is here today but changed by growth tomorrow, and gone when the body dies, like the characters in a play when the curtain closes. Through it all, I remain untouched.

This response appears to capture the shift in awareness from identification with the highest expressions of individual self-development to identification with the universal Self, the foundation of higher stages of consciousness. According to the parallels of development stages and levels of the mind outlined in Table 2.1, such a shift is the next predicted milestone markedly extending self-development beyond its ordinarily conceived endpoint.

In her chapter in this volume, Cook-Greuter describes her independent observation of extremely rare SCT responses that she believes express a transcendence of conceptual self-identity. She explains that this new Universal stage constitutes "a qualitatively different, higher cognitive integration of the self" beyond the Integrated stage described by Loevinger. After blindly scoring the self-development tests for our research, Cook-Greuter reported to us (personal communication) that there was a much higher concentration of such Universal responses among our subjects (using the modified SCT format) than in any prior sample.

We believe that results of the comparative longitudinal study of university alumni and the modified-format study of advanced practitioners strongly support the hypothesis that through the process of transcending during TM, development naturally continues beyond typically achieved limits. Our research suggests that in the process of realizing the transcendental or universal Self, the individual self also becomes fully actualized.

Conclusion

In this chapter we explored how the Vedic Psychology of Maharishi Mahesh Yogi addresses the challenges of scientifically investigating transcendental experiences. Vedic Psychology contributes a theoretical framework which describes the nature and sequential unfolding of higher states of consciousness and explains the dynamics through which advanced development can be facilitated. We then provided a connecting conceptual model to show how higher states of consciousness transcend the representational domain in a no more mystical way than representation transcends the domain of action, and suggested that these states met criteria for momentous advance posed by developmental psychology. To verify that these higher states extend the unfolding of inherent developmental potentials, we used Loevinger's measure to assess longitudinal self-development in adults practicing technologies of Vedic Psychology. An unprecedented proportion of these subjects scored at postconventional stages, and also reported growth toward the further advanced stages predicted by Vedic Psychology.

Maharishi's Vedic Psychology clearly has theoretical and practical implications which merit further investigation. Since the endpoint of any normative stage theory shapes the understanding of all development leading up to it (Kohlberg & Armon, 1984, p. 391), the concept of unity consciousness has fundamental implications for developmental theory which have not been previously explored. The evidence of technologies which can promote development to higher stages has equally fundamental practical implications, because the depth of knowledge, the effectiveness of action, and the character of collective life all depend upon the level of development of every member of society (Kohlberg, 1969; Torbert, 1991). Through the utilization of such technologies, it may be possible to have a society in which a majority are achieving self-actualization, or further still, are realizing higher states of consciousness once enjoyed by those exceptional individuals who historically blessed their cultures with lasting wisdom.

Notes

1. Maharishi explains that over the long course of time as precise knowledge of meditation was lost, techniques began to involve increasing mental effort in the form of concentration (controlling the mind) or contemplation (consideration of the meaning of thoughts). In contrast, he describes the Transcendental Meditation technique as a completely effortless mental procedure. It is learned through a standard course of seven steps, and is practiced 20 minutes twice a day sitting comfortably with eyes closed. An accumulated body of more than 500 research studies has shown that TM produces distinctive physiological, psychological, and sociological effects (Orme-Johnson & Farrow, 1977; Chalmers, et al., 1989).

2. Cognitive and self-development levels as interpreted in contemporary psychology do not necessarily fully correspond to unfolding of deeper mental levels in our connecting model. Piagetian formal operations are often defined in a rather restricted way in terms of the ability to perform well on certain scientific reasoning tasks (which may be rather culture-specific). We hold that the developmental unfolding of the intellect is indicated in a broader way by the kinds of cognitive advances that would distinguish a typical adult (in any culture) from a relatively young child, such as the capacity to reason more systematically, and organize resources to achieve goals. Similarly, we would broadly construe more advanced postformal operations in terms of growth of cognitive flexibility, creativity, and wisdom (rather than narrowly in terms of advanced hypothetico-deductive reasoning). The full capacity of any level of the mind, however, may not be available until all stress is neutralized and transcendental consciousness can be permanently maintained.

3. Because structural-developmentalists (e.g., Piaget, 1970; Kohlberg, 1969) theorize that fundamental cognitive structures are only gradually "constructed" through continuous interaction with the external physical world, they would be less likely to believe that such fluid movement between levels was possible.

Acknowledgments

The authors gratefully acknowledge the editorial assistance of Maxwell Rainforth, Janis Langstaff, Alex Heaton, and Eva Zimmerman.

References

Alexander, C. N. (1982). Ego development, personality and behavioral changes in inmates practicing the Transcendental Meditation technique or participating in other programs: A cross-sectional and longitudinal study. Doctoral dissertation, Harvard University. *Dissertation Abstracts International* 43 (2B): 539.

Alexander, C. N. (1993). Transcendental Meditation. In R. J. Corsini (Ed.), *Encyclopedia of psychology* (2d ed.). New York: Wiley Interscience.

Alexander, C. N. & Boyer, R. W. (1989). Seven states of consciousness: Unfolding the full potential of the cosmic psyche in individual life through Maharishi's Vedic Psychology. *Modern Science and Vedic Science* 2: 324–372.

Alexander, C. N.; Cranson, R. W.; Boyer, R. W. & Orme-Johnson, D. W. (1987). Transcendental consciousness: A fourth state of consciousness beyond sleep, dreaming and waking. In J. Gackenbach (Ed.), *Sourcebook on sleep and dreams* pp. 282–315. New York: Garland.

Alexander, C. N.; Davies, J. L.; Dixon, C.; Dillbeck, M. C.; Druker, S. M.; Oetzel, R.; Muehlman, J. M. & Orme-Johnson, D. W. (1990). Growth of higher stages of consciousness: Maharishi's Vedic Psychology of human development. In C. N. Alexander & E. J. Langer (Eds.), *Higher stages of human development: Perspectives on adult growth* pp. 286–341. New York: Oxford University Press.

Alexander, C. N.; Rainforth, M. V. & Gelderloos, P. (1991). Transcendental Meditation, self actualization, and psychological health: A conceptual overview and statistical meta-analysis. *Journal of Social Behavior and Personality* 6 (5): 189–247.

Alexander, C. N.; Robinson, M. P. & Rainforth, M. V. (1993). Treating and preventing alcohol, nicotine, and drug abuse through Transcendental Meditation: A review and statistical meta-analysis. *Alcoholism Treatment Quarterly* 11.

Alexander, C. N.; Swanson, G. C.; Rainforth, M. V.; Carlisle, T. W. & Todd, C. C. (in press). A prospective study on the Transcendental Meditation in two occupational settings: Effects on stress-reduction, health, and employee development. *Anxiety, Stress, and Coping: An International Journal.*

Bower, T. G. R. (1987). *Development in Infancy* (2d ed.). New York: W. H. Freeman.

Bruner, J. S. (1972). The nature and use of immaturity. *American Psychologist* 27: 687–701.

Carpenter, E. (1921). *The art of creation: Essays on the self and its power.*

London: Allen & Unwin.

Chalmers, R. A.; Clements, G.; Schenkluhn, H. & Weinless, M. (Eds.) (1989). *Scientific research on Maharishi's Transcendental Meditation and TM-Sidhi programme: Collected papers* (vols. 2–4). . Vlodrop, The Netherlands, MVU Press.

Chandler, H. M. (1991). Transcendental Meditation and awakening wisdom: A ten-year longitudinal study of self development. *Dissertation Abstracts International* 51 (10B): 5048.

Chandler, H. M.; Alexander, C. N. & Heaton, D. P. (in preparation). Transcendental Meditation and advanced self development: A ten-year longitudinal study.

Commons, M. L.; Richards, F. A. & Armon, C. (1984). *Beyond formal operations: Late adolescent and adult cognitive development.* New York: Praeger.

Cranson, R. W. (1989). Intelligence and the growth of intelligence in Maharishi's Vedic Psychology and twentieth-century psychology. Unpublished doctoral dissertation. Maharishi International University, Fairfield, IA.

Cranson, R. W.; Orme-Johnson, D. W.; Dillbeck, M. C.; Jones, C. H.; Alexander, C. N. & Gackenback, J. (1991). Transcendental Meditation and improved performance on intelligence-related measures: A longitudinal study. *Journal of Personality and Individual Differences* 12: 1105–1116.

Dillbeck, M. C. & Orme-Johnson, D. W. (1987). Physiological difference between Transcendental Meditation and rest. *American Psychologist* 42: 878–881.

Eppley, K.; Abrams, A. & Shear, J. (1989). Differential effects of relaxation techniques on trait anxiety: A meta-analysis. *Journal of Clinical Psychology* 45: 957–974.

Farrow, J. T. & Hebert, J. R. (1982). Breath suspension during the Transcendental Meditation technique. *Psychosomatic Medicine* 44 (2): 133–153.

Flavell, J. (1985). *Cognitive development* (2d ed.). Englewood Cliffs, NJ: Prentice-Hall.

Fowler, J. (1981). *Stages of faith: The psychology of human development and the quest for meaning.* New York: Harper & Row.

Fromm, E. (1960). Psychoanalysis and Zen Buddhism. In D. T. Suzuki, E. Fromm & R. De Martino, *Zen Buddhism and psychoanalysis* (pp. 77–141). London: Allen & Unwin.

Gambhirananda. (1977). *Eight Upanishads,* vol. 2. Calcutta: Advita Ashrama.

Gaylord, C.; Orme-Johnson, D. W. & Travis, F. (1989). The effects of the Transcendental Meditation technique and progessive muscle relaxation on EEG coherence, stress reactivity, and mental health in black adults. *International Journal of Neuroscience* 46: 77–87.

Gilligan, C.; Murphy, J. M. & Tappan, M. B. (1990). Moral development beyond adolescence. In C. N. Alexander & E. J. Langer (Eds.), *Higher stages of human development: Perspectives on adult growth*. New York: Oxford University Press.

Haan, N. & Stroud, J. (1973). Moral and ego stages in relationship to ego processes: A study of "hippies." *Journal of Personality* 41: 596–612.

Husserl, E. (1970). *The crisis of European sciences and transcendental phenomenology*. Evanston, IL: Northwestern University Press. Original work published 1954.

James, W. (1902). *The varieties of religious experience*. New York: Longmans, Green.

Jephcott, E. F. N. (1972). *Proust and Rilke: The literature of expanded consciousness*. New York: Barnes & Noble.

Jung, C. G. (1969). Psychology and religion: West and East. In H. Read, M. Fordham & G. Adler (Eds.), *The collected works of C. G. Jung* (vol. 11). Princeton, NJ: Princeton University Press.

Jurich, J. & Holt, R. R. (1987). Effects of modified instructions on the Washington University Sentence Completion Test of Ego Development. *Journal of Personality Assessment* 51: 186–193.

Kohlberg, L. (1969). Stage and sequence: The cognitive developmental approach to socialization. In D. A. Goslin (Ed.), *Handbook of socialization theory and research*. Chicago: Rand McNally.

Kohlberg, L. & Armon, C. (1984). Three types of stage models used in the study of adult development. In M. L. Commons, F. A. Richards & C. Armon (Eds.), *Beyond formal operations* (pp. 383–395). New York: Praeger.

Kohlberg, L. & Ryncarz, R. A. (1990). Beyond justice reasoning: Moral development and consideration of a seventh stage. In C. N. Alexander & E. J. Langer (Eds.), *Higher stages of human development: Perspectives on adult growth*. New York: Oxford University Press.

Koplowitz, H. (1984). A projection beyond Piaget's formal-operational stage: A general system stage and a unitary stage. In M. L. Commons, F. A. Richards & C. Armon (Eds.), *Beyond formal operations*. New York: Praeger.

Loevinger, J. (1976). *Ego development: Conceptions and theories*. San Francisco: Jossey-Bass.

Loevinger, J. (1979). Construct validity of the Sentence Completion Test of Ego Development. *Applied Psychological Measurement* 3: 281–311.

Loevinger, J. (1985). Revision of the Sentence Completion Test for Ego Development. *Journal of Personality and Social Psychology* 48: 420–427.

Loevinger, J.; Cohn, L. D.; Bonneville, L. P.; Redmore, C. D.; Streich, D. D. & Sargent, M. (1985). Ego development in college. *Journal of Personality and Social Psychology* 48: 947–962.

McAdams, D. P. (1984). Scoring manual for the intimacy motive. *Psychological Documents* 14, no. 2613.

Maharishi Mahesh Yogi (1966). *The science of being and art of living.* Los Angeles: International SRM.

Maharishi Mahesh Yogi (1969). *On the Bhagavad-Gita: A new translation and commentary.* Harmondsworth, Middlesex, England: Penguin.

Maharishi Mahesh Yogi (1972). *The science of creative intelligence.* Videotaped course manual. Fairfield, IA: Maharishi International University Press.

Maharishi Mahesh Yogi (1973). *Brahman consciousness.* Videotaped lecture, 16 January 1973, La Antilla, Spain.

Maharishi Mahesh Yogi (1976). *Creating an ideal society: A global undertaking.* Rheinweiler, Germany: MERU Press.

Maharishi Mahesh Yogi (1978). Internation Conference in EEG at Maharishi European Research University: Perception and cognition in higher states of consciousness: Maharishi's inaugural address. Videotaped lecture, 1 April 1978, Seelisberg, Switzerland.

Maharishi Mahesh Yogi (1986). *Life supported by natural law.* Washington, DC: Age of Enlightenment Press.

Mair, V. H. (1990). Afterword. In Lao-tzu, Tao Te Ching (V. H. Mair, Trans.) (pp. 119–161). New York: Bantam Books.

Maslow, A. (1971). *Farther reaches of human nature.* New York: Viking Press.

Mason, L.; Alexander, C. N.; Travis, F. T. & Gackenbach, J. (1990). EEG correlates of witnessing during sleep: A pilot study. *Lucidity Letter* 9 (2): 85–88.

Nidich, S. I.; Ryncarz, R.; Abrams, A.; Orme-Johnson, D. W. & Wallace, R. K. (1983). Kohlbergian cosmic perspective, EEG coherence, and the Transcendental Meditation and TM-Sidhi program. *Journal of Moral Education* 12: 166–173.

Orme-Johnson, D. W. (1973). Autonomic stability and Transcendental Meditation. *Psychosomatic Medicine* 35: 341–349.

Orme-Johnson, D. W. (1988). The cosmic psyche—an introduction to Maharishi's Vedic Psychology: The fulfillment of modern psychology. *Modern Science and Vedic Science* 2: 113–163.

Orme-Johnson, D. W. & Farrow, J. T. (Eds.) (1977). *Scientific research on Maharishi's Transcendental Meditation program: Collected papers* (vol 1). Rheinweiler, Germany: MERU Press.

Orme-Johnson, D.W. & Haynes, C.T. (1981). EEG phase coherence, pure consciousness, creativity, and T.M. Sidhi experiences. *International*

Journal of Neuroscience 13: 211–217.

Patanjali (1978). *Yoga Sutras* (R. Prasada, Trans.). New Delhi: Oriental Books Reprint Corporation.

Pelletier, K. R. (1974). Influence of Transcendental Meditation upon autokinetic perception. *Perceptual and Motor Skills* 39: 1031–1034.

Piaget, J. (1970). Piaget's theory. In P. H. Mussen (Ed.), *Carmichael's manual of childpsychology* (vol. l). New York: Wiley.

Plato. (1961). *The Collected Dialogues of Plato* (E. Hamilton & H. Cairns, Eds.). New York: Pantheon.

Raine, K. (1975). *The land unknown*. New York: Braziller.

Rest, J. R. (1986). *Moral development: Advances in research and theory*. New York: Praeger.

Rest, J. R.; Turiel, E. & Kolberg, L. (1969). Level of moral development as a determinant of preference and comprehension of moral judgement made by others. *Journal of Personality* 37: 225–252.

Rosen, A. & Nordquist, T. A. (1980). Ego development level and values in a yogic community. *Journal of Personality and Social Psychology* 39: 1152–1160.

Russell, B. (1977). *The problems of philosophy*. London: Oxford University Press.

Smith, H. (1976). *Forgotten Truth: The Primordial Tradition*. New York: Harper & Row.

Snarey, J. R. & Blasi, J. R. (1980). Ego development among adult kibbutzniks: A cross-cultural application of Loevinger's theory. *Genetic Psychology Monographs* 102: 117–157.

Sutton, P. M. & Swensen, C. H. (1983). The reliability and concurrent validity of alternative methods for assessing ego development. *Journal of Personality Assessment* 47: 468–475.

Torbert, W. R. (1991). *The power of balance*. Newbury Park, CA: Sage.

Travis, F. (1979). The TM technique and creativity: A longitudinal study of Cornell University undergraduates. *The Journal of Creative Behavior* 13: 169–180.

Wallace, R. K. (1993). *Physiology and consciousness*. Fairfield, IA: Maharishi International University Press.

Werner, H. (1957). The concept of development from a comparative and organismic point of view. In D. Harris (Ed.), *The concept of development* (pp. 125–148). Minneapolis: University of Minnesota Press.

White, M. S. (1985). Ego development in adult women. *Journal of Personality* 53: 561–574.

CHAPTER THREE

Cognitive Development and Transcendence: An Emerging Transpersonal Paradigm of Consciousness

L. Eugene Thomas
University of Connecticut

Psychologists as diverse as Jung (1933), Rank (1941), Maslow (1971), and Kohlberg (1990) have concluded that the highest levels of psychological development are nonegoic, and have characteristics commonly associated with advanced spiritual development ("a cosmic perspective . . . at which self and the universe seem unified," Kohlberg & Ryncarz, 1990, p. 206). Unlike Freud and other reductionists, they do not see these unitive states as being pathological or regressive, but rather see them as the logical continuation and extension of mature rationality.

A long philosophical tradition, from Hegel to Berdyaev and Teilhard de Chardin, has posited a similar type of development beyond the rational level (Wilber, 1982a). These approaches have been admittedly "speculative," dealing principally with ontological issues, and only indirectly referring to individual psychological development. In particular, they have not given attention to the "deep structures" by which the individual comes to know these larger dimensions of reality. Because of this, Kohlberg, although in sympathy with the position, labels this level of functioning (which he designates as the seventh stage of his model) as "metaphorical."

Wilber, in a series of publications over the past decade and a half (1977, 1979, 1980, 1981, 1982a, 1983, 1986, 1990), has attempted to extend the cognitive developmental model beyond the rational level by identifying the "deep structures" which underlie the higher or transpersonal levels of consciousness. In effect, he has attempted the ambitious task of integrating the "perennial philosophy" (Huxley, 1944) of the world's great philosophical and spiritual traditions with the cognitive-developmental perspective of

Western psychology.

Colleagues and I have found Wilber's model very useful and provocative in our analysis of the cross-cultural data of life history interviews with elderly respondents (Thomas et al., 1993). Western developmental theories, when applied to mature persons from other cultural traditions, come off as one-dimensional, and appear to miss important dimensions of lived reality (Thomas, 1991; Thomas, 1992). Wilber's theory has provided an alternate way of viewing these data that is sensitive both to spiritual dimensions of experience and cross-cultural differences in values and assumptions that are glossed over by much of our Western psychological theory.

As conceptually seminal as we have found Wilber's theory, we experienced difficulties with it when we tried to apply it to actual cases from our sample. Only after reworking his stage descriptions in terms of other developmental theorists, as well as returning to some of the original perennial philosophical sources, were we able to develop satisfactory coding procedures. This resulted in a clarification of Wilber's theory, and in some cases, modification of his stages, though the main thrust of his model has been retained.

In this paper I will examine the underlying assumptions of Wilber's model, highlighting the way it builds on and extends existing developmental psychological theories. I will then describe the modifications made to the model, particularly in seeking to explicate the deep structures underlying the transpersonal stages of consciousness. Finally, in evaluating the contribution that Wilber's theory makes to our understanding of life-span development, I will explore the possibility that this formulation represents a scientific paradigm shift, as formulated by Kuhn (1962).

Levels of Development: Content and Process

Wilber's model is based on the concept of hierarchical development of stages of consciousness through successively more integrative levels. As an overview he summarizes this development as "going from subconscious to selfconscious to superconscious, or prepersonal to personal to transpersonal" (1990, p. 119). He sees consciousness as being made up of a number of separate dimensions, including cognitive capacity, motivation, moral sense, interpersonal capacity, etc. These developmental lines can evolve somewhat independently, he suggests, but the developmental sequence is led by the cognitive dimension, hence putting his theory in close affinity with Kohlberg's (1981; 1983) cognitive-developmental model, in which levels of cognitive development are seen as necessary, but not sufficient for successive levels of moral judgment.

For Wilber each successive stage of consciousness is based on a "deep" cognitive structure, "which consists of all the basic principles embedded at that level" (1990, p. 40). This deep structure serves as a kind of paradigm through which the world is viewed. Wilber utilizes Piaget's levels of cognitive functioning in defining the structures of the lower level of the hierarchy. For the higher or transpersonal stages of development, Wilber turns to the perennial philosophy in identifying potential deep structure. As will be seen, Wilber only sketches these deep structures in brief outline, with the understanding that their full development remains a task for future scholarship.

The surface structure of each stage consists of the sense of self which develops from the deep structure. Stated more precisely, the potential for a self-system (made up of various dimensions, such as motivation, interpersonal capacity, etc., as noted above) exists when the new deep structure develops. But growth of these other dimensions may lag, since self or surface structures are learned and are culture-specific. The deep structures, on the other hand, are "remembered" (in the Platonic sense of anamnesis) and are universal in nature.

In addressing the issue of changes in levels of consciousness, it is necessary to note the distinction Wilber makes (again following Piaget) between "translation" and "transformation." Translation refers to changes in surface structure of a particular level of development. That is, the world is viewed within the same basic paradigm (or deep structure), but changes may be "assimilated" (to use Piaget's term) within one's self-system. Transformation occurs when there is a change in basic structures of consciousness (cf. Torbert's and Alexander's chapters in this volume for a further discussion of important implications of the assimilation and transformation concepts).

Kegan's (1982) developmental-constructive theory provides a useful illumination of Wilber's model. Kegan sees individual development as "an ongoing conversation between individuating organisms and the world" (1982, p. 44), in which there are periods of dynamic "meaning-making," i.e., the way of knowing the world is a dynamic balance. Each stage is the manifestation of a "distinct, separate reality, with a logic, consistency, and integrity of its own" (p. 28). There is, he suggests, a built-in tendency for the organism to maintain this balance by "digging in and defending against movement" (p. 266).

But Kegan's contribution is not, he insists, so much about static stages, as about the ongoing process of evolution of meaning. The end of each evolutionary truce involves a gestalt shift, a transformation in structure, which involves "the death of the old self that is about to be left behind" (p. 266). Like Kegan, Wilber suggests that in order to grow, the self must accept the "death" or negation of the lower self in order to move on to the next higher level. One remains at a given stage as long as "translation" is possible, "as long as Eros outweighs Thanatos" (Wilber, 1980, p. 307).

When translation is no longer possible, when "Thanatos outweighs Eros," only then does the organism move to the next level of development.

So great is the temptation to remain fixated at each level, Wilber maintains, that there are particular pathologies associated with each level of development (Wilber, 1986). At the lower level of development Wilber (1982b) identifies the Oedipus complex as the residue of inadequate transition from the emotional-sexual level to the mental level of consciousness. The "Apollo complex" is the term he uses for transition problems encountered between the mental-egoic and the beginning transpersonal level. Finally, the "Vishnu complex" is the pathology associated with transition from the low transpersonal to the high transpersonal level. Westerners are likely to experience the transition from the personal (mental-egoic) to the transpersonal level as being particularly difficult, he suggests, because this transition represents a move beyond the conventional level of culture, and hence beyond normal societal support structures. It is at this point, Washburn (1988) argues, that the individual experiences what mystics call the "dark night of the soul."

Higher Levels of Consciousness

Wilber, in seeking models for postrational levels of consciousness, draws on the Advaita Vedanta theory in identifying the major levels of consciousness. Thus he terms his postpersonal stages the "Subtle," "Causal," and "Ultimate," all taken from the Advaita Vedanta tradition. But he draws on other traditions of the perennial philosophy, particularly Buddhism, in seeking to make explicit the deep structures or "ways of knowing" that are implicit in the Advaita Vedanta model (cf. Wilber, 1982a).

As indicated earlier, when colleagues and I attempted to use Wilber's theory in coding cross-cultural interview protocols, we found his description of the higher-level deep structures too brief and vague to be of much use. We found it necessary to go back to the Vedantic model, as well as Western sources, in our attempt to flesh out his stage descriptions, particularly in coming to an understanding of the underlying deep structure.

Advaita Vedanta philosophy (Deutsch, 1969), following Shankara, posits three levels of consciousness beyond the rational, or waking state: the state of sleep in which there is dreaming; the state of dreamless sleep; and an ultimate state beyond dreamless sleep, *turyiva* or "fourth state."

Shankara's analysis of the waking state is remarkably close to that of present-day existential phenomenology. Waking consciousness is seen as intentional (i.e., it must have an object) and it is time-bound. Therefore we can only see things one at a time, and we do not see them in their totality. The self, which is attached to this waking consciousness, identifies with the physical body. In thus taking itself as an object among other objects, the self is estranged from its being. This concern with objects and seeking to find enjoyment from objects, prevents it from ever being satisfied and happy (an analysis of the human condition not unlike that made by Spinoza, the seventeenth-century Dutch philosopher [cf. Kohlberg & Ryncarz, 1990]).

Given this starting point, Shankara, surprisingly, turns to the dreaming state of sleep as the analogue for the next higher level of consciousness. In the dream state the individual "creates a subtle body of desire, and shapes his dreams according to the light of his own intellect" (Deutsch, 1969, p. 57). The quality of dreaming that is central for Shankara, however, is the degree of independence the subject experiences from its object—one is involved in one's dream, while at the same time being witness to it. One is thus enabled to "dis-identify" with the objects of one's consciousness to a certain extent.

The dream state is called "subtle" because it subtly influences subsequent waking life, and its contents are less gross than those of the waking state. The individual in the waking state is unable to be free from influences of the dream state, which means that it, like the dream state, is largely involuntary. Thus the dream state serves as an analogue to the true nature of the waking state, which is missed in waking state observation. *Avidya*, or ignorance, is thus pervasive in both states, though more easily seen in the dream state. In addition to this important teaching, the dream state illustrates the important concept that there is a continuity of consciousness underlying both the waking and the dream state, which, by implication, persists into higher states.

Dreamless sleep is taken as the third level of consciousness in the Advaita Vedanta system. Deep sleep consciousness is one in which the self is unified and integrated. This state serves as the ground for future action, hence it is called the "Causal" level of the self. Bliss is the characteristic quality of this state because in it there is a harmonization of desires and activity. It is also blissful because the self (*jiva*) is said to perceive ignorance (*avidya*), the cause of all distinctions for the first time at this level.

The highest level of consciousness does not lend itself to the sleep (or any) analogy, and is referred to in the Advaita Vedanta system as pure or transcendental consciousness, or *turiya* (literally, the "fourth" state or level). The attainment of this level of consciousness leads to self-realization and freedom (*moksha*). In this state there is complete nonduality, characterized as *savikalpa samadhi*, in which the self is aware of the presence of Reality only, and, in fact, the self passes into *Atman*.

In some ways the Vedanta sleep analogy might be considered a poor metaphor for describing the higher levels of consciousness. In everyday language we equate sleep with lack of consciousness and awareness. Hence we associate it with drowsiness and lack of attention, and say of someone who is unreflective that they are "sleepwalking." Buddhism, in the same vein, uses the image of awakening from sleep as the metaphor for enlightenment.

Perhaps the reason Shankara uses the sleep analogy is to indicate the process or "deep structure" underlying the higher levels of consciousness, particularly the arational qualities of what Wilber calls "vision logic." Buddhism, on the other hand, in using the awakened state as the analogy for higher levels of consciousness, focuses more on the surface qualities of the state. As will be indicated below, Bateson's formulation of the unconscious ascribes far more importance to nonrational states, and helps provide a firmer rationale for Shankara's typology. But first it is necessary to explore the issue of deep structures in greater detail, since this is crucial to Wilber's cognitive-developmental theory.

Vision Logic

Wilber is able to draw on Piaget's cognitive theory in identifying deep structures of the conventional levels of consciousness, but when he moves to the transpersonal levels he faces relatively uncharted territory. Although there has been recent work on developing models of postformal operations (Basseches, 1984; Commons et al., 1990; Sinnott, 1984), underlying deep structures comparable to Piaget's levels of cognitive functioning, the nature of these higher stages is far from clear. Therefore Wilber is able to sketch only in broad outline what the deep structures underlying transpersonal levels of consciousness are, and he has to leave the details to be worked out in the future.

The deep structure underlying the first transpersonal level, "vision logic," is of special importance to Wilber's model, since it is pivotal to the movement from the personal level of consciousness to the transpersonal level. Wilber gives more attention to this dimension than to subsequent deep structures, but even here the treatment is sketchy. Fortunately, the work of several other authors bear on the concept and can help flesh out the description Wilber has provided.

Briefly, Wilber sees vision logic as the next step beyond formal operations. Whereas in formal operations propositional statements are utilized ("if a, then b"), in vision logic networks of these propositional concepts can be apprehended simultaneously, rather than serially. This, Wilber concludes, is the beginning of a higher-order synthesizing capacity, "a system of truth-seeing at a single view" (1982a, p. 27). In describing vision logic further, Wilber quotes from the writing of the twentieth-century Indian mystic, Sri Aurobindo: "Its most characteristic movement is a mass ideation, a system of totality of truth-seeking at a single view; the relations of idea with idea, of truth with truth, self seen in the integral whole" (Wilber, 1982a, p. 27).

When my colleagues and I sought to clarify the nature of vision logic we found it instructive to return to the second level of consciousness in the Advaita Vedanta system, which is likened to the state of dreaming. Commenting on dream consciousness, Deutsch (1969) notes that it is "the state of fancy and wish-fulfillment" (p. 57). As indicated above, it appears odd that Shankara should liken a higher state of consciousness to that of dreaming, which today is thought of as being more primitive and magical. Gregory Bateson (1973), in an important paper on the universal quality of art, helps clarify this issue. He argues that our Western preference for linear rationality has obscured the importance of the arational (as distinct from irrational). Suggesting an image similar to vision logic, he paraphrases Pascal, "the reasons of the heart must be integrated with the reasons of the reason" (p. 235).

Bateson does not hesitate to use the term "primary process" as the means of this integration. In his use of this Freudian term, it should be noted that Bateson views the unconscious far more positively than did Freud. Rather than seeing the unconscious as containing mainly material that once was conscious but has been repressed, Bateson sees the unconscious as containing essential metarules and programming that enable the individual to operate with maximum efficiency, particularly in handling complex relationships. And the primary processes communicate this information in nonlinear, nontemporal pictures and images.

Wilber may have avoided Shankara's sleep analogy because he has been at pains to insist that transpersonal levels of consciousness are qualitatively different from prepersonal, more primitive functioning (the confusion of the two, he defines as the "pre-trans fallacy"). The young child can believe in magic ("an unrestrained and unrefined belief in action at a distance," 1983, p. 240) because he or she is unable to distinguish image from reality. Rather than representing a high level of holistic synthesis (vision logic), which in some ways it resembles, Wilber suggests that "magic does not unite subject and object; it fuses and confuses them" (1983, p. 240).

Although there is a danger that the prepersonal will be confused with the transpersonal, Bateson's approach seeks to rescue the concept of primary process from the primitive connotation it received from Freud. The primary processes described by Bateson are more like the waking state of synchronicity that Jung speaks of, in which one sees a meaningful coincidence of a psychic state (dream, vision, or premonition) and a physical state or event. Such events "have no causal relationship with one another," Jung suggests, "but seem to be connected primarily with activated archetypal processes in the unconscious" (1963, p. 400).

Nor is vision logic simply gut-level (i.e., emotional) intuition of the type exhibited by the young child. Bernadette Roberts, a contemporary mystic, has observed that as one enters the unitive state (her term for Wilber's transpersonal level of consciousness), the affective state is modified such that emotions are no longer the center of one's attention, and "clarity of the mind takes precedence, so that doing stems from knowing and seeing, not from feeling" (1985, p. 94). There evolves at that time what she calls a "non-conceptual way of knowing, of experiencing reality and truth" (p. 17), which is very similar to Wilber's vision logic. Roberts clarifies what she means by this way of knowing, pointing out that it "has no true counterpart in concepts, ideas, images, or even vocabulary" (p. 18). This corresponds to Wilber's position that the term used for this stage, *vision logic*, should not be taken to suggest that it refers to what is usually thought of by the word "logic," but rather that "this level is above language, logic and culture" (1980, p. 59).

Roberts makes a distinction between "below the neck" and "above the neck" experiences related to the unitive way of knowing. The "below experiences," she contends, have to do with a sense of presence, love, peace, and joy. These intuitions, or "supernatural infusions," do not arise from emotions, but if emotions enter in, they only dissipate the experience. Much of the work of the mystic is devoted to "below the neck" experiences, she believes, because this is the area most in need of transformation. When there is no longer work to be done at this level, there is a "radical change in consciousness" with a shift from "below" to "above the neck."

"Above the neck" experiences have to do with higher consciousness and the mental faculties. "Here," she states, "we encounter the cloud of unknowing, self-forgetfulness, and the true origin of ecstasy" (p. 19). Finally, there can be the coming together of the two types of experience, to give a holistic experience which can "take us out and beyond our self . . . to the unity of God" (p. 18). She continues, "When this dichotomy falls away, God is realized as pure subjectivity, closer than close, the Eye seeing Itself without reflection" (p. 23).

We will come back to these distinctions shortly when we examine the different levels of consciousness which these deep structures make possible. For the present purpose, it is sufficient to note that it is possible to broaden the concept of vision logic to include primary processes, without falling into the pre-trans fallacy; that is, the mistake of confusing the prepersonal, more primitive experiences of childhood (and pathological mental states) with advanced, transpersonal levels of functioning.

Stages of Consciousness

Moving from a consideration of underlying issues related to Wilber's theory, we will now consider the levels of consciousness posited by the theory. It should be noted that Wilber has made slight modifications in his designation of the stages of consciousness over the years. In his later work (cf. 1986) he has focused more on the deep structures of consciousness, utilizing a "tree" model of presentation. In this discussion we will focus more on the "self-system," or personality manifestations of the various hierarchical stages. For this purpose we will utilize the terminology of one of Wilber's earlier works (1982a), in which he focused particularly on the religious "self" implications of his structural-developmental model.

It should be noted that we diverge slightly from Wilber's designation of the Piagetian deep structures of the conventional stages at several points (as will be indicated below). And we diverge more substantively from Wilber's model in positing a final conventional stage, the Interindividual/Conjunctive, which is based on the work of Kegan (1982) and Fowler (1981). Finally, it should be pointed out that less time is spent describing the lower stages, simply because they are least likely to be represented in samples of normally functioning adults.

1. *Archaic.* Wilber uses this stage to encompass three lower levels of development: physical, sensoriperceptual, and emotional-sexual (1982a). Kegan (1982) fleshes out the self aspects of this level, pointing out that the individual's sense of self is seen through the lenses of one's impulses and perceptions, since the individual is limited in perspective by the deep structure of sensorimotor cognition. Both authors note the similarity of this stage to that of other developmental theorists: Kohlberg's Punishment and Obedience orientation, Loevinger's Impulsive stage, and Maslow's Physiological Satisfaction orientation. It should be noted that this level of consciousness would underlie Fowler's (1981) "Intuitive-Projective" stage of faith development as well.

2. *Magic.* The concepts the individual uses at this stage are magical because they "display condensation, displacement" (1983, p. 20). Wilber identifies the deep structure of this stage as preoperational, but we are inclined to agree with Kegan that it is based on concrete operations (although there may still be vestiges of preoperational cognition present). This stage corresponds closely with Kohlberg's second stage of Instrumental Hedonism, which Kohlberg sees as being based on concrete operations. At this level there is an absence of shared reality, an inability to take the role of others, and the individual is characterized by the absence of guilt or conscience (he may worry about potential consequences if he is found out, but does not experience guilt). One's identity at this stage is not differentiated from one's needs, interests, and wishes (Kegan, 1982).

Religion for persons at this level is likely to be primitive (magical) and superstitious. This stage would correspond with Fowler's "Mythic-Literal" stage of faith development, where religious stories and beliefs are taken literally and uncritically. It should be noted that Kegan's formulation diverges from Fowler's at this stage regarding role-taking ability. Fowler suggests that there is an increasing ability to take the role of the other at this stage, while Kegan holds that this ability doesn't develop until the next stage. Kegan's formulation seems more likely in view of the fact that individuals at this stage have not moved beyond concrete operations, and are not likely to be cognitively sophisticated enough to be aware of the role of others (hence the term Instrumental Hedonism in Kohlberg's model).

3. *Mythic-Membership.* This is the stage of conformity in which "there is no self independent of the context of 'other people liking me'" (Kegan, 1982, p. 96), because there is no self-coherent sense of "identity." At the personal level the question the person asks at this stage is "Do you still like me?" At the social level, the question would be "Am I still a member in good standing?" This is the stage of Kohlberg's Interpersonal Concordance orientation, Loevinger's Conformist stage, and Maslow's Love-Affection-Belongingness orientation. In terms of Kegan's object-relations formulation, issues of the interpersonal and mutuality become the lenses through which one views the world.

Wilber identifies the deep structure of this level as that of concrete operations, but we are inclined to agree with Kegan and place it higher, at the beginning of formal operations. In coding interview protocols, my colleagues and I were perplexed by individuals who were obviously conforming and group-membership oriented, but who were equally obviously not limited to concrete operational thought. Kegan's identification of his third stage with the lower level of formal operations allowed us to clear up coding difficulties we initially experienced. It is interesting to note that this designation fits with the formulations of other significant stage theorists (e.g., Kohlberg and Loevinger), who see persons at this level functioning beyond concrete operations. Overall, at this level we would expect the emotional dimension to be primary, whereas at the next level the rational would be primary.

In terms of religious behavior, persons at this level would see their primary identity in their religious group (with other groups, this might well take the form of patriotism or loyalty to some other primary group). Or the loyalty and identification could be with a charismatic leader. In any case, individuals at this stage would be conforming, conscientious, and duty-bound, whatever the group they identified with. It should be noted that Fowler's (1981) "Synthetic-Conventional" stage of faith, which extends a person's experience beyond the family, would correspond to Wilber's Mythic-Membership level.

4. *Rational.* Based on full formal operations, the individual is able to "think about thinking," and hence, this stage "is the first structure that is clearly self-reflexive and introspective" (Wilber, 1983, p. 20). This stage

corresponds to Kohlberg's Societal orientation of moral judgment and Loevinger's Conscientious stage. It corresponds to Erikson's stage of Identity/Diffusion in which ideology is a central focus. Kegan identifies this stage as the point of "Institutional Balance" in which the individual attains a sense of identity across situations, with authority (i.e., a sense of self, self-independence and self-ownership) as its hallmark. Emotional life is internally controlled; regulation, rather than mutuality, is ultimate.

This level corresponds to Fowler's "Individuative-Reflective" stage of faith development. When a person reaches this level he or she begins to differentiate themselves from previous group-shared values and beliefs. This is seen as a "demythologizing" period in which one's self-identity and world outlook are differentiated from those of others.

5. *Interindividual/Conjunctive.* Here we found it necessary to depart from Wilber's model, both in substance and terminology, in identifying the next level of development. In order to focus on the "self" (rather than the deep structure) aspect of the stage, we adopted Kegan's self-stage, "Interindividual" (coupled with Fowler's fifth stage of faith development, the "Conjunctive"). It should be noted that Kegan posits a deep structure of postformal operations as the basis of this stage, which corresponds, at least to a degree, with Wilber's beginning structure of "vision logic."

Kegan focuses on the self-characteristics that emerge at this stage, particularly issues of identity and ideology. Rather than being the foreground in defining who one is, as was the case at the previous stage, at this stage these self-characteristics recede into the background and become an object of reflection. No longer encased in one's ideology or "institution," the individual can envision community as "universal," in which all persons are eligible for membership. At the personal level, the individual is open to genuine intimacy for the first time, which springs from the ego's "capacity to be intimate with itself" (p. 106).

This level is, of course, similar to Erikson's level of Intimacy/Isolation (and probably Generativity/Stagnation). It corresponds to Kohlberg's Principled level of morality, Loevinger's Autonomy stage, and Maslow's level of Self-Actualization.

The name we assigned this stage indicates its affinity with Fowler's fifth stage of "Conjunctive" faith, in which the individual moves beyond dichotomized thinking to an awareness of interrelatedness. This involves integrating one's past into one's deeper self. Specifically, in terms of faith, there is a new openness to contradiction and an openness to new depths of inner and spiritual connection.

It should be noted that this is the last of the "conventional" stages of consciousness which correspond to the recognized stage models in Western psychology. Beyond this level it is necessary to turn to the religious and mystical traditions of the perennial philosophy for guidelines.

6. *Psychic.* Wilber sees this stage as providing a transition to the transpersonal level of consciousness. He notes that this stage has been characterized by the "third eye," which is said to include psychic events and "lower forces of mysticlike experiences" (1983, p. 92). Although paranormal experiences may occur at this stage, they are not seen as necessary. Wilber notes that the stage "is defined simply by its intensification of consciousness and the beginning of the opening of the eye of contemplation" (p. 92). It is at this point that an individual "begins to learn to very subtly inspect the mind's cognitive and perceptual capacities, and thus to that extent begins to transcend them" (1986, p. 72).

Wilber suggests that at its most panoramic, vision logic can enable the individual to experience intense insight, "that seems to go beyond thought into a type of vision, noetic, numinous, inspiring, often enstatic, occasionally ecstatic" (1982a, p. 29). This can result, he observes, in experiences of nature mysticism or "cosmic consciousness."

In seeking to further understand this first transpersonal stage, and in particular the deep structure on which it is based, i.e., vision logic, we turned to the Advaita Vedanta tradition and the analogy to dreaming in the sleeping state. Having distinguished this level from primitive magical thinking, utilizing Bateson's (1973) broadened definition of primary processes, the noncausal nature of "knowing" at this level seems quite similar to Jung's concept of acausal "synchronicity." It also resembles Bernadette Roberts's "unitive state," a "non-conceptual way of knowing, or experiencing reality and truth" (1985, p. 94). The Psychic stage would seem to correspond to her "below the neck" type of experience in which there was a bodily sense of presence.

In order to establish that a person had attainted this level of consciousness and the higher levels, there would have to be evidence that the individual had a fully developed sense of identity, was capable of intimacy and generativity, such that he or she would see themselves as part of the larger collective, as well as being able to relate to individuals in a caring and mature way. Beyond that, in order to qualify for the transpersonal level, there would have to be clear evidence of vision logic, i.e., of a sense of knowing beyond traditional logic. This might well be manifested in nature mysticism, or a firm awareness and knowledge of a higher-order working and moving in the world. We have found that people for whom this was true reported frequent experiences of synchronicity and sometimes paranormal experiences. If they had had paranormal experiences, however, they made it clear that they were not interested in trying to control events, as would be true at the Magical level, but simply acknowledged their presence with gratitude and wonder.

7. *Subtle.* The deep structure of this level is that of "archetypal form," and is marked by "transmental illumination, intuition and gnosis" (1983,

p. 92), and "symbolic visions." Wilber further describes this stage as being based on "a truly trans-rational structure . . . not emotionalism or merely felt meaning . . . or hunch" (1982a, p. 30). This description closely parallels Bernadette Roberts's experience of "above the neck" unitive consciousness, which follows a radical change in consciousness beyond the "below the neck experience." In this state, one's sense of consciousness moves from the body into the higher mental faculties, leading to illumination. Or to use Wilber's term, this is "intuition in its highest sense."

Wilber notes that people at this stage of development display transcendent insight and absorption, experiencing a sense of God's immanence beyond the more generalized mystical awareness at the psychic level. Wilber quotes Hixon concerning this state of mystical awareness: "Gradually we realize that the Divine Form or Presence is our archetype, an image of our own essential nature" (Wilber, 1983, p. 95). At that point, "The self dissolves into archetypal Deity" (p. 97). Persons at this stage are likely to be looked on as saints, and sought out by other people. Indeed, they might be thought of as charismatic in this sense.

It should be noted that the qualities of this and the previous stage are implied in Fowler's sixth stage, "Universalism." Fowler doesn't really describe the inner processes of this stage of development, but focuses more on the outward ethical behavior related to it, observing of persons at this stage that "they created zones of liberation from the social, political, economic and ideological shackles we place and endure on human futurity" (1981, p. 200). He never fully describes what it is about this "special group" that makes them "more lucid," "more simple," and "somehow more fully human than the rest of us" (p. 200).

Fowler's position perhaps reflects traditional Protestant suspicion of mysticism (as expressed, e.g., by Niebuhr [1951] and Tillich [1951]), in which "radical monotheism" allows little possibility for a sense of God's immanence. (Wilber observes, regarding this tradition, "God and man are forever divorced. . . . The only contact between God and man is by airmail: by covenant, pact, or promise" [1981, p. 3].) Wilber's theory, based on the broader "perennial" tradition, makes the mystical dimension central, of course.

The nonmystical, and hence nontranspersonal nature of Fowler's model is suggested by the fact that his faith stages correlate so highly with Kohlberg's stages of moral development as to be almost a tautology. For example, correlations of .75 have been found between the two sets of stages, which Kohlberg notes, "is almost as high as one would find between two alternative forms of the moral dilemma instrument" (1990, p. 203). Kohlberg further observes, "Fowler's broad definition of faith, which does not distinguish it from moral judgment, leads to confusions that make the study of the relationship of ontological development to morality difficult"

(p. 204). It seems equally clear that the lack of distinction of Fowler's faith stages from conventional cognitive development leads to confusion in the study of transpersonal levels of spiritual development as well.

8. *Causal.* Concerning this state, Wilber says it does not involve any particular experience, but rather "the dissolution or transcendence of the experiencer himself, the death of the watcher principle. That is, the subject-object duality is radically transcended" (1982a, p. 31). Or to put it in more traditional terms, this stage is characterized by nondualistic mysticism. In another context Wilber describes the Causal level in the following way: "This is total and utter transcendence and release into Formless Consciousness, Boundless Radiance. There is here no self, no God, no final-God, no subjects, no thingness, apart from or other than consciousness as Such" (1983, p. 97).

This description is remarkably similar to accounts given by the contemporary mystic Bernadette Roberts, who describes the final unitive state when the dichotomy of "below" and "above the neck" falls away as the time when "God is realized as pure subjectivity" (1985, p. 23).

The image of the still center as the source of outward action is another aspect of the Causal level (as suggested by the name given this level of consciousness). Thus Lao-tzu, the ancient Chinese philosopher whose writings reflect the Causal level of consciousness, observes, "The world is governed by no acts at all" (Bynner, 1944, p. 65). And more specifically, "Men knowing the way, do without acting" (p. 65). Individuals who realize this state of consciousness are known as sages, Wilber suggests.

Discussion and Conclusion

As has been illustrated in the preceding sections, Wilber's theory articulates well with cognitive-developmental theory and object-relations personality formulations, combining the two to suggest a conceptualization of advanced nonegoic states that is more than "metaphoric" (Kohlberg, 1990). Wilber's concept of vision logic, in particular, was found useful as providing the "deep structures" underlying the movement to these nonegoic transpersonal stages. This examination of Wilber's theory suggests that although at places it stands in need of further development (as he acknowledges), it displays enormous scope and comprehensiveness, and appears to have remarkable heuristic value for further conceptualization and research.

If one can take Wilber's theory as exhibiting qualities of a new paradigm, it well suits Kuhn's criterion of providing scientists "not only with a map but also with some of the directions essential for map-making" (Kuhn, 1962, p. 108). Paradigms, he suggests, are like lenses through which the world is viewed, and to adopt a new paradigm, to change metaphors slightly, is like being transported to another planet. The change from one paradigm is thus a kind of gestalt shift in which the same data is viewed in a new and different way, such that "after a revolution scientists are responding to a different world" (p. 110). (Cf. Miller, Chapter 6, for a discussion of world views—a structural concept which he uses in a manner similar to my use of the term "paradigm.")

In order for a new paradigm to be seriously considered, Kuhn suggests, it is necessary: 1) that it resolve outstanding problems that can be met in no other way; and 2) that it preserve a great deal of the past achievements of the discipline (p. 168). Novelty alone, though desirable in the creative arts, is not sufficient to establish a new paradigm.

It is far too early to make a judgment concerning the merits of Wilber's transpersonal theory at the present time. It literally will take years of work to begin to evaluate its implications. But an impartial reading of the present situation can give assurance that it meets Kuhn's second criterion. That is, it maintains and integrates a great deal of previous psychological theory (particularly of cognitive-developmental psychology). Whether the theory does in fact resolve outstanding problems that the normal science paradigm fails to handle is a more complicated question whose answer depends on the very paradigm that one accepts in making the decision. In other words, its answer depends on the paradigmatic lenses through which one views the world.

Viewed from a broader perspective, it may be that rather than constituting a scientific paradigm shift, Wilber's transpersonal theory is more in the nature of a cultural paradigm shift. Unlike scientific paradigmatic revolutions that were of concern only to specialists in the field (e.g., whether light is a wave or a particle), the transpersonal theory might well constitute a cultural paradigm shift, challenging broader cultural assumptions about reality. It may be more akin to the Copernican revolution in which laymen as well as specialists were called on to view the world through a new paradigm.

In any case, if Kuhn's documentation of previous scientific revolutions can serve as an indication of future experience, we may well have to wait for the final decision until we see the response of new professionals in the field. Kuhn uses the image of Darwin's "survival of the fittest" to suggest that, in the end, the more adequate paradigm will prevail. To put it more poetically, we can trust the outcome, remembering the adage that "truth is the daughter of time." With the benefit of historical perspective, perhaps the winnowing process can take place without the acrimony that so often accompanied earlier scientific revolutions and paradigm shifts.

86 *Chapter Three*

References

Basseches, M. A. (1984). Dialectical thinking as a metasystematic form of cognitive organization. In M. L. Commons; F.A. Richards & C. Armon (Eds.), *Beyond formal operations* (pp. 216–238). New York: Praeger.

Bateson, G. (1973). Style, grace and information in primitive art. In A. Forge (Ed.), *Primitive art and society* (pp. 128–152). Oxford: Oxford University Press.

Bynner, W. (Trans.) (1944). *The way of life according to Lao Tzu*. New York: Capricorn.

Commons, M. L.; Armon, C.; Kohlberg, L.; Richards, F. A.; Grotzer, T. A. & Sinnott, J. D. (Eds.) (1990). *Adult development,* vol. 2. New York: Praeger.

Deutsch, E. (1969). *Advaita Vedanta: A philosophical reconstruction.* Honolulu: East-West Center Press.

Fowler, J. (1981). *Faith stages: The psychology of human development and the quest for meaning.* New York: Harper & Row.

Huxley, A. (1944). *The perennial philosophy.* New York: Harper & Row.

Jung, C. G. (1933). *Modern man in search of a soul.* New York: Harcourt, Brace.

Jung, C. G. (1963). *Memories, dreams and reflections.* New York: Random House.

Kegan, R. (1982). *The evolving self.* Cambridge, MA: Harvard University Press.

Kohlberg, L. (1981). *Essays in moral development: The philosophy of moral development,* vol 1. New York: Harper & Row.

Kohlberg, L. (1983). *Essays in moral development: The psychology of moral development,* vol. 2. New York: Harper & Row.

Kohlberg, L. & Ryncarz, R. A. (1990). Beyond justice reasoning: Moral development and consideration of a seventh stage. In C. N. Alexander & E. J. Langer (Eds.), *Higher stages of consciousness.* Cambridbe, MA: Harvard University Press.

Kuhn, T. S. (1962). *The structure of scientific revolutions.* Chicago: University of Chicago Press.

Maslow, A. H. (1971). *The farther reaches of human nature.* New York: Viking.

Niebuhr, R. (1951). *The nature and destiny of man.* New York: Scribners.

Rank, O. (1941). *Beyond psychology.* New York: Privately printed.

Roberts, B. (1985). *The path to no-self.* Boston: Shambhala.

Sinnott, J. D. (1984). Postformal reasoning: The relativistic stage. In M. L. Commons, F. A. Richards & C. Armon (Eds.), *Beyond formal operations* (pp. 298–325). New York: Praeger.

Thomas, L. E. (1991). Dialogues with three religious renunciates.

International Journal of Ageing and Human Development 32 (3): 211–227.

Thomas, L. E. (1992). Review article: Religion and aging in the Indian tradition. *Aging and Society* 12: 105–113.

Thomas, L. E.; Brewer, S. J.; Kraus, P. A. & Rosen, B.L. (1993). Two patterns of transcendence: An empirical examination of Wilber and Washburn's theories. *Journal of Humanistic Psychology* 33 (3): 66–81.

Tillich, P. (1951). *Systematic theology,* vol. 1. Chicago: University of Chicago Press.

Washburn, M. (1988). *The ego and the dynamic ground.* Albany, NY: State University of New York Press.

Wilber, K. (1977). *The spectrum of consciousness.* Wheaton, IL: Theosophical Publishing House.

Wilber, K. (1979). *No boundary.* Boston: Shambala.

Wilber, K. (1980). *The atman project.* Wheaton, IL: Theosophical Publishing House.

Wilber, K. (1981). *Up from Eden.* Boston: Shambhala.

Wilber, K. (1982a). *A sociable God.* New York: McGraw-Hill.

Wilber, K. (1982b). Odyssey: A personal inquiry into humanistic and transpersonal psychology. *Journal of Humanistic Psychology* 22 (1): 57–90.

Wilber, K. (1983). *Eye to eye.* New York: Doubleday.

Wilber, K. (1986). The spectrum of psychopathology. In K. Wilber, J. Engler & D. P. Brown (Eds.), *Transformations of consciousness.* Boston: Shambhala.

Wilber, K. (1990). Two patterns of transcendence: A reply to Washburn. *Journal of Humanistic Psychology* 30 (3): 113–136.

CHAPTER FOUR

The Structure of Mind and Its Resources

Phil Nuernberger
President, Mind Resource Technologies, Inc.

*"I salute her, the Samvid Kala who shines in the
form of Space, Time and all objects therein."*
Yoginihrdaya Tantra

This paper presents, in very brief part, the conceptual framework of the
Tantric tradition of Shaktism. However, I must admit to some degree of
hesitancy. I am willing and happy to share the experience of my personal
research of the last 23 years, but do so with the realization that I have
merely scratched the surface of the tradition which so absorbs me. I hope
to present in a clear and simple fashion the results of my experiments and
journey. I must also warn the reader that this paper is a distillation of a
Tantric practice, and not an academic exercise of compare and critique. The
validity of the tradition is only experienced within the practice, and not in
logical discourse or analysis.

Contrary to popular misconceptions, the Tantric tradition, like all Eastern systems of self-discipline and self-mastery, is based on the most critical
elements of science. It is an experimental, verifiable, and highly empirical
introspective science in which the object of study is not a "thing"—an
external object or behavior—but is instead one's self, one's mind and
consciousness. The knowledge base is grounded in personal experience
rather than academic theories. The entire realm of human capacity is the
field of study; the body and mind are the laboratory; self-knowledge and
self-discipline are the foundation; and the goal is complete knowledge of
human functioning, from the most mundane physiological activity through
the more subtle mental activities to the highest expression of human con-

sciousness. And, like any science, achieving results requires significant effort and patience.

Tantra is an oral tradition, steeped in cultural mythology and symbols that do not necessarily speak to our technological Western culture. However, these myths and symbols are not the knowledge itself, but only the medium. The explanatory systems—theory, beliefs, and philosophy—are attempts to translate personal experience, and are secondary to the science and technology of self-mastery. This inner science can be effectively translated only if the individual is willing to undertake the discipline and training necessary to acquire the experiential knowledge. Studying philosophy, critiquing theories, analyzing and comparing various meditative systems—even setting up laboratory experiments—do not constitute an effective translation of this tradition and inner science. We gain the knowledge and skill inherent in meditative traditions only by engaging in the discipline itself.

I will supplement my experience with the voice and authority of the teachings of my tradition in those areas that I do not yet command. I do not wish to convince, nor am I an apologist, nor do I need to defend. If I seem enthusiastic, it is because of my own joy of discovery, and the fascination that I continue to find in my research within this tradition. Please take what you find helpful, explore what you find of interest, and leave that which is of no use to you.

Philosophical Perspectives

I draw from the philosophy of Advaita Vedanta as expressed in the writings of Shankara, and in particular, from the Tantric scriptures as expressed through Shaktism. Shankara (A.D. 686–718) is considered to be India's greatest logician and philosopher. A simple, gentle, and joyous man, he reformed Indian philosophy and founded ten monastic orders which are the foundation of Hindu spirituality today. In the seven major systems of philosophy of India, Advaita Vedanta is considered to be the philosophical expression of mankind's most profound experience, that of complete mystical union with the Divine. The practical, or methodological, foundation is Tantra Yoga, and in particular, Shaktism. As you might suspect, this presents a radically different approach to understanding human functioning relative to Western traditions.

Contrasting Philosophical Perspectives

We can briefly contrast the relevant philosophical positions in the following manner (see Miller, Chapter 6 this volume, who also has discussed contrasting Western and Eastern philosophical positions):

Materialistic Reductionism: The dominant philosophical approach of Western science posits that the only reality is a material reality. Any complex phenomenon can be broken down into its component parts. Psychological phenomena can be explained through biology, and biology through chemical and genetic events. Within this tradition, the word "mind" serves a vague philosophical purpose, and all behavior is ultimately understood in terms of brain functioning or genetic determinism. Consciousness is a function of neurological activity, and there is no "ghost in the machine." This model dominates Western psychology, expressed in behaviorism, psychoanalytic theory, general psychiatry, mainstream academic psychology, and most recently, genetic determinism.

Humanistic: The primary thrust of humanistic psychology is to deny that human experience can be reduced to biology and chemistry. Humanistic psychology holds human experience as unique, and asserts that each human being has an innate potential for fulfillment. Railing against the mechanistic determinism of behaviorism and the Freudians, the humanistic psychologist emphasizes the value and dignity of mankind. Focused on the experience of self in the waking consciousness, humanistic psychology holds a position somewhat between reductionist and dualist positions. It does not, however, offer a coherent framework of human functioning or the mind. Its importance is its opposition to reductionism, and in serving as the birthing ground for Transpersonal Psychology.

Western Dualism: Psychologies based on dualism are far older than the reductionist systems. The most prominent of modern dualist theories are Jungian psychology and Systems Theory. The most recent dualist framework relevant to our discussion of the mind is represented by what has loosely been called the Emergent Theorists (Brown, 1980). Their position is that human behavior is far too complex and rich to be explained merely on the basis of brain functioning. They argue that the "mind" is a powerful force, an intelligent, cohesive energy field that arises from the neuronal activity of the brain, but becomes a separate, independent reality superior to the brain. Consciousness is the consequence of the interaction of this energy field and the brain. Representative theorists include Roger Sperry, Sir John Eccles, Wilder Penfield, and Barbara Brown.

Eastern Dualism: The dualistic philosophy of Samkhya and its practical application found in the Yoga Sutras of Patanjali offer a stark contrast to the materialistic approaches of the West. Samkhya, one of the oldest philosophical traditions, postulates two irreducible principles: Consciousness (*Purusha*) and Matter (*Prakrti*). It is the interplay of these two principles that leads to the manifestation of the Universe. In radical contrast with Western approaches, consciousness is not considered a derivative of anything. It is an independent eternal reality. *Purusha*, the limitation of consciousness into individual form, corresponds to what we might call a soul. Much of what is presented here relative to the structure of mind is also found in Samkhya philosophy.

Nondualism: Advaita Vedanta and Tantra: Advaita Vedanta posits an underlying unity to all phenomena—a unity that can be verified only through direct experience. This pervasive, eternal reality is pure Consciousness. The phenomenal world is an apparent reality, real enough in its momentary existence, but it is momentary. Made of energy, this manifest reality undergoes constant change, death, and decay. Only Consciousness is unchanging; only Consciousness is Real. Yet, it is from Consciousness that the manifest world arises to express its temporary existence. In the words of Sri Ramana Maharshi, "The world is illusory; Brahman [Consciousness] alone is real; Brahman is the world." Tantra Yoga provides the methodological science that verifies this unchanging reality.

The overall framework is represented by the summary given in Table 4.1. As shown in the table, the following discussion will include the various levels of the persona, from the central concept of Consciousness to the relatively primitive level of the body, and briefly touch upon innate capacities (power functions) of each level, the type of knowledge obtained, as well as the experience of each level.

Consciousness—Alpha and Omega

We begin our exploration with what might appear to be a statement of belief: The power that underlies our human nature is infinite and eternal. This power is without beginning and without end, and thus immeasurable. Called by various names in different cultures—God, Brahma, the Tao—it remains beyond all names and forms. It is the final cause of all change, and yet, itself, remains changeless. It is the one Reality from which all realities evolve, the one Truth from which all truths evolve. It is pure Intelligence, indestructible, and ever-present.

This one Reality is pure Consciousness (Merrell-Wolff, 1973). It is all pervasive, and cannot be categorized, broken into parts, analyzed, or detected by the most sophisticated technology. It is nonmaterial, without form or structure. This impermeable Reality is the fundamental ground of all being, including our unique human expression. It is not the mind, nor the limited consciousness of the mind. Without Consciousness, the mind is an unconscious field of energy. Pure Consciousness is our ultimate resource, the hidden, subtle Self inside every creature. Without realization of this power, we cannot gain accurate insight into the structure of human nature.

In a radical departure from the materialist's view, Tantra begins with *samadhi*, the realization (direct mystical experience) of pure Consciousness.

The term "realization" is critical as it signifies to comprehend fully and correctly. Consciousness is a "Transcendent and Immanent Reality" that exists beyond time, space, and states of mind. It is the "stuff" of the soul, but exists far beyond individual soul or individual sense of "I."

For most, the above statement remains simply a belief. Westerners, such as materialist philosopher Dennett (1991), author of *Consciousness Explained*, argue that ultimately any statement about consciousness is a matter of faith or belief. This statement belies his dependence on analytic reasoning to solve every question and puzzle of life. It does not apply to realization, or mystical knowledge, created through direct apprehension or awareness. The materialist's ignorance of mystical knowledge achieved through direct apprehension does not nullify or negate this knowledge. It only reflects the limited experience of the materialist. (See Alexander, this volume).

To those skilled in disciplined introspection, Transcendent/Immanent Consciousness is verified through realization, through direct experience. No argument or intellectual discourse, however clever, can alter or minimize that direct, primary experience. Once the experience is gained, then philosophy and scientific models are used by the introspective scientist to communicate their experience and knowledge gained as clearly as possible.

Clarifying Terms

Transcendent/Immanent Consciousness (which for purposes of clarity and brevity we refer to as Consciousness with a capital *C*) should not be confused with the term "conscious awareness" of a particular object, event, or process, or conscious mind. This awareness, or personal consciousness, is dominated and limited by individual ego. I may be conscious of my thoughts and emotions, conscious of a conflict; I may even get involved in a consciousness-raising group to become more aware of certain issues.

The term consciousness with a small *c* refers to a degree of limited awareness, with focus on a particular thing or process. This consciousness is in a continuous state of flux. I may be very conscious of my surroundings, or I may be conscious only of my own thoughts, oblivious to my environment. I may be aware of my heartbeat, but it would be highly unusual if I were conscious of my spleen.

We also use the term "conscious" when referring to levels of awareness in our mind. We speak of the "conscious mind"—the elements of our awareness of the moment; the "subconscious mind"—the mental, physiological, sensory, and behavioral experiences that we bring to present awareness; and an "unconscious mind"—the elements and experiences of mind which remain outside of awareness. We don't really have three minds. These terms represent different degrees of awareness within the same mind.

Table 4.1

The Structure of Mind and Its Resources

Level	Computer Analogy	Power Function	Experience	Knowledge Base	Practical Resource
I. Individual Consciousness (*Purusha*)	Owner/operator	Spiritual knowledge, vision, recognition of Divinity within all	Mystical, resolution of all duality, experience of complete knowledge	*Nirbija samadhi, sri vidya*—highest level of experience	Love, joy, tranquility, complete fearlessness, perfect will
II. Balanced Mind (*Anandamaya Kosha*)	The potential of the computer language before specified in written form	Experience of inner harmony and peace	God's in the heavens, the absence of any stress or conflict	*Samadhi*, all knowledge in latent form	Absolute self-confidence, dynamic will, equanimity
III. Discriminating Mind (*Jnanamaya Kosha*)	Computer language	Discrimination, the ability to discern cause/effect relations	Intuition, clarity of thought, no emotional distraction	Intuition, critical thought	Intuition, decisiveness, critical thinking

IV. Sensory Mind (*Manomaya Kosha*)	Software programs	Perceptual organization, habits; language, emotions	Mind chatter, habitual reactions, memory, emotionality	Instinct, critical thought	Creativity, instinct, imagination
V. Energy (*Pranamaya Kosha*)	Electricity	Breath	Various forms of energy experienced as color, form, movement, or vibration	Transmitting agency, link between body and mind	Control mechanism for body/mind balance, enhance concentration
VI. Body (*Anamaya Kosha*)	Hardware	Health, wellness, information resource	Sensory experience: pain/pleasure, health/disease	Information, sensory data	Health and wellness, tool to enhance awareness

Consciousness with a capital *C* is the unlimited reservoir from which we draw personal, ego-centered awareness. Our individual Consciousness is an infinitesimal spark within the eternal flame of Universal Consciousness. Like sunlight refracted through a prism into the rainbow of colors, ego consciousness is a colored (limited) expression of Consciousness. Through ego consciousness, we experience limitations of time and space, and pleasure and pain. To the degree that we free ourselves from the limits of personal awareness, we experience more of the vast expanse of Consciousness which lies beyond the boundary of individual identity, beyond the limitations of time and space.

History contains the wisdom of those who have transcended the limitations of personal consciousness. The insight and wisdom generated from the experience of Consciousness is not limited to Eastern mystics. A great deal of Western thought, beginning with the ancients (for instance, Plato and Plotinus) and well into modern times (Spinoza, Whitman, William James), has indicated another form of knowledge beyond the logic and rationality of the individual mind. The great spiritual leaders and mystics of all cultures and time—Christ, Buddha, Shankara, Lao-tzu—all speak of the power of direct knowledge, of reality beyond the capacity of the logic and rationality of an individual mind. Expressed in religious terms, we say that we exist eternally in the Divine, or in God. There is no separation between humans and God, nor can there ever be. What appears as separation is an artifact of our limited consciousness.

This ability to experience and know the deepest mystery of all, the God-head of existence, defines the highest human capability and allows us to explore human nature in depth. To ignore this Reality because it doesn't fit a certain paradigm, because it cannot be detected with advanced technology, or because it isn't found through analytic reasoning, is destructive. Logic and rationality, though necessary, are limited parts of the whole. To explore the totality of human nature and capacity, we must go beyond rationality into direct knowledge and awareness.

Consciousness and Descriptive Models

Our model of human nature begins with Consciousness. As the uncaused cause of manifest reality, Consciousness is ever-present. God is not an absentee landlord, but the ever-present, pervasive ground of our reality, including ourselves. While the religionist might be comfortable leaving this statement as an article of faith, the Tantric wants to verify this fact with his or her own experience. The Tantric is not content with having a mystical experience, and letting it go at that. He or she wants to know the specifics, the details of the connection, and utilize these details to derive greater harmony and personal fulfillment.

There are necessarily different models or explanations of mystical experience. The fundamentalist, whether a scientist or religionist, argues that there is only one truth, that one of these models must be right and the others wrong. It is true that only one eternal reality exists, whether we choose to call it God, Cosmic Consciousness, the Tao, or something else. However, it is also true that all experiences, even mystical experiences which transcend the mind, are filtered through individual minds conditioned by personal history, learning, and culture. While the experience of Consciousness is irrefutable, and is its own validity, how that experience is communicated is quite another matter. There are as many models and descriptions as there are different minds.

Furthermore, the "mystical experience" is not an all-or-nothing event. Different degrees of introspective skill allow different degrees of enlightenment. Just as not all astrophysicists are equal in their skill and knowledge, not all introspectionists are equally skilled. The concepts, the models, the ways of communicating and explaining one's transcendent knowledge differ according to culture, depth of experience, even personal skills of logic and communication.

There are, consequently, different philosophical positions, different approaches to the psychology of transcendence, and even different names for the same experience. To judge which is right or wrong is irrelevant, though we may critique and disagree with the logic of any philosophical position. Our task is to explore our own inner reality, using the models as guides, and to verify the primacy of Consciousness through experience.

What follows is not intended to be a description of the final truth of human nature. It is a model based on the author's meditative and contemplative experience as well as his studies of Eastern and Western systems of psychology. It is a way of describing mystical experience that makes sense of our human capacities and provides a way to access and refine our inner resources in order to become more skilled human beings. My goal is psychological, not philosophical. I do not intend to provide a comprehensive ontology, but rather sketch a practical model of the mind.

Consciousness: One Reality with Two Aspects

From this single reality of Consciousness emerges the world of intelligence, life, and form. Although it is a unitary reality, Consciousness has a dual aspect, just as a coin has two sides. One is the transcendent aspect, the "background Reality," the pure illumination or intelligence. In the Tantric tradition of India, this "ground of action before action" is seen as the masculine aspect, or Shiva. It is the Universal Consciousness without an object, the experience of completeness in and of Itself.

There is also the immanent aspect of Consciousness, its power to express

**Figure 4.1. The Unity of Shiva and Shakti
in the Androgenous Ardhanarisvara**

itself through limitation into manifest form, to create and project the
universe of material reality out of Itself. It is the power of I-consciousness,
of self-illumination. In the Indian Tantric traditions, this aspect of
Consciousness is called Shakti, the feminine aspect. Pure Consciousness
(Shiva) does not exist without this power (Shakti), and this power cannot
derive out of non-Consciousness. Consciousness and Consciousness-power
are one and the same Reality. As the great Western Tantric author Sir John
Woodroffe states, "When the one Reality or Brahman is regarded as the
Changeless Consciousness it is called Shiva: when it is regarded as the
Power of Consciousness or Consciousness-Power which projects the

Universe from out itself, it is called Shakti" (Woodroffe, 1974). Let's use the analogy of a spoken word. The silence both before, buried beneath the sound, and again apparent after the sound is the unchanging potential, or Shiva. The force which brings about the sound is Shakti. Shakti is the effort, the power to move, which allows the energy to take form. The form, the spoken sound, emerges from the potential through determination (called Samkalpa Shakti) and returns again to potential after expression. The sound itself is a manifest form of energy. It is neither Shiva nor Shakti, but an expression involving both. Without Shiva and Shakti, the sound would not occur. Both the unformed, unmoved transcendent Consciousness, and the immanent power to manifest, to limit in an expression, are one and the same Consciousness.

This unity of Shiva and Shakti is often symbolized as the androgenous form of Shiva (Ardhanarisvara; Figure 4.1), a hermaphroditic image, half male and half female, illustrating the dual principles in harmonious unity. Perhaps a more familiar image for the Westerner is the Taoist image representing Yin and Yang shown in Figure 4.2, signifying unity in diversity.

Figure 4.2. Taoist Symbol of Unity in Diversity

Energy: The Movement of Consciousness into Form

Central to our understanding of mind and body is knowing the relationship of energy and Consciousness, and the primary, relational role energy plays in the formation of mind, the life force, and matter. When Consciousness limits itself, and creates form, it does so through the use of energy. Energy itself is not Consciousness, nor is it Consciousness-power (Shakti). It is the signature of Consciousness, emerging from the inherent power (Shakti) of Consciousness. In its most fundamental and subtle state, this energy is called *prana* in Yoga science.

Modern physics and ancient mystical sciences agree that existence is dependent on energy. Thoughts, objects, even the life force itself, are all energy. Energy is the foundation for empirical reality, and this includes the world of thought. However, modern physics limits itself to sensory phenomena, or matter. The modern scientist speaks of the four fundamental forces of physics—strong and weak nuclear, electromagnetic, and gravitational—and denies the existence of anything beyond these four fundamental forces. We should note, however, that not one of these, nor any combination, will create life. Nor do these four "fundamental forces" explain the nature of thought. The mystical sciences go much further in their research, and explore the energy structures of the life force and thought. To the Tantric, all manifest reality—the world of objects, the life force, and the world of thought—are forms of energy existing in various degrees of subtlety.

For the Tantric, the connecting link to all forms of matter is energy. There is no dichotomy, no unbridgeable gulf, between the world of thought and the world of objects. The difference is one of degree, not kind. Thoughts are a subtle expression of energy, while objects are a crude or gross expression of energy. Both exist along the same energy continuum from the very subtle to the very gross. They are related and connected to each other through this common source.

The Tantrics do not accept Subjective Idealism. They are empiricists, accepting the reality of material things independent of our perception of them. Matter, while related to thought because it is also a form of energy, has its own independence, just as thought, also a form of energy, is independent of matter. However, both matter and thought, as forms of energy, share a common thread and a definitive relationship.

Thoughts and matter are both real, but they are ephemeral. Energy is movement, and what is made of energy is in a constant state of transition—emergence, change, and decay. These three forces—creativity, maintenance, and destruction—characterize the material world of energy and the forms it creates. But the final cause is still the eternal, unchanging Consciousness, and as such, underlies all material (body and mind) existence. What we experience as thought, as life force, as an object (such as our bodies), is ultimately there because of Consciousness. In the Judeo-Christian tradition, this reality is expressed by the words "In the beginning was the Word." The Taoist states that "The nameless is the beginning of heaven and earth." The Tantric expresses that "All this is verily Myself, eternal there is no other." The only unchanging, eternal Reality is Consciousness, the source of energy, and thus of all manifest reality.

The Three Paths of Energy

In the emergence of energy out of Shakti, or Consciousness-power, there is a differentiation in the form in which energy will express itself. Three interactive tendencies, inherent in the operation of Shakti, determine whether energy finally becomes thought, life-force, or material object. These three tendencies (referred to as *gunas*) are named *sattvas*, *rajas*, and *tamas*.

Sattvas (essence) is the revealing tendency, the tendency for the operation of Shakti to lead back to pure Consciousness, or Shiva. To reveal is to clarify, to make something known by bringing its aspects or functions to awareness. To understand is to be aware of relationships. Awareness, then, is the necessary condition of knowledge. This *sattvas* tendency is the basis of personal intelligence. We understand something when part or all of its nature is revealed to us. When Consciousness is enveloped and acted upon by its power (Shakti) with the revealing tendency (*sattvas*) predominant, what eventually emerges is the individual mind, which is called the *antahkarana*, or inner instrument.

Rajas (active principle) is the energizing tendency, the tendency of Shakti to activation. When Consciousness is enveloped and acted upon by Shakti with the energizing tendency (*rajas*) predominant, what eventually manifests is the life force. It is this subtle form of energy that sustains what we call life in all living things, from the tiniest one-celled amoeba to the most complex form, the human being.

Tamas (inertia) is the veiling tendency, the tendency of Shakti to limitation. When Consciousness is enveloped and acted upon by Shakti with the veiling tendency (*tamas*) predominant, what eventually emerges is matter in the Western sense. This is the world of dense physical form. It is this veiling form of energy that Western science has become so proficient in understanding.

All manifest reality is comprised of these three qualities of energy. Within Consciousness, these three are perfectly balanced. In the phenomenal world, imbalance prevails, and one tendency predominates, leading to a particular manifestation or condition. The entire manifest reality, from the subtle level of mind to the dense world of objects (such as the body) consists of energy dominated by one quality or the other. The diversity of phenomena results from the various combinations of the three qualities of energy (*gunas*) which constantly unite and separate.

Mind and Body: The Limitation of Consciousness

The human being is a complex mixture involving all three qualities of energy. At the level of mind, the revealing (*sattvas*) tendency is dominant; at the level of life force, the energizing (*rajas*) tendency is dominant; and at the level of the body, the veiling (*tamas*) tendency is dominant. Between Consciousness and its expression in human form, there are a number of intervening steps or levels. (For those interested in this conceptual framework, read Basu, 1986).

The individual expression of Consciousness (called *Purusha*, or soul) suffuses the persona with awareness and intelligence. Both mind and body are objects of Consciousness, and in and of themselves are unconscious forms of energy. The mind, like the body, is part of the material world, a manifestation of energy. But since the revealing tendency of energy (*sattvas*) predominates, the mind remains in subtle form, and does not become part of the sensory world of objects.

With this brief conceptual introduction, we can state some of the more important principles relative to the structure, functions, and resources of the mind:

1. The mind is a subtle field of energy, a unique reality, separate from and superior to the brain. The brain is a physical organ, part of the body, which serves as the control room for the mind. The brain functions as a transducer, translating the subtle energy modifications of the mind into biochemical and neurological events in order to activate the body.

2. The energy of the mind is modified in its contact with the world of objects through sensory activity, and through the various functions occurring in the mind, such as emotional reactions, beliefs, and memory.

3. The mind is an integrated whole. At all times, all of the mind and its functions are operational. Categories, functions, and faculties are only descriptive, as a map is descriptive of reality, but they are not the reality itself.

4. The mind is the instrument of knowledge. It is a tool designed to create knowledge of the world and events around us. It is the nature of the sattvas guna, which predominates in the mind, to reveal and to bring to awareness.

5. As a field of subtle energy, the mind is not limited by the structure of the body. As the most subtle energy form, mind permeates the entire persona. The Yogic saying "All of the body is in the mind, but not all of the mind is in the body" characterizes the relationship between mind and body.

The Levels of Human Functioning

The Vedantic concept of sheaths (*koshas*) provides a structural framework for delineating the relationships between Consciousness, mind, life force, and body. Each level is seen as a layer of functioning imposed over the core of individual Consciousness (*Purusha*, or soul). It is as if the different levels of the persona are colored filters of crystal overlying the light of Consciousness. The persona (mind, life force, body) is viewed as a hierarchical, interpenetrating organization, formed of increasingly subtle forms of energy and function as we move towards the core identity of individual Consciousness (*Purusha*). Each level, more subtle and more powerful than the preceding one, contributes various practical and powerful resources to the persona.

We can use a computer system to help define the relationships of the various levels to each other. When we use a computer, we enter data through a variety of ways, such as a keyboard, modem, or scanner. Inside the computer, the hardware and software work together to manipulate the data and provide an intelligent outcome. We will refer to these functions as "power functions." The more you know how to manipulate the power functions inside the computer, such as the ability to program, the more creative use you get out of the computer. If you have little knowledge, you are limited to the software packages you buy. The same is true of our persona. Each of the levels of the persona has particular power functions. We can live without having much knowledge about how they work, but then we are limited to whatever habits (programs) have been created.

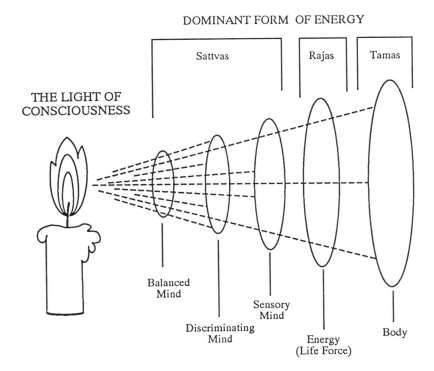

Figure 4.3. Consciousness and the Five Levels of Human Functioning

"I AM"—The Spiritual Core

Our core identity is the individual expression of Consciousness, the *Purusha*, or soul. This spiritual identity is beyond the persona, and cannot be known or understood by the mind. There is a great body of mystical knowledge and wisdom that is most often ignored, particularly by academics and scientists. This knowledge is not intellectual or rational, but stems from the deepest insights and intuition into the nature of life itself. It is Truth experienced within a variety of cultures and times, but each expression is fully coherent and consistent with all others. We hear the voice of Christ in the mystical gospel of St. John saying, "I am the Way, the Truth, and the Life; no one comes to the Father except through me" (John 14:6). He then quickly explains, "I am not myself the source of the words I speak: it is the Father who dwells in me doing his own work" (John 14:10).

In other words, Jesus is clear that he is not referring to his personality, the mind/body complex that makes up the ego, but the spiritual core that is the essential nature of our human existence. Out of ignorance, religious materialists identify the "I AM" as the physical Jesus, not realizing that it represents the same spiritual "I AM" found in every human being. This is the same spiritual "I AM" found in the Vedic mantra "OM TAT SAT" or "That Thou Art," as well as in all great mystical spiritual traditions, whether it is Taoism, Sufism, or the Kabbalah of Judaism. It is the experience of God within as well as without, and the realization that this is our fundamental identity.

Spiritual knowledge is singularly experiential. In Tantra, we find a systematic developmental process to expand personal awareness in order to experience this spiritual core identity of Consciousness. This direct experience is called *nirbija samadhi*, or enlightenment in common parlance. Through discipline involving physical, psychophysical, and mental practices, the Tantric develops mastery at achieving *nirbija samadhi*. With identity grounded in the eternal Self, the mind now becomes an object of awareness, and the various levels and resources of the mind are available for full development. Exploration of the mind as well as the rest of the persona occurs only through relentless objectivity and fearlessness.

The Mind and Its Functions

With our identity firmly rooted in consciousness, we can now explore the mind and the rest of the persona. Using the Vedantic framework of overlying sheaths (*koshas*), we will start from the inside out. The inner three sheaths constitute the mind, or inner instrument (*antahkarana*). There is a related conceptual framework in Tantra that helps define the mind and its resources that is relevant here. Tantra talks of four faculties of the mind:

sensory organization (*manas*); discrimination (*buddhi*); ego (*ahamkara*); and memory (*chitta*). Two of these, the sensory and discriminating faculties, overlap with the Vedantic concept of overlying sheaths. They are action centers, so to speak, where many different functions occur. The other two, ego and memory, are much broader in scope and are involved in all the activities of the mind.

I Am, Therefore I Think: The Ego Faculty

The Tantric concept of ego is much broader than that found in Western psychologies. In Tantra as well as other Yoga systems, the ego signifies a boundary function, and it provides a unique center on which all other mind operations depend. Without the limiting frequency of the ego, the energy field called mind would dissipate and could not retain a cohesive form. There would be no personality for us to relate to.

The ego provides the "sense of I-ness," a central identity for the persona, which allows perception to have a personal impact and create a personal reality. If what you perceive has no relevance or meaning to you, it will not make a lasting impact on the mind, and you will not remember it. Similar to Western concepts, the Tantric ego includes the management role of supervising the operations of the mind in order to sustain and enhance the total organization. (See Funk, Chapter 1, this volume.)

Probably the most critical difference between Tantric and Western concepts of ego is that in Tantra, the core identity of Consciousness allows us to step out of ego entirely. There is no "observing ego" as we find in psychoanalysis, for example. Western systems deny any objective, non-involved observation of the ego. The ability of the Tantric to step completely outside of the persona provides the "objective introspection" necessary for accurate knowledge of one's ego states and functions. Only by establishing an identity separate from the ego can you gain objective, accurate knowledge of the games that the ego plays in order to maintain control. Without knowledge of the spiritual core, there is nowhere to stand.

This failure of objectivity is the reason introspection failed as a reliable and valid tool in the early days of Western psychology. The inability to break free of ego identity turned introspection into neurotic imagination, while self-delusion introduced too much error, and prevented reliable data. It takes great discipline to establish identity in the spiritual core and break the hold of ego identity, but it is this discipline that characterizes Tantra and other meditative sciences.

Memory: The Shape of Things to Come

The second general faculty of the mind is called *chitta* and corresponds to memory. However, it is a much broader concept. *chitta* includes both long- and short-term memory, but it also includes the template function that structures the shape of the energy field we call mind. The experiences we have modify the energy field of our mind, literally shaping the overall structure of the field itself. This, in turn, not only determines how we interpret our reality, but even what experiences are possible for us.

Our ability to focus attention plays a critical role in how the mind is structured. In more common parlance, our minds become what we pay attention to. In Tantra and other meditative sciences, great care is given to choosing experiences, and thus systematically creating the mind structure that is most useful.

Balanced Mind: The Source of Inner Strength

The first overlying sheath to individual Consciousness (*Purusha*) is called the Balanced Mind, or *Anandamaya Kosha*. The term *ananda* signifies bliss, the experience we have when we are completely free from any kind of stress or disharmony. The names of all the sheaths end with the term *maya*, signifying that they are part of the illusory (unstable, changing) material world.

The Balanced Mind represents the most subtle level of the personality. This level corresponds to the potential of a computer language before it is written into specific instructions. At this level, the revealing quality (*sattvas*) dominates with only the very slightest coloration from the other two qualities. Like a crystal mirror, this clear state of mind reflects the spiritual core of individual Consciousness. At this level, the mind's energy exists in pure or latent form, unchanged or unmodified by contact with the world around it.

This sheath is the purest condition of mind, before knowledge has formed. Only the ego function exists to maintain boundary. As there is no modification of the mind's energy field, there is no stress (in the engineering sense) within the field, and consequently, there are no distortions or conflicts. When we become conscious of this level, we experience it as "bliss." Bliss does not mean happiness or pleasure. In fact, this balanced state has nothing to do with our emotions or our senses at all. We experience bliss when we free ourselves of all inner conflicts or compulsions, needs, drives, or anxieties. At the moment, we are entirely at peace with ourselves and the world. This tranquility is the critical power function of this sheath.

This is not an uncommon experience. It happens occasionally when we are out for a walk and respond to the calm and beauty of our surroundings. Suddenly, we feel great contentment, completely free of any worry or compulsion. It is, in Browning's words (1841), a time when "God's in his heaven, All's right with the world." This experience of tranquility lasts only a few moments, but leaves quite an impact.

This inner harmony wasn't created by a change of external conditions or by drugs. What we experienced was our inner balance, a source of strength for the persona. The practical outcome of the Balanced Mind is absolute self-confidence. Conscious ability to utilize this resource provides psychological balance and a profound equanimity, the ability to face whatever life has in store with a clear and confident mind.

Discriminating Mind: Forming Pure Knowledge

Deep within the mind, the second sheath overlying individual Consciousness is called the Discriminating Mind (*Jnanamaya Kosha*). To discriminate means to distinguish between things, to discern cause/effect relationships directly. The Discriminating Mind is where the energy of the mind is first modified into knowledge states. In our computer analogy, this level corresponds to the language used by the computer.

At this level, the sophisticated knowledge of energy acquired by the Tantric plays a critically important role. To the Tantric, there is no essential difference between a thought or image in the mind and an object in the world. Both are forms of energy. Where Westerners find a fundamental difference between an object and a thought of that object, Yoga science recognizes that both are forms of energy.

Within the Discriminating Mind (*Jnanamaya Kosha*), the harmony found in the Balanced Mind is altered as the mind's energy is modified in its contact with the reality around it. In order to form knowledge, the mind goes out to (apprehends) the object. The mind's subtle field of energy, unlimited by physical restraints, can go wherever we have the capacity to direct it. Knowledge forms when the energy field of the mind is modified by contact with an object. At this time, part of the mind's energy is modified to form the same energy pattern as the object. It is this energy modification which is the knowledge, not a label, name, or concept.

Wherever we have the power to direct our minds, we have the power to create knowledge and understanding. Direct knowledge is our awareness or experience of this modification of the mind's energy. This knowledge is pure, unalloyed by sensory input, language, learning, emotional reactions, and other more superficial events in the mind. This ability to discern things as they are is the power function of this level.

This is not as strange as it first may seem. We know from modern physics that there are different levels of reality. For example, our senses operate on one level of reality, while an electron microscope operates at another. Every object has a particular energy pattern on the subatomic level as well as its secondary characteristics on the sensory level. While we are aware of sensory stimulation, we are typically not aware of the more subtle level where the modification of the mind's energy takes place.

We perform essentially the same operation with a computer when we copy a file from one disk to another. We experience the file on the screen as a complex ordering of different images, such as words, numbers, or graphics. The fundamental structure of the file, however, is a consistent field of electromagnetic energy. When we copy the file, we make an exact replica of its energy field. Now the original and replication are identical. This is essentially what our mind does through the power of discrimination.

Each modification of our mind's energy represents a particular knowledge event as yet unaltered and undistorted by sensory input. This knowledge event is free of the limitations suffered by sensory data, such as conditioning and emotional distortion. When this power of discrimination is directed internally, we achieve awareness of our spiritual core identity. When this power is directed externally, we gain intuitive knowledge about the world.

As each pattern is formed, certain processes in our mind embellish and complicate the original form, resulting in complex models of the surrounding reality. In other words, we further modify the original modification of the mind's energy. The pure pattern formed within the discriminating mind is altered by the processes occurring within the next level, the Sensory Mind.

Sensory Mind: The Processing Domain

The most familiar part of our mind is the Sensory Mind, or *Manomaya Kosha*, where we organize sensory data. This sheath, with its habitual patterns of behavior, corresponds to the software programs of a computer. We use our five senses to gain information about our world. Our Sensory Mind collects, organizes, and interprets this sensory data, creating meaningful patterns. This function serves as our personal reality generator, and in the Yogic view, we have total responsibility for creating our personal world of meaning. Our emotions, past experiences (memory), beliefs, expectations, worries, fears, and anxieties, as well as constitutional and genetic factors, state of health, stress, and environmental and cultural or social factors all have an impact on how we structure and interpret our sensory experience.

The first power function of the Sensory Mind is perceptual organization. Two of its most powerful operations—time/space and pleasure/pain—have extraordinary impact on our actions, thoughts, and beliefs. Without these two, sensory data would be a meaningless jumble of sensation. Outside our Sensory Mind, we do not know what time and space are. Even the most sophisticated atomic clock, which measures the infinitely subtle decay of atoms, is understood through sensory experience.

These two operations combine to form habits, the most powerful function of the Sensory Mind. Conditioning begins at least as early as three months after conception, when the nervous system has matured enough to begin to function as a system. By the time we are five or six years old, the basic patterns of our personality have pretty well formed within our Sensory Mind, and regulate the three outer sheaths—Sensory Mind, Energy, and Body.

Our habits also channel our emotional energy, the third power function within the Sensory Mind. Four primitive biological urges—self-preservation, food, sleep, and sex—are not only an important part of the body's innate mechanism for survival, but are the wellsprings of our emotional energy. These powerful streams of energy, when directed with discrimination and clarity, allow us to accomplish whatever we set out to do. But they can just as easily be destructive—distorting our perceptions and thinking in unconscious ways.

Still another power function of the Sensory Mind is language. Our personal reality is not the event itself, but the meaning we assign to it. Once our mind assigns words to describe the event, these words, and not the event, become the reality to which we react. For example, a particular event in our life is perceived as being either good or bad, engaging or tedious, awful or wonderful. We are not describing the actual event, but what it means to us.

The Four Types of Knowledge

The Balanced Mind, Discriminating Mind, and Sensory Mind, along with the two general faculties of ego and memory, constitute the basic structure of the mind. For the Tantric, these sheaths are the inner instrument whose sole job is to create knowledge through the modification of the mind's energy field. We can identify four types of knowledge:

1. Spiritual Knowledge: (Primary access is through Balanced Mind.) This is often referred to as mystical knowledge and consists of direct experience (awareness) of individual Consciousness and Universal Consciousness. It is awareness of the Divinity within oneself and others. A transformational experience, it alters the identity of the individual and eventually leads to wisdom, complete fearlessness, and the objective awareness of mind and its resources.

2. Intuitive Knowledge: (Primary access is through the Discriminating Mind.) When we gain insight into the real consequences of our actions, we call that experience "intuition." This is the power to discern cause/effect relationships and the subtle movements of change. Based on awareness of the primary modifications of the mind, intuitive knowledge is the purest form of knowledge. Both the formation and access of intuitive knowledge depend on the ability to focus attention. Errors result from incomplete modification of the mind field or from incomplete attention. Four critical factors define intuitive knowledge:

• Intuition is pure awareness of cause/effect relationships. It does not depend on analysis, logic, or intelligent guessing. Thinking may facilitate or interfere, but is not a necessary component.

• Intuition is free from time/space restrictions. It is not fortune-telling, but direct awareness of subtle cause/effect relationships as they exist in the moment. As these relationships change, intuitions change.

• Intuition is free of sensory pleasure or pain. As a consequence, emotions neither influence nor distort intuitive knowledge.

• Intuitive knowledge is unconditioned knowledge. It uses experience without being limited by it. It remains spontaneous, in tune with reality as it is, not as we have learned to see it.

3. Instinctual Knowledge: (Primary Access is through Sensory Mind and the body.) Instinctual knowledge is based on subliminal perception directly related to our personal well-being. Our persona, a sophisticated receiver, responds to a wide range of energy patterns, many of which lie beyond the range of our sensory limits. If we understand our sensitivity to subtle changes in the energy fields that surround us, then instinct is simple to understand. These changes may be physical events, such as changes in barometric pressure, in the electromagnetic spectrum in sunlight, even gravity. Changes in the emotions of individuals around us create an impact on us long before we are aware of any sensory information. Most of us have had the experience of walking into a room where the tension is so thick "you could cut it with a knife." We responded to a definite energy in the atmosphere that no instrument in physics can measure. We can be misled by our instincts when we confuse them with emotional needs, wants and fears, or through lack of awareness.

4. Analytic or Sensory Knowledge: (Primary access is through Sensory Mind and Discriminating Mind.) This is our most familiar knowledge. Our Sensory Mind creates the context in which we view the world. The quality of sensory knowledge depends on how well we manage our Sensory Mind and the sophistication of our concepts. Sensory knowledge is based on probabilities and convention, where right or wrong depends on the most convincing argument. The quality of sensory knowledge also depends on the quality of the operating systems. Distorted emotions, poor memory, even faulty sensory mechanisms, may limit sensory knowledge. Beliefs, attitudes, emotions, memory, education—all play critical roles in determining the quality of sensory knowledge. Logic may help us think in a consistent manner, but it does not guarantee the right answer.

While the mind is the primary source of knowledge, two remaining sheaths play a vital role. These two sheaths, energy and the body, constitute the outer instrument and complete the persona.

Life Force: The Connecting Link

Prana

Prana, the elementary unit of energy, is the life force of the persona. In our computer analogy, our life force is like the electricity that allows the computer to run. This life force constitutes the Energy sheath (*Pranamaya Kosha*), and plays a critical role as the mediating link between body and mind. The spectacular control of physiological functioning demonstrated by Swami Rama at the Menninger Clinic is a result of knowledge and control of this *pranic* sheath (Green, 1977; Green, 1974; Britannica Yearbook, 1973). Just as blood, the nerves, and glandular discharges are distributed throughout the body, this life force energy is distributed through specific channels. Eastern systems of medicine and psychology give sophisticated descriptions of these energy channels. Japanese and Chinese medicine call energy channels meridians, and use them as the template for acupuncture. Yoga science calls these same energy channels *nadis*, and uses sophisticated techniques to develop awareness and control of them. The major vehicle for *prana* is the breath, and breathing exercises play a central role in Tantra and other forms of Yoga. The primary power function for this sheath is the breath.

The Physical Body: A Fluid Picture of the Mind

The most primitive and least powerful part of the persona is the body (*Anamaya Kosha*). In our computer analogy, the body corresponds to the hardware of the system. Two power functions are found in this outer sheath—balance/health and information. The body is used as a valuable source of information and as a vehicle for action. In Tantra, the body plays the role of facilitator, and effort is made to maintain a healthy, balanced body. It provides an enormous amount of data about the world around us and about our own inner knowledge states. The body is used as a tool to enhance inner awareness and expand direct knowledge and self-control. Through Hatha Yoga and meditative postures, the body becomes a sensitive instrument, and leads to a greater awareness of the levels and functions of the mind.

The various levels and functions presented above are innate resources of the human condition. From the Tantric viewpoint, the problems we face as human beings are not caused by insufficiency, but stem from our lack of self-awareness and self-mastery. The Tantric discipline, as well as other meditative disciplines, is directed not towards change, but rather towards transformation, a process of discovery and skill based on self-awareness and self-mastery.

Attention: The Secret Power

The Tantric realizes that our greatest handicap is ignorance. Ignorance doesn't mean stupidity, or a lack of education. It means exactly what it says—to ignore, to be unconscious of. It is well known that the power and potency of our mind lies primarily in the unconscious, a vast storehouse of knowledge. But few recognize the even greater power that lies undeveloped in our conscious mind. Our conscious mind has one unique power—the ability to direct attention, to focus the energy of the mind. Through attention, our conscious mind can direct the entire mind and all of its resources—knowledge, creativity, will, emotional energy, even habits. We gain the power to command whatever we become aware of.

Biofeedback is a classic example of the power of increased awareness. Many think that biofeedback is a process of conditioning. This is not true. We already know how to control the body. Everything that happens in the body is regulated by the mind, but it happens on the unconscious level. Through biofeedback, we become more conscious of both the physical event and the thoughts and feelings associated with it. By bringing the physical event out of the unconscious mind into our conscious mind, we have more choices. We take control of the physical event by choosing our thoughts and feelings.

Concentration: Key to the Inner Resources

Of all the skills, the Tantric knows that the power of attention is the most crucial. Using a variety of techniques, the most sophisticated of which is meditation, Tantrics achieve deep states of inner concentration. This concentration focuses the energy of the mind into a single point, making the mind powerful in its activities, such as perception, forming knowledge, and taking action. Concentration also expands awareness of heretofore unconscious elements in the mind, increasing access to subtle resources of the mind, such as creativity, intuition, and confidence.

The laser is an excellent analogy for the power of the mind. When light photons are scattered, light has little power. But when the photons are focused, all moving in the same direction at the same time, you have a laser. The laser is so powerful it penetrates a steel plate, so precise that it is used for eye surgery.

The same is true of the energy of the mind. Typically, our mind is scattered. When we pay attention, we focus the mind's energy. The more focused we become, the greater our concentration, the more powerful our mind becomes. Concentration is the central skill by which all other knowledge and resources of the mind are accessed. Concentration plays a critical role in performance, in learning and memory, in our ability to pull out the vital elements in a mass of information. Key opportunities are often missed because someone was not paying attention. The relationship is simple and direct. If you cannot concentrate, you will not function well.

The Empowered Mind:
Practical Consequences of Concentration

Unfortunately, few Westerners realize the powerful and practical consequences of training the mind in introspective discipline. By gaining awareness of the full range of our inner resources, we can become skilled in the use of the power functions inherent in the different sheaths of the persona. Briefly (for more detailed development, see Nuernberger, 1992), these resources can be defined as:

- *Health and Wellness Skills:* The ability to live without stress and its diseases, enhanced capacity for optimism and joy, and emotional balance;
- *Perceptual Skills:* The ability to use instinct as a reliable skill, enhanced creativity and problem-solving skills, increased clarity of thought;
- *Visionary Skills:* The ability to use intuition as a conscious skill, direct imagination for practical outcomes, enhance decisiveness;
- *Command Skills:* The ability for dynamic will, the skill to consciously direct energy (as opposed to "will power," which involves conflict, dividing the mind's energies), access to unlimited self-confidence, and self-discipline;
- *Spiritual Skills:* Arise out of the mystical experience of Consciousness and allow us to experience wholeness and community, humility and selfless love; brings recognition of the Self in others, allowing us to step beyond petty ego needs and live in harmony with ourselves and others.

For a summary of the relationships of the various sheaths, power functions, and practical resources, refer to Table 4.1 presented earlier.

This chapter is just a brief sketch of the rich and sophisticated conceptual framework contained in Advaita Vedanta and the Tantra scriptures. In Tantra and other Eastern meditative disciplines, it is the obligation of the practitioner to experiment and verify the inner truths. The conceptual framework is not "the truth," but a cohesive explanation of inner experience. To the Tantric, academic theorizing may be entertaining, but fruitless without inner discipline. Unless one develops awareness of the inner reality, logical argument remains simply that, and knowledge remains rhetoric. Nothing is given or taken on faith. One must be willing to suspend all judgments, beliefs, and preconceptions about the nature of self. Intellectual knowledge plays an important role, but alone cannot provide insight into the complete nature of humankind. To achieve the highest knowledge, called *sri vidya* in Tantra, one must be skilled in mystical knowledge as well. It is the most difficult of journeys, but it has the greatest of rewards—self-knowledge and self-mastery.

References

Basu, M. (1986). *Fundamentals of the philosophy of Tantras*. Calcutta, India: Mira Basu, Publishers.

Britannica Yearbook of Science and the Future, Encyclopedia Britannica. (1973). Chicago: William Benton Publishers.

Brown, B. (1980). *Supermind: The Ultimate Energy*. New York: Harper & Row.

Browning, Robert. (1962). Pippa Passes. In *The Norton Anthology of English Literature,* vol 2. New York: Norton and Co. Original work published 1841.

Dennett, D. C. (1991). *Consciousness explained*. Boston: Little, Brown and Company.

Green, E. & Green, A. (1977). *Beyond biofeedback*. San Francisco: Robert Briggs Associates.

Green, E. & Green, A. (1974). The ins and outs of mind-body energy. In *Science Year: The World Book Science Annual,* (pp. 137–199). Chicago: Field Enterprises Educational Corporation.

Merrell-Wolff, F. (1973). *The philosophy of consciousness without an object*. New York: The Julian Press.

Nuernberger, P. (1992). *Increasing Executive Productivity*. Englewood Cliffs, NJ: Prentice-Hall.

Woodroffe, J. (1974). *The World as Power*. Madras, India: Ganesh & Co.

PART III

Theories of Mature Development
Based on Empirical Research

CHAPTER FIVE

Rare Forms of Self-understanding
In Mature Adults

Susanne R. Cook-Greuter
Harvard University

This chapter describes two postautonomous ways of understanding the self and reality that go beyond the integrated stage defined in Loevinger's ego development theory (1976). It documents how scarce data can suggest new ways of looking at an existing paradigm. It is argued that a careful and receptive reading of even a single "telling" sentence completion can lead to fresh questions and a restructuring of an existing paradigm. In this case, unusual responses to the Washington University Sentence Completion Test (Loevinger & Wessler, 1970) provided clues to cognitive changes in self-conceptions beyond the autonomous stage. A basic tenet of constructive-developmental psychology is that the more differentiated and objective, that is, the less distorted one's self-view, the closer to truth one gets (see Kegan, 1982). So far, the level of accurate, nondistorted self-knowledge achieved has been one of the chief criteria in ego development theory that distinguishes the postconventional stages. I will argue that the very assumption of an "objective self-identity" becomes questionable and is finally rejected at the most advanced stage of ego development. Instead, the self-experience described and cherished at the universal stage is fluid and open-ended. It is suggested that this kind of postrepresentational awareness, though gained through cognitive development, is consonant with the initial transcendent self-awareness as experienced through spiritual or meditative paths.

But before launching into the various cognitive distinctions at the highest ego stages, a clarification of what is meant here by ego development is in order.

Traditional Ego Development Theory

Ego development theory describes a sequence of consecutive stages of how human beings make sense of themselves and their experience. It explains both the strengths and the limits of a given meaning-making system and shows the next "logic" of experience that a developing person will enter into. The need for coherent meaning seems to be a fundamental and driving force in human life. Whenever we are not quite certain of things because they are beyond the scope of our present understanding, most of us begin to feel anxiety. We want closure and certitude. One of the main functions of the ego is to provide this closure and to generate coherent meaning.

According to Funk (see Figure 1.1, this volume), the "ego" itself is best understood as having two main aspects: The representational ego (Funk's ERep-I and ERep-M) can be defined as that sense of separate self in a person which is identified with the terms "I" and "me." It is constructed out of remembered and internalized images of self-other interactions. The ego as process (Funk's EPro) processes (perceives, organizes, judges, and synthesizes) input from both external and internal sources and executes actions to secure a stable self-sense. The more differentiated persons are, the more elements from more diverse sources they can simultaneously process and integrate into a coherent structure of meaning. At the highest levels elements can be whole systems of knowledge or experience that are related, contrasted, and synthesized into a new whole (see Commons & Richards, 1984). Ego development theory explains how people form such systems of coherent meaning through a series of increasingly abstract and differentiated reinterpretations of self and object. For a more detailed description of the whole sequence of ego stages see Cook-Greuter (1990). Ego development theory explains the dynamic interconnection between one's conception of the self and one's conception of reality. Since the question of how one forms and defines the self-concept is at the core of this paper, the dynamic interplay with the conception of reality is de-emphasized, yet implicit.

In order to communicate with each other, humans codify experience in various ways. Of all symbol systems, natural language is the most elaborate and widely shared. It structures the otherwise unlimited number of stimuli into manageable and communicable objects and arranges them into a map of reality accepted by a group through the process of mutual consensual validation. The problem is that language is internalized so completely and at such an early age that it acts as an unconscious exclusionary filter for a vast number of stimuli.

When individuals become conscious of phenomena that do not fit their already existing maps of reality, they often screen them out by selective inattention (Sullivan, 1953) or defense mechanisms. On the other hand, they can learn to accommodate them in either of two ways. Most growth in adulthood seems to occur *within* a given stage, i.e., *laterally*. The current way of viewing reality is refined, enriched, and modified to include more diverse domains, more cases and detail, and to establish more connections among them. The higher the stage, the more room for such horizontal expansion exists. This is one of the reasons why Miller (this volume) did not find much upward change in ego stage in his longitudinal study despite some indications that individuals grew in their overall capacity to understand and reflect. Alexander (this volume) cites several studies that show little or no change in ego stage even after interventions to raise it. Although rare, *vertical* change does occur. In that case, the whole previous meaning system is transformed and restructured into a new, more expansive and inclusive self-theory.

In summary, ego development theory postulates an invariant, hierarchical sequence of distinct views of reality and subject-object integrations which comprise operative, cognitive, and emotional aspects of living. Roughly 10% of adults are at the three preconventional ego stages, 80% at the conventional ones (stages 3, 3/4, and 4), and 10% function at the postformal or postconventional ego stages (stages 4/5, 5, 5/6, 6).[1] The two highest ego stages, stages 5/6 and 6, are rare (<1%, Cook-Greuter, 1990). The description of the underlying self-concept or self-identification of these two highest stages will be the focus of this article. Since data from the Washington University Sentence Completion Test were used to define these higher stages, a brief description of the instrument follows below.

The Washington University Sentence Completion Test (SCT)

The SCT was introduced by Loevinger and Wessler (1970) and Loevinger, Wessler, and Redmore (1970) to measure the different stages of ego development. It now exists in several forms generally consisting of a scoring guide and manuals for specific items. The SCT is based on the fact that language is so much a part of our unconscious behavior that we reveal our underlying interpretation of who we are and what we believe reality to be when we express ourselves verbally. For each ego stage there is a list of categories and representative responses in the manual.

The written test consists of a set of 36 sentence stems on two pages that subjects are to finish in whichever way they like. Alexander (this volume) points out two problems with the two-page form: Postformal respondents may need modified instructions[2] as well as a longer form. Otherwise they may choose to respond in terms of appropriateness to the task rather than from their more complex level of actual understanding, especially since there is little room to be comprehensive on two pages.

Whatever the form, the completions are next matched as closely as possible to examples in the manuals and given 36 separate item ratings. The rater determines the distribution curve for all items and assigns a final overall ego stage score to the whole protocol according to a predetermined psychometric algorithm.

Postformal Ego Development

At the postformal level, ego development theory deals with people's ability to represent the self and its environment with increasing accuracy and objectivity. At stage 4, individuals use a rational, *formal-operational logic*. Their salient time frame is the recent past and the predictable future. Energy is spent to realize and cement one's personality and to fulfill the traditional societal roles and norms as expertly as one can. The parameters for action are the perception that time and causality are linear, that observer and object are separate and have clear boundaries, and that the whole can be understood by analyzing its parts.

In contrast to the conventional world view, the time frame at the autonomous stage 5 includes one's whole life project from birth to death. As a result, adults at this stage focus on discovering and actualizing their overall, long-range potential. They have a well-developed *psycho-logic* which enables them to analyze both their own and others' thoughts, behaviors, and feelings and to gauge their reactions to and impact on others. Cognitively, they perceive self and environment as several interdependent systems. They expect to deal with many variables which interact in a nonlinear, organismic mode. They are aware of their multiple roles in society with often conflicting demands and of contradictory aspects, needs, and perceptions within themselves. What is more, they become aware that their values and beliefs are culturally conditioned and therefore relative. They begin to uncover self-protective motives and instances of self-deception within their own behavior. That greater self-awareness makes them definitely more objective and knowledgeable about human affairs than conventional adults. Because they have found a relative balance between inner and outer life, thought and feeling, self-reliance and dependency, they often display high self-esteem. In SCT protocols, they like to demonstrate how well they function, and how much they know about themselves and others. They truly relish their unique selfhood. Furthermore, they believe in human perfectibility and advocate rigorous self-scrutiny which can lead to deeper and truer insight into the self. The autonomous stage has been identified, described, and documented by several developmentalists (Maslow, 1971; Perry, 1968; Kegan, 1982; Loevinger, 1976). A strong, well-developed ego with clearly established boundaries is at the core of the autonomous individual's striving for self-realization and an objective self-identity.

In addition to the autonomous stage I-5, Loevinger and Wessler (1970) proposed an integrated stage I-6. They see the *preoccupation with "objective" identity* as the distinguishing milestone for the achievement of this stage I-6: "The problem of identity appears in terms of reconciliation of roles, striving for one's autonomy, individuality, and self-fulfillment, and recognizing other people's right to theirs" (p.108). To rate a person at stage 6, they look "for responses that integrate inner and outer life, immediate and long-term concerns, personal and social, trivial and important, and particularly responses that integrate several of the foregoing" (p. 132). "Perhaps the only general rule that can be given is that these [I-6 responses] combine several thoughts that would separately be rated at I-5" (p. 107). The lack of a set of propositions that define stage I-6 on its own terms rather than in terms of stage I-5 is a serious flaw of Loevinger's ego development theory and the assessment instrument. If there are self-theories beyond the autonomous stage, they must be defined uniquely and differ qualitatively from previous stages to qualify as stages in an invariant, hierarchical sequence. Besides, there is a scoring rule just for such compound responses. It states: "Where the combination of two or more elements in a compound response generates a more complex level of conception, rate the response one-half step higher than the highest element" (p. 115). According to this rule, most stage 6 responses in the manuals should be scored at a hypothetical stage 5/6. That there are so many more instances where this scoring rule applies at the autonomous stage than at any other is in itself an interesting phenomenon. The following discussion seeks to address these inconsistencies and offers a new interpretation of positive growth and self-understanding beyond Loevinger's stage 5.

The Challenge of Unscorable Responses to the SCT

Soon after I began rating SCT's in 1979, I came across several unusual responses. They did not match anything in the manuals, nor did they seem to fit the existing theory of ego stages. As a rule, such completions are dismissed by rating them at stage 3, category 5. But these particular responses, although unusual, seemed authentic and meaningful, so that they could not be simply dismissed.[3] Their specific structure and sometimes their content as well seemed to carry within them the seeds for clarification. They also generally came from postformal protocols. Consequently, I wanted to find out how they were unique and qualitatively different from the high completions discussed in Loevinger's theory and scoring manuals.

Sample

Since 1980 I have been systematically collecting such unusual, seemingly high completions. Each response (R) is identified with a running number in the data base in order of its original entry. At present, the data base has 844 postautonomous completions. These represent about 0.8% of all 103,000 responses (3,374 protocols) scored. The protocols originate from 85 different research projects, a wide range of ages (11 to 84) and subject populations, and many test forms. Since they were rated blindly, only the gender of the subjects was usually known. However, no postautonomous responses from individuals younger than 26 years were found.

Method of Analysis

Each time a meaningful, but unmatchable response was spotted, it was recorded and analyzed. The responses often differed both in content and structure from the ones given for a particular stem in the manuals. For each such response, the following questions were posed: What is the central theme or preoccupation in this response? Or conversely, what kind of ideas or beliefs does it question or reject? What is the complexity of the sentence structure and how differentiated is the vocabulary used to express the ideas? In which way does it differ from the examples in the manuals? And most crucially: What kind of experience and view of reality would make this response possible? Starting out with a few striking completions, I looked for patterns and similarities and ventured some preliminary propositions. These were followed up by applying them to other similar pieces of original data. The conjectures were tested in several ways: First, by trying to locate other instances of the observed phenomena in the data base as more data were collected, as well as among the responses rated at stage I-5 and I-6 in the manuals. Second, by actively searching for protocols from other research projects judged by their raters to be at stage 6 and then examining whether there was any evidence for the proposed patterns.[4] Third, by checking them against the overall evolutionary paradigm of continuing cycles of differentiation and integration observed in human development. And ultimately, the generated explanations were also evaluated by checking them against the personal life experience of available research subjects who were openly searching for meaning beyond separate, objective individuation. An overall hypothesis was generated by creating a feedback loop between empirical data and initial propositions till a sufficient match between observation and explanation was found. I was satisfied with the new stage distinctions and categories when there were no more completions that could not be classified with the revised theory. Because this is a theory based on empirical data, it is sensitive to limitations outlined in notes 2 and 3.

Hypothesis 1

The overall paradigm of individuation and self-actualization shows increasingly deeper levels of self-knowledge and self-awareness concomitant with increasing levels of cognitive, affective, and behavioral differentiation and integration. At each stage the balance between differentiation (setting boundaries) and assimilation (connecting with others) is renegotiated. Stages Δ, 3/4, and 4/5 represent a balance in favor of separation and differentiation, stages 3, 4, and 5, one in favor of participation and assimilation (see Cook-Greuter, 1990). To continue this evolutionary pattern, individuals at stage 5/6 would have to reiterate an attempt to define themselves apart from the previously held notions and to disengage themselves from the prior autonomous holding environment. Instead, they would have to assert their unique differences and question the very assumptions that constitute the autonomous reality.

Procedure 1

In order to test this prediction, I separated the data collection into sets with common features. The first category contained responses that fit the rule for compound sentences and was put at a hypothetical stage 5/6. It includes completions with a complex matrix of abstract thoughts, feelings, and ideas. Second, I ordered the rest of the completions into three other categories. There is one for completions which seemed to be more spontaneous and comprehensive and/or showed deeper psychological probing into self-knowledge and understanding of others than at stage 5. To check whether there was evidence of a critique of stage 5 beliefs at stage 5/6, I examined responses to item 8: *What gets me into trouble—* and item 25: *My main problem is—* from the data bank. If my hypothesis that 5/6 protocols are characterized by uncertainty about the previous way of assessing oneself is correct, then I could expect to find indications of this in the above items. And, indeed, several such instances were found.

Analysis 1

Postautonomous persons seem to feel even more compelled than those at stage 5 to give comprehensive responses in an attempt to be as objective as possible in representing reality in its full complexity. The one-sentence completions rated at stage 5/6, category 1, because of the rule for compound sentences, are often several lines long. They employ a great variety of stylistic devices and punctuation marks in order to mirror and express the complex matrix of experience they perceive.

R#206 When I am with a woman—how can I generalize? Sometimes I am overwhelmed, sometimes bored; sometimes incredibly aware of a sexual electricity, often times primarily involved in business dealings; sometimes arguing, sometimes enjoying her company and sometimes wishing I were somewhere else.

R#616 Crime and delinquency could be halted if—Since both these are "shortcuts" to fulfilling one's desires they could be solved if 1) people could understand the purpose and benefit to everyone in the long term of conforming to society sanctioned channels for fulfilling desires—Employment, Marriage, etc., and 2) People could be more fulfilled self-sufficiently from within, independent of outer circumstance.

Many of the complex responses are also more spontaneous, less sanitized, than those at stage 5. They often reveal the thoughts and feelings of a person as they actually occur. Conflict and contradictions are expressed directly without apology or from hindsight. The completion below illustrates this postautonomous flavor of psychological differentiation and immediacy.

R#392   Crime and delinquency could be halted—oh fuck! it can't be halted; it can possibly be ameliorated, and the question seems trivial as I sit here in a country where terrorists are killing whole villages and leveling homes with bulldozers, and [. . .] army officers are possibly raping [. . .] women—anger and despair are responses to these realities, and to crime and delinquency, too.

In spite of the profanity, this woman has a highly developed understanding of the issue. She rejects the stem as presented. What is more, she is struck by the incongruence between the mundane task of completing the SCT and the civil war raging in her current reality both in the outside world and within.

Next I noticed marked similarities in content and sentence structure in the responses to the two self-critical items. There is a repeated concern with thinking, and thinking as projection in the following examples:

R#4   What gets me into trouble is—Thinking that I am in trouble?

R#37   What gets me into trouble is—messages I give myself—not interpreting things as they are, but rather as I am afraid they might be.

R#318   What gets me into trouble is—letting what *is* become obscured by what *I am afraid is*.

R#11   My main problem is—seeing things as they really are and not expecting them to be different.

R#212   My main problem is—thinking I "know" when the "answer" isn't the appropriate response.

R#321   My main problem is—thinking about being instead of just being.

R#48   My main problem is—undulating with life so that I don't need it to be different than it is.

First, "undulating" in R#48 suggests a dancelike motion that is not geared towards any specific destiny. Whereas "the journey of life" and "being the master of one's soul" were the preferred images for stage 5 self-actualizers, we are now listening to a different tune in R#48, that of life as a dance.

Second, these individuals seem to say that too much thinking gets in the way of genuine experience (R#4, 11, 212, 321). They show a heightened awareness that the mental habits of thinking, expecting, defending, and fearing are problematic in themselves. While the autonomous ego effectively, but unconsciously, coordinated external and internal experiences, the postautonomous ego is no longer sure that it really is and wants to be in control. It sees itself trapped by automatic mental procedures which on a deeper level it has found inadequate. How does this bear on one's self-understanding? R#26 and R#28, when read in the context of each other, provide insight into a woman who realizes the dilemma between old mental habits and a new level of awareness. She writes:

R#26   I am—simple and complex. Medium and small, (oh yeah? what does that mean?) Everything, if I believe I create my reality.

R#28   My main problem is—noticing when I'm beginning to see myself as vulnerable.

She knows that by defining herself as vulnerable she creates her vulnerability. But the habit of labeling experience is so ingrained, that it traps her in spite of her recognition of the danger. As a first step in overcoming this habit, she wants to at least "notice" when it happens. Loevinger offers no examples or explanations for this kind of cognitive insight into linguistic conditioning and mental habits. At her stages I-5 and I-6 persons take for granted that proper reflection and rational analysis will eventually lead them to discover the underlying truth in spite of the obvious differences in interpretation at the surface level. The above samples suggest that at the postautonomous stage, rational thought and reflection are no longer accepted as automatic givens, but become themselves objects of intense questioning and exploration.

Numerous completions in the data pool refer to the sustained concern with thought and language and how they affect one's understanding. At this juncture people often become entranced by their inner world and the workings of the mind and start to watch the intricate proceedings with great curiosity and absorption. Stage 5/6 persons don't just notice that they always think about things; that feat is possible earlier. Now they want to know the underlying mechanics of how they think and interpret reality while they are doing so. More important, they realize how impossible it is for them not to think and analyze at every waking moment. The question of identity changes from a question with a possible answer to a question about such questioning itself. The question "Who am I truly and fundamentally?" changes to "What is the meaning behind the experience of continually yearning for a more accurate self-definition?" To some, the paradox of trying to find out the nature of thought by using thought becomes obvious. Others become conscious of the process of successive approximations in their endeavors to create coherent self-identity and of the futility of ever getting at the source through further intensive self-scrutiny.

At stage 5 (and stage I-6) one thinks of oneself as a separate individual with a unique mission. One automatically thinks, feels, assesses, labels, coordinates, and interprets experience and in doing so creates a stable, enduring sense of self. At the postautonomous level, a more critical stance towards these automatic processes has been developed as the following groups of examples demonstrate. The most common group indicates that labels and definitions are arbitrary conventions that make reality appear fixed and static in a way it never is.

> R#205 A man's job—has traditionally been the role of "breadwinner," but such simplistic labeling ignores an almost infinite number of possibilities, limited only by that man's conceptual model of himself and his world.

Such responses mirror an insight that Koplowitz (1984) presented in defining his unitary or postsystemic concept of reality: "Reality is undifferentiated. The process of naming or measuring pulls that which is named out of reality, which itself is not nameable or measurable" (p. 289). Other examples like the following are less explicit, but still show a palpable concern with issues of definition:

> R#409 "I feel sorry"—(meaning remorseful) is often confused with "I feel sorry" (meaning sympathy)—both important to feel, to speak, and to clarify.

> R#411 People who step out of line at work—sometimes are only that—out of line—and other times can help by how and when they step, to redefine a more workable + appropriate line.

Symbolic representations are abstractions; they pull things out of the phenomenological continuum. They thus simplify everyday experience by presenting a preselected map of what to attend to and what not.

The following two responses use items on the SCT itself to point out that any verbal stimuli or test questions act as filters which preshape the responses.[5] The authors of the instrument must have been unaware (as are most subjects who take the test) that the SCT, too, limits in a fundamental way the range of possible responses for all but the most alert and insightful individuals.

> R#157 Raising a family—is a misnomer. A family is not raised, it grows as a group process given mutually shared attitudes of affection, respect and wish to communicate.

> R#507 I just can't stand people who—what "can't stand"?! That's too strong. How about "I prefer people who . . ." enjoy silence, are gentle, kind and happy, are positive and intelligent, etc. People in the opposite direction I can stand as needed.

> R#401 "If my mother"—begins some lingering treasured fantasies I'd love to give up.

When respondents mention the process of how they construct meaning and reality in their minds, they give yet another clue that they are now conscious of the constructed nature of everyday reality. They can imagine multiple realities, not only many interpretations of the same reality as at stages 4/5 and 5.

> R#2 Rules are—amazing structures to me, sometimes. We create order and force it to last.

> R#673 When people are helpless—when they lose touch with who they are— creators of their own experience.

> R#694 When people are helpless—I feel it is because they have *created* this state, or *allowed* this to happen to them—"we create our own reality"— always.

> R#565 At times he worried about—anything + at times he worried about nothing, and the worry was in his mind not in its object.

Another group of responses refers to meaning making as an ongoing process.

> R#20 Education—means, to me, at this moment, an unfolding process of coming to make sense of the world.

> R#38 Education—means so many different things to different people. I think of it as a never-ending process of restructuring one's views of the world.

> R#329 I am—always thinking, always questioning, always struggling with meaning—not in some abstract form, but meaning in a concrete, everyday

sense, between people, as we all struggle to make sense of the world.

Because the need to make sense is fundamental in humans beings, the subject below looks for coherence even among the seemingly unrelated items on the SCT:

R#526 I am—trying to look beyond each individual sentence in this exercise to establish some meaningful connection or theme that will help me overcome my current stage of "stuckness."

Other responses deal with perception and frame of reference[6] as crucial elements in meaning making.

R#266 Raising a family—is an important choice, and the relative (actual) importance which it is given in a society determines many of that society's basic values.

R#663 I just can't stand people who—oppose positive values in life and actively pursue negative goals. Actually, though, in a broader context I can appreciate that each man does what he feels is best according to his perception of reality.

R#396 People who step out of line at work—are sometimes acting out of idiosyncratic motives or counterdependency, and sometimes responding to stupid or unartful management, and sometimes kindly [?] challenging history. You have to know the context to make a judgment and even then the judgment is filtered by your frame of reference.

These responses are different from those at stages 4/5 and 5, where subjects are only aware of the general relativity of points of view. The first part of the following stage 5/6 completion reflects this earlier, more superficial recognition. What makes this a postautonomous completion, however, is the awareness of the ongoing process of restructuring one's world view.

R#38 Education—means so many different things to different people. I think of it as a never-ending process of restructuring one's views of the world.

Discussion 1

As people grow and are able to perceive and process more information from more and more diverse sources, they become increasingly aware of how complex reality is. Starting at the autonomous stage, they try to describe this experience through ever more intricate complex arrays of abstract thought, reflection, and interpretation. The sudden increase of responses that fit the higher complexity rule for compound sentences[7] at stage 5 is probably a result of this intensified search for accuracy and a defense against a budding sense of reality's illusiveness. Subjects at the postautonomous level of differentiation seem to become conscious of the fact that language is not only a wonderful tool, but imposes fundamental limits. The attempt to pin down reality with more precise language and distinctions inevitably brings unsatisfactory results because language is always and only an abstraction. Language (or any other form of symbolic codification) constitutes a map that can never fully reflect the underlying territory.

Once this is realized, the ego no longer *unconsciously* organizes coherent meaning from experience, but becomes aware of itself as an organizer and as a temporary, though necessary and useful construct. This stage is therefore referred to as ego-aware or construct-aware. Only when a stable, autonomous self-sense is achieved can adults become fully aware of the human activity of meaning making through the delineation, objectification, and labeling of reality. Now, concepts can be seen for what they are: potentially effective but nevertheless arbitrary codifications, representations, summaries of the flux of sensory data.

At stages 3/4 and 4, one experiences one's current view as a final and sufficient explanatory principle for how the world is, for how everything makes sense. With postformal development, one becomes more conscious of growth and change over time. Finally, at the construct-aware stage, people understand the whole psychological process of the continual transformation of one's self-view and reality perception. This includes an awareness that all abstract concepts and maps of the self are essentially impermanent.

Even though this discovery is in part "hypothetical-deductive," it mainly results from a systematic deconstruction of the formal operational assumptions. At least for ego development, postformal stages represent not just "more complex patterns of already available forms of formal operational thought" (Commons & Richards, 1984; see also Alexander, this volume). Rather, postautonomous conceptions represent new ways of thinking and experiencing.

On the one hand, construct-aware individuals know empirically and intuitively that there is no clear subject/object separation, no either/or, yet they are stymied by trying to express their unease about this state of affairs. This can be seen in the following completion:

R#356 I am—a confusing complex of contradictions—both good/bad, assured/self-doubting, aloof/warm at the same time. There are no easy formulations to the way I am.

At stage 5, the identification with polar opposites is still linear (sometimes I am good, and sometimes I am bad) or context dependent. But now these dichotomies are integrated, and nondefensively appreciated as two sides of the same coin (I am good and bad at the same time), because each concept can only exist through the other. This is understood on an intellectual level only, and a desire to lift the confusion can still be heard in the above response.

As was shown, some postautonomous adults know that there are "no easy formulations" for describing one's self-experience. For one, trying to do so is felt to be a limiting mental habit. And second, meaning is seen as each individual's personal and temporary construction of reality. These insights constitute a new level of cognitive insight entirely different from that of ego stage 5. At the ego-aware stage 5/6, the previous way of rational analysis is rejected and a new kind of self-understanding is sought.

Since postautonomous adults are by definition already autonomous and familiar with the possibility of self-deception and defensive maneuvers, they don't need to deny the value of the concept of the self and of rational behavior once they recognize their limitations. Instead, human mental activity and language are valued as essential tools for human adaptation and interaction, but no longer unexamined and taken for granted as they were earlier. In the representational realm, we always create paradox. By labeling, comparing, measuring, analyzing, and predicting, attention is automatically taken away from what is, to what we presume there is because of cultural and personal bias. Responses R#37, R#318, R#11, and R#48 (shown above) illustrate this insight.

Once individuals realize that their sense of a coherent self has been built on a partial, filtered perception of reality, they naturally desire to experience the underlying, unfiltered reality. They want to be liberated from the bondage of rational "thought" and the pseudo-grounding afforded by the ego. They wish to be free from restricting self-definitions. They desire to see life afresh, without the preconceived ideas and mental behaviors that have been perfected through lifelong habit and conditioning. But as their construct-aware completions demonstrate, they also become aware of how difficult it is to transcend automatic rational behavior. An inkling of this postautonomous dilemma comes across in the following response:

R#25   At times she worried about—holding on too tight to any particular idea of how she or the world should be.

The very desire for freedom from any particular idea of how the world should be keeps one fettered within that frame of reference. A genuine openness—an openness that is completely detached from any desired outcome—would have to be the essence of a different mode of experience. The next completion grapples with this issue of radical openness:

R#527 My main problem is—finding the courage to live with uncertainty, "unanchoredness," and the discomfort of not knowing what lies ahead or how well I will respond, and how I will affect others and be affected by their responses.

Yet living with uncertainty is clearly a desire of this man. If he can get accustomed to it, unanchoredness promises to be a more adequate and satisfying stance towards living than striving for predictable order. The idea of becoming unanchored, unattached from a specific self-view hints at the potential transformation from an identity based on a complex, objective self-theory to a process-oriented, unfiltered mode of experiencing that will be addressed in the next section.

Hypothesis 2

These last two responses anticipate a fundamental change in the evolution of self-awareness. Stage 5/6 subjects seem to realize that their self-identity is always and only a temporary construct. Thus they become less invested in the idea of an individual ego that serves the unconscious function of creating a stable self-identity. They see through the mental habits of analyzing (cutting apart), comparing, measuring, and labeling as a means to reify and map experience. They understand the need for a different approach to knowing, one which relies on the immediate, unfiltered experience of what is. But this requires an attitude of complete openness: One has to free oneself from wishing for any particular outcomes, as well as from the automatic habits of representational thought. In short, the next step requires that one's objective self-identity, that is, the ego as representation,[8] be transcended and that one's way of knowing be transformed.

An entirely new kind of self-representation constitutes one of the elements of the next projected stage, the universal stage 6. It must have some of the following characteristics. In this new self-balance, the continuous flux of changing perceptions, thoughts, feelings, and sensations is acknowledged. The immediate witnessing of the ongoing processes is found to be more satisfying than orienting oneself with maps of whatever level of complexity. Mental activity is experienced as active when it opens towards such witnessing, and as passive or automatic when it is unaware of itself (see Torbert, this volume). The affirmation that one is *nothing* is at the core of this new self-perception. No-"thing" implies that there are no definite boundaries and therefore no clear identifications. When one is aware of the subtlest shifts in one's self-experience from moment to moment, one is more attuned to what actually is (including one's inner life) than is possible through rational interpretation and reflection. Thus, one can act with greater spontaneity and harmony to the demands of any given situation. A fluid, postobjective, metaconceptual self-view would therefore constitute a qualitatively different, higher cognitive integration of the self at the next predicted stage. Several instances of this postobjective or transcendent way of understanding the self have been found on SCT protocols as will be shown next.

Procedure 2

I will forever appreciate response R#10 below because it made me question early on whether existing ego development theory was adequate to account for all possible self-representations that the SCT elicits. More than any other it has triggered my inquiry into higher ego stages.

Of the 36 stems on the SCT, stem #23 "I am—" is the only one that requests a direct self-description or definition. I therefore went through the data base looking for other indices of an ego-transcendent self-view among the 28 postautonomous completions for this stem. By studying them, I hoped to elucidate the nature of the underlying cognitive transformation that seemed to make the following, unique response possible.

R#10   I am—finally, in the long run, mostly unfathomable, but I enjoy the process of trying to fathom.

Analysis 2

Do we know any concrete things about this woman? Do we know what personal interests or desires she has, what roles she sees herself playing, what conflicts she experiences? Does she present us with an objective, non-distorted self-definition of the sort that Loevinger or Kegan are looking for in their highest stages? On the other hand, is this the response of an undifferentiated or a sick individual or of someone who doesn't know how to express herself? The answer to all these questions has to be no. Of course, the 1970 manual presents other reasons why people don't respond with an explicit self-definition. Examples from the manual indicate that they may lack self-differentiation or simply evade the task which is common to stage 3, or they may be unwilling to choose from among several competing possibilities, as illustrated by the third example below (Loevinger et al., vol. 2, 1970, pp. 279-286):

I am—nothing (I-3) [evasion]. (p. 279)
I am—what I am (I-3) [evasion, cliché]. (p. 279)
I am—impossible to describe by any one adjective or noun. (3/4) (p. 281)

However, R#10 does not sound like any of these, nor does it fit into one of the higher stages of Loevinger's theory. The following is the only example given at stage I-6 for item #23 in the 1970 manual:

> I am—aware of human frailty and weaknesses, yet I believe that man can, thru his own efforts, improve his own lot. (p. 286a)

Although this subject professes a relatively tolerant awareness of human nature, she is still firmly embedded in the autonomous conviction that one is master of one's destiny and can (and should) better oneself. This completion is a little more distanced and inclusive than is common for stage 5, but there is nothing in it that indicates a higher than stage 5 cognitive integration. On the other hand, the same manual also lists an unclassified completion at stage I-5 which seems uniquely different from all the other examples given.

> I am—at times a question mark, at times just a period, but many times an exciting exclamation mark. (p. 286b)

Now this person uses a surprising metaphor to convey a vivid sense of her changing self-experience. She does not refer to conventional formulations of identity, nor does she feel confusion like R#356 (see page 135). On the contrary, the completion has a playful quality. It would seem to be a more likely candidate for a postautonomous rating than the one cited above (p. 286a), which was actually rated at stage I-6.

R#10, however, differs from this response and any other examples given in the manual by suggesting a fluid self-experience. The author of R#10 declares that she is no thing that can be fathomed, assessed, or identified. Nonetheless, she does not seem to experience any of the anxiety or distress that is symptomatic of individuals at earlier stages when they find themselves unable to figure out who they are. Kegan (1982) gives a careful account of the different depressions caused by "the not-knowing" or "the no-longer knowing" who one is at each transition in the evolution of the self. R#527 attests to this awareness. Instead R#10 acknowledges that one cannot and—what is more telling—need not "in the long run" know and describe who one is. Witnessing the process is gratifying—not pursuing the always-fleeting answer. There is no need, because this woman has realized that the sense of the permanent individual self is an illusion. The self is created and experienced anew at every moment.

At stage 5/6 individuals intellectually recognized the pattern of forming self-identities by consecutive, integrative approximations driven by the underlying human need for certitude and stability. At stage 6, the fundamental instability of self-representations is both experienced and acknowledged on a deeper level. Because the above subject has no need for

Table 5.1

Comparison of the Three Highest Stages of Understanding: Autonomous, Construct-Aware, and Fluid

Name of Stage	Autonomous Stage 5	Ego-Aware Stage 5/6	Universal Stage 6
Goal	To be the most one can be	To be aware	To be
Example from SCT	I am—a well-balanced professional human being, definitely on the path of self-actualization and self-fulfillment	I am—simple and complex. Medium and small, (oh yeah? what does that mean?) Everything, if I believe I create my reality. (R#26)	I am—finally, in the long run, mostly unfathomable, but I enjoy the process of trying to fathom. (R#10)
Focus	Self-realization, self-actualization: to create a complex, meaningful, coherent and objective self-identity and to maximize a sense of individuality	Exploring the habits and processes of the mind and the way one makes sense of experience by constructing ever more complex theories and maps via cognition and language	Nonevaluative, integrative witnessing of ongoing process of experience and meaning making; deepening one's sense of connectedness and appreciation
Self-definition	Autonomous, multiple roles; self-generated core-identity; aware of many defenses and expression of some inner conflict. Sense of self-esteem, empowerment	Complex matrix of self-identifications, at the same time aware of its construction and stages (approximations); critique of conventional labeling	Description of self as in constant flux and transformation; transcendent awareness: I am no-body, no-thing
Dominant center of awareness	Rational mind and intellect; thought as mediated through language (symbolic codifications); unique self as master of one's destiny	Ego as process and meaning-making center; rational mind plus intimations (vision) of transcendent awareness during peak moments	Subtle transpersonal self; immediate, metarational, postrepresentational awareness and direct experience of what is

Range of awareness	Aware of body/mind as system; aware of cultural conditioning, context and interpretation in human experience; continuous search for more accurate map of experience	Aware of the limits of symbolic codifications and rational thought; aware of ego and conventional reality as constructs; possibility of other planes of reality gleaned; keenly aware of difference between map and territory	Witnessing the perceptional flux and changing states of consciousness; unfiltered, direct experience; rational mind seen as one possible way of experiencing; aware of "illusion" of permanent individual self
Method of knowing	Reasoning, careful rational analysis aided by feeling and intuition: one assesses, evaluates, judges; compares, measures, contrasts experience from many angles and integrates into larger whole	Rational analysis of limits of logical reasoning, its inevitable paradoxes; insight into the nature of symbolic codifications, thought, and the construction of meaning; contemplation of limitations of present way of knowing	Contemplation, witnessing of continuous flux; subjective experience of nonsymbolic mode of direct knowing and apperception of deeper level of reality; intellect and intuition are used, but not overvalued
Loevinger's ego development theory*	autonomous stage I-5 (E-8), integrated stage I-6 (E-9)		

*Loevinger, 4/92: unpublished, revised manuals for scoring the Washington University Sentence Completion Test premature closure, she can relish "the process of trying to fathom." In Keats's words she possesses the "negative capability, that is when a man [or woman] is capable of being in uncertainties, mysteries, doubts, without any irritable reaching after fact & reason" (Keats, 1817/1962). It is this ability to abstain from automatically trying to name and explain everything which characterizes self-understanding at stage 6. Below are four more responses that reflect this openness to process at various levels of depth and awareness.

R#288 I am—alive, trundling along, making sense as best as I can, diversifying & expanding while consolidating & contracting

R#410 I am—which is pretty wondrous to me all by itself as it unfolds

R#511 I am—I believe life is an exploration of this question

R#26   I am—everything I imagine myself to be and more (and less)

Discussion 2

The above completions to item 23 express a self-experience free from the need of previous stages to reach after fact and reason. "Objective" self-knowledge no longer satisfies the need for constancy as it does for the highest stages in Loevinger's theory. Instead the unfiltered experience or the perception of ongoing process, rhythm, and flux provide inner stability and affirmation. The self-sense of this different stage is fluid, "undulating," based on one's trust in the intrinsic value and processes of life. According to the axioms of cognitive-developmental theory, one can truly speak of a different, higher-stage integration here. A whole logical/psycho-logical system (the rational, symbolic domain in human development) has become the content—an element in a higher-order, postrepresentational integration.

In this new self-experience, individuals see through the function of the representational ego to objectify and reify the self by defining (delimiting) it. They experience the self in its moment-to-moment transformation and therefore consciously decline to satisfy the implicit demand of item 23: *I am*—for an objective identification. They understand that the striving for individual permanence is an impossible and unnecessary dream in the face of their experience of continuous flux and change in states of awareness. Now, the ego—with its striving for independence and for permanent, objective identity—is just one way among others of how one is conscious of being. In that sense, the symbolic, representational self has been deconstructed and transcended and a whole new mode of self-perception and understanding has opened up.

In contrast to the preceding stage 5/6, individuals at stage 6 have replaced the habitual, unconscious mental processing by learning to immerse themselves in the immediate, ongoing flow of experience. The awareness of their thoughts, feelings, behaviors, perceptions, and states of alertness is consistently maintained, not just occasionally experienced. They have become, primarily, nonjudgmental witnesses of their own being-becoming who observe the many roles they, secondarily, play out on the stage of life. The following response from one subject illustrates this witnessing and the recognition of the touching folly of all temporary identifications.

R#772 I am—increasingly able to play many roles without becoming the role(s)—doctor, farmer, father, husband, carpenter, friend, judge, student, advisor, business man (and many more)—and do so while all the while watching myself do it (and laughing).

Overall, the above examples from the SCT suggest that there is at least one stage of self-awareness beyond the postautonomous stage 5/6 described earlier. Its openness to the flux of experience, combined with a conscious refusal to reify and codify experience, makes this stage fundamentally and structurally different from all previous ego stages. In addition, people with a fluid self-sense seem to be free from the anxiety accompanying "not-knowing" that characterizes other ego stages.

Conclusion

A careful reading of a small sample of unusual completions to the SCT reveals evidence of two forms of self-description beyond the "objective self-identity" of stages I-5 and I-6 in Loevinger's scheme: a postautonomous self-description at an ego-aware or construct-aware stage 5/6, and a fluid, ego-transcendent self-experience at the universal stage 6.

An autonomous, well-integrated ego is the prerequisite for the cognitive development to these higher forms of self-cognition. Jack Engler (1986) said it concisely: "You have to be somebody before you can be nobody" (p.17). Autonomous/integrated individuals see themselves and are usually experienced by others as "somebody." They show high self-esteem. Stage 5/6 individuals become aware of the anthropocentric self-importance of the stage 5 stance. They may feel torn between high and low self-esteem. They feel skilled and powerful when comparing their highly developed mental capacities and their ability to analyze and create meaning with those of most others. But, at peak moments, when they see through the illusion of the stable, independent self and the dysfunctional, unconscious aspects of rational behavior, they may feel annihilated, that is, "like nothing." A more detailed analysis of the stage 5/6 existential paradox is given in Cook-Greuter (1990). The drama is the more salient, because at stage 5/6 individuals have achieved a measure of insight that most outside observers tend to admire. But ego-aware subjects know that they are fettered within deep-rooted mental habits that prevent them from developing the different kind of self-experience and knowing for which they yearn. They struggle valiantly to abdicate control, wishing, and attachments, but inevitably fail left to their own devices. For the essence of the new way of knowing is effortlessness, noncontrol, nonattachment, and radical openness.

By stage 6, individuals no longer attempt to consciously break the rational mental habits, but have relaxed enough to be open to both the naked experience and the mental activities as they unfold.

Self-identifications at stages 5/6 and 6 are structurally different from Loevinger's highest stages as well as from each other. In each case, the dominant structure of awareness of the lower stage becomes an element in the next stage. First, individuals become conscious of their own development in terms of stages. They can look back and describe and compare the changing ways of their understanding and the mechanics by which they create meaning and reality. In a step beyond, they are able to transcend the representational realm and immerse themselves in the fluid, nonevaluative mode of direct experience as exemplified in R#10 and R#288.

Based on the above evidence from the SCT, it is proposed that some initial form of transpersonal awareness seems to be an *inevitable and natural outcome* of the completed journey of the self through the stages of cognitive, rational development in the symbolic realm. So far, there are few signs in the completions to the SCT that subjects develop on their own beyond a preliminary, though constant awareness and tolerance for uncensured perceptual input from both external and internal sources.

By all accounts, some training in one of the many forms of spiritual development, meditation, or meta-awareness is necessary for individuals to develop to subtler, more differentiated stages of transcendence as described by proponents of consciousness theory (see Wilber, 1986; Washburn, 1988, Alexander et al. 1990; and Nuernberger, this volume). What is more, the training must be mediated by a catalyst, i.e., an individual who functions from a more advanced and refined level of perception than the trainee. This contingency is reminiscent of early language acquisition, which also requires years of extensive conditioning, more knowledgeable external catalysts, and cultural support to succeed.

A unique response (1 out of over 103,000) from an advanced meditator, who was rated as a compromise at stage 5/6, hinted at a possible further level of cognitive-symbolic deconstruction. On first impact, his completion sounds "deranged," but is it?

R#580 I am—infinite unbounded at times I think how far can one see through muddy water muddy with the infinite laws of nature lively in the infinite unbounded I'm binding the infinite how infinite can it be absolutely full with unsullied by the infinite laws of nature.

The administrator of the project also had doubts. He sent a note to the subject asking him whether he might want to edit this response for the possible sake of clarity. The man's written response was:

This response can and should be edited in a number of different ways—by the reader, to get a taste of my experience: Sometimes I know, sometimes I don't. — Eg: [sic] "I am. I am infinite unbounded. I am infinite unbounded at times. I am infinite unbounded at times, I think. at times I think, at times I think how far? At times I think how far can one see?" — It's muddled but it's fun and it captures the essence of my experience.

A response like R#580 may not be enough to further refine the cognitive-developmental paradigm in terms of further deconstructions of the representational self in ego development theory, but it certainly points in that direction. According to SCT scoring instructions, such a response must be dismissed because it doesn't fit the theory or the manuals. But can any developmental psychologist dismiss evidence that indicates there are as-yet-uncharted cognitive modes in his/her data?

This paper is the result of 12 years of collecting and analyzing unusual postautonomous responses that came from mature adults. Looking at the evidence from their "unscorable" completions, two ego stages beyond Loevinger's stages I-5 and I-6 can be identified. Each, in turn, hierarchically integrates the previous way of meaning making. The construct-aware stage 5/6 is the highest observed self-perspective in the rational/representational realm of cognition. The universal stage 6, with its fluid, deconstructed self-view, belongs to the postrepresentational, metaphysical or spiritual domain of higher consciousness (see Figure I.1, Introduction).

Koplowitz (1989) argued that both in method and purpose, spiritual development and cognitive development always remain distinct. The very existence of transcendent awareness from differentiated adults who are not concerned with spiritual development *per se* indicates a different possibility. Developing through the full range of ego stages and the concomitant cognitive, emotional, and behavioral transformations can be regarded as an inevitable, legitimate, and nonmeditative path through the gates of rationality towards a higher, postsymbolic consciousness (see also Funk's analysis of the relationship between the paths of self-actualization and self-transcendence, Chapter 1). The radical openness to uncensored experience, the absence of anxiety in the face of "not-knowing" and the deconstructed, fluid self-understanding found in the universal stage 6 responses are evidence of it.

Notes

1. In order to distinguish Loevinger's highest stages from mine, I-5 and I-6 are used to refer to her highest stages, and stage 5, stage 5/6, and stage 6 for my own stages.

2. In my experience, individuals who are determined to give an extensive response usually find ways to do so by writing in the margins or on the back of the test forms. What seems more critical in this context is that a short form may be interpreted as a subtle hint that complex responses are not welcome. In order to make sure that conventional individuals are not tempted to just carry on (and some do anyway), an even less fortunate bias has been introduced into the test form. Whereas it is quite easy to disqualify a wordy, conventional response from a high rating, it is impossible to judge what postformal persons might have said if they had been encouraged to express themselves to their own, fullest satisfaction. This technical detail is an important one if one plans to construct a theory which includes higher stages and is based on the empirical data gathered through such an instrument.

3. It is possible that these types of responses did not appear in the original data sets from which ego development theory was constructed either because of their rareness (less than 1%) or possibly for the mechanical reasons outlined above. Even if they did occur, they may not have been recognized by the theoreticians because of their own level of awareness (see explanation of rater bias: Loevinger & Wessler, p.125, 1970).

4. By 1985 there was enough evidence to suggest that self-awareness was the basic structure that underlies all ego stages. In addition, the unmatched data could be more systematically accounted for by revising the paradigm at the highest level into a transitional, ego-aware stage 5/6 and an ego-transcendent stage 6 (see Cook-Greuter, 1990). A set of new scoring criteria for these postautonomous stages was then introduced (Cook-Greuter, 1987) and used alongside the less refined distinctions found in the manuals to score postconventional protocols. So far, the new categories seem to be both necessary and sufficient to account for the data gathered hitherto.

5. It is for this reason that especially probing interviews have to be examined for hidden messages, hidden in most cases from both the interviewer and the subject.

6. Frames of reference range from limited to comprehensive. The frame of reference one might have in a specific profession like that of a farmer can be partially or fully conscious. The frame of reference that encompasses a whole cosmology such as one's language or the Western mind-set is almost always unconscious. For definitions see Miller, this volume.

7. Even though completions that fit the rule for compound sentences at stage 5 [they generate a more complex level of conception than their elements] are rated in a separate stage 5/6 category, a protocol should be rated at stage 5, if there is no other evidence of postautonomous awareness.

8. Funk (Chapter 1 in this volume) gives an extensive review of the different functions of the ego. Generally, the synthetic function continues to operate even at higher stages of consciousness, whereas the representational aspects are sequentially deconstructed.

Acknowledgments

I sincerely wish to thank Jane Loevinger for her seminal work in ego development theory and measurement. It has been the springboard for many of my own ideas and certainly for this paper. I am also deeply grateful to my husband, Craig Cook, for his loving and generous moral support over so many years of our life together.

I addition, I want to thank Michael Commons, Bill Torbert, Skip Alexander, and Mel Miller. They have challenged me and provided me with excellent editorial advice. Their friendship and support are very much valued.

Appendix A: Scoring Categories for Stages 5/6 and 6

Stage 5/6 Categories:
1. Complex matrix of possibilities, reasons, feelings, and contrasts, often rational, abstract, distanced in an effort to accurately describe the complexity of reality as perceived.
2. Wide range of thought with self as referent including complex relationships and deep insights into own and other's multilayered psychological functioning.
3. Aware of existential and psychological paradoxes, thinking about own thinking process and thought habits, aware of loops, recursions, and logical paradox as inherent in any symbol system (not as instances), stream of consciousness, free associations, comments on various levels of own awareness or experienced lack thereof.
4. Explicit awareness of perceptions, definitions, labeling, assumptions, frame of reference, paradigms, and structure in meaning making. Aware of the constructed nature of self and reality.

Stage 6 Categories:
1. Wide range of thought on human relationships (self not as center) often with unique, positive affect and gratitude.
2. High tolerance, acceptance of self and world "as is," openness to life, change, process, rhythm, self in flux.
3. Universal connectedness, nontrivial expression of self as part of larger world, humankind, history, ongoing creation.
4. Fundamental feelings, thoughts and reflection about human existence, fate, life, death, joy and suffering, conscience and consciousness, mystery of being, etc.
5. Instances of unitive thought or metaphor: Shifting focus effortlessly between near and far, mundane and sublime, temporal and eternal, serious and ridiculous, individuated self and transcendent self, as well as fluid transition between different states of consciousness.

References

Alexander, C. N.; Davies, J. L.; Dixon, C. A; Dillbeck, M.; Drucker, S.; Oetzel, R.; Muehlman, J. M. & Orme-Johnson, D. (1990). Growth of higher stages of consciousness: Maharishi's Vedic Psychology of human development. In C. Alexander & E. Langer (Eds.), *Higher stages of human development: Perspectives on adult growth* (pp. 286-341). New York: Oxford University Press.

Commons, M. L. & Richards, F. A. (1984). A general model of stage theory. In M. L. Commons, F. A. Richards & C. Armon (Eds.), *Beyond formal operations: Late adolescent and adult cognitive development* (pp. 120-140) New York: Praeger.

Cook-Greuter, S. (1987). *Defining and measuring postconventional ego stages, especially stages 5/6 and 6.* Paper presented at the annual meeting of the Society for Research in Adult Development, Cambridge, MA.

Cook-Greuter, S. (1990). Maps for living: Ego development stages from symbiosis to conscious universal embeddedness. In M. L. Commons, C. Armon, L. Kohlberg, F. A. Richards, T. A. Grotzer & J. D. Sinnott (Eds.), *Adult development, models and methods in the study of adolescent and adult thought*, 2 (pp. 79-104). New York: Praeger.

Engler, J. (1986). Therapeutic aims in psychotherapy and meditation: Developmental stages in the representation of self. In K. Wilber, J. Engler & D. Brown (Eds.), *Transformations of consciousness* (pp.17-51). Boston: Shambhala.

Keats, J. (1817/1962). Letter to George and Thomas Keats. In *The Norton Anthology of English Literature*, vol. 2, p. 571. New York: Norton and Co.

Kegan, R. (1982). *The evolving self: Problem and process of human development*. Cambridge, MA: Harvard University Press.

Koplowitz, H. (1984). A projection beyond Piaget's formal operations stage: A general system stage and a unitary stage. In M. L. Commons, F. A. Richards & C. Armon (Eds.), *Beyond formal operations: Late adolescent and adult cognitive development* (pp. 272-295). New York: Praeger.

Koplowitz, H. (1990b). Development of mind and discipline of mind in the workplace. Unpublished manuscript. Paper presented at the Fifth Adult Development Symposium. Cambridge, MA: Harvard Medical School Department of Psychiatry.

Loevinger, J. (1976). *A theory of ego development*. San Francisco: Jossey-Bass.

Loevinger, J. & Wessler, R. (1970). *Measuring ego development*, vol. 1: *Construction and use of a sentence completion test*. San Francisco:

Jossey-Bass.

Loevinger, J.; Wessler, R. & Redmore, C. (1970). *Measuring ego development*, vol. 2: *Scoring manual for women and girls*. San Francisco: Jossey-Bass.

Maslow, A. H. (1971). *The farther reaches of human nature*. New York: Penguin Books.

Perry, W. G. (1968). *Forms of intellectual and ethical development in the college years*. New York: Holt, Rinehart & Winston.

Sullivan, H. S. (1953). *Interpersonal theory of psychiatry*. New York: W. W. Norton & Company.

Washburn, M. (1988). *The ego and the dynamic ground*. Albany, NY: State University of New York Press.

Wilber, K. (1986). The spectrum of psychopathology. In K. Wilber, J. Engler & D. Brown (Eds.), *Transformations of consciousness*. Boston: Shambhala.

CHAPTER SIX

World Views, Ego Development, and Epistemological Changes from the Conventional to the Postformal: A Longitudinal Perspective

Melvin E. Miller
Norwich University

The adulthood years provide some individuals the opportunity to use their intellectual abilities and awareness in ways that differ from those dictated by mere formal operations. Postconventional thinking (Kohlberg, 1983), postformal operations, dialectic thinking (Basseches, 1984), and meta-systematic reasoning (Commons et al., 1984) are among the descriptors used to characterize the kinds of intellectual activity which may take place during these years.

This paper attempts to understand how both formal and postformal thinking interplay with certain personality and cognitive variables to form belief systems and world views (Miller, 1982, 1988; Miller & West, 1993). It also investigates how these world views—and their interrelated cognitive structures—are involved when individuals attempt to make sense of new information about their worlds and their lives in general. Likewise, it addresses the question of how world views influence the decisions people make, and the ways in which they conduct their lives.

In addition to looking at cognitive and personality variables, questions relating to the development of an individual's world view will be investigated. How much awareness do some bring to this process? Do many individuals strive for ongoing development? How diligently do people work at developing a world view? Is there a way that world views can be system-atically articulated and organized? How do world views—and the personalities of those who embrace them—change during adulthood?

Questions such as these will be addressed in this paper. I shall begin, though, with an attempt to arrive at a workable definition of a world view or philosophical frame of reference.

World Views, Weltanschauungen, and Philosophical Frames of Reference: Definitions, Descriptions, and Background

A world view can be thought of as a particular set of mental constructs used to make one's world meaningful. World views and their concomitant constructs are like structural "filters" through which phenomena are perceived. They are basic sets of presuppositions that are molded, for the most part, by words and concepts and serve as a frame of reference for one's thoughts and behaviors (Miller, 1988). In fundamental terms, one's world view or philosophical frame of reference is a set of conceptual rules used to guide one's life and to make sense of one's world. They enable one to make meaning in a variety of ways and contexts.

This definition of a world view is based, in part, upon a Piagetian notion of cognitive structure. However, the structural demands are not as restrictive as Piaget's and are more in line with those posited by Loevinger (1976), Kegan (1982), Basseches (1984), and others. This definition involves more of a "soft stage" (Kohlberg & Armon, 1984) or "existential stage" (Gibbs, 1979) conceptualization of structure which invites the postformal, and includes the possibilities of metasystematic and dialectical kinds of thinking. It is a notion of stage which transcends the limitations of formal operations as interpreted in a strict Piagetian context. Within the World View Classification Grid discussed below, it offers the possibility of changes which move in a horizontal fashion as well as stage transitions which progress in a vertical one.

Discussions of global and philosophic notions such as world views, Weltanschauungen, and philosophical frames of reference are rare in the traditional literature of psychology. It might be conjectured that such constructs are viewed as being too broad and vague to lend themselves to the more conventional modes of scientific investigation. Given the dearth of such writings, background investigations into fields such as philosophy, sociology, and theology were pursued in order to establish a theoretical foundation for this study.

One of the more apt descriptions of the role—and importance—of world views is set forth by Kaufman, a contemporary theologian, in his book *The Theological Imagination* (1981). Kaufman states:

An overall framework of interpretation of this sort, [in reference to a theological world view] which gives meaning to existence, is indispensable to humans. We cannot gain orientation in life and cannot act without some conception or vision of the context within which we are living and moving—and without some understanding of our own place and role within that context. Such a framework of interpretation is like the air we breathe: it does not easily or quickly become an object directly perceived or noticed. In consequence, it is seldom realized that the terms or foci, which structure the framework and give it its peculiar pattern of meaning, in fact function only within and as a part of the framework itself. (p. 27)

Kaufman has speculated at length about the importance of world views, and how they must change over time. His focus on *theological* world views is more theoretical than empirical. Nonetheless, his understanding of the role of world views and his emphasis upon the need to consciously and constantly review and update them contribute substantially to the orientation of this project.

In the field of sociology, an interesting exploratory study on world views was accomplished by three sociologists who were interested in frames of reference as related to professional thinking and behavior. Holzner, Mitroff, and Fisher (1980) interviewed six distinguished professionals in the fields of psychology, psychiatry, sociology, and law. They found that each of these individuals had world views or frames of reference which could be articulated with varying degrees of clarity, and that some subjects more consciously reflected upon the specifics of their world views/frames of reference as they conducted their professional lives. Holzner et al. (1980) defined a frame of reference as "a *structure* of (a) taken-for-granted assumptions and a set of preferences for certain symbol systems, (b) analytical devices, and (c) the availability of and the preference for certain cognitive skills, within which inquiry proceeds" (p. 2). A content analysis of the tape-recorded interviews with their subjects revealed that nine categories were sufficient to characterize the various frames of reference of these people. These nine categories according to Holzner et al. are:

1) Intellectual Commitments, 2) Problem Selection and Formation, 3) Strategies of Problem Solution, 4) Rules of Inquiry and Analytical Devices, 5) Conceptions of the Nature of Facts, 6) Reality Tests, 7) Delimiting the Domain of Inquiry, 8) Articulation and Codification of the Frame of Reference, and 9) Reflectivity. (1980, pp. 18–19)

Their focus on world views includes commitments, reflectivity, and the matter of codification. And, in this vein, it informs the goals and objectives of this current study. On the other hand, it does not address in any systematic way a connection to personality variables. Their approach does acknowledge that nonacademic and nonprofessional people may also have frames of reference, but their preference was to construct a study which sampled the variety of frames of reference subscribed to and upheld by academicians and professionals. Given their respective orientations as sociologists, Holzner et al. (1980) stress that anyone's frame of reference, professional or lay, is "always situated in the context of a social structure" (p. 2).

A recent study which seems even more pertinent to the project at hand was conducted by Shapiro (1989) and presented in an article entitled "Exploring Our Most Deeply Held Belief about Ultimate Reality." In this study, Shapiro (1989) encouraged a group of individuals who studied and/or practiced the "consciousness disciplines" to talk about "their most deeply held belief[s] about ultimate reality" (p. 15). Shapiro makes the argument that we "have models of the world that we utilize as organizing principles . . . and these models inform our efforts at scientific understanding of such topics, perhaps causing us to selectively attend to certain information and to discard or reframe other information" (1989, p. 16).

There is an implied Piagetian and/or structuralist orientation in Shapiro's study. In addition to the structural approach, which is similar to the one taken here, Shapiro is also attempting to analyze how individuals use their more mature intellectual capacities and expanded awarenesses. He is aware of a reluctance in some to articulate world view notions, while—at the same time—he recognizes that individuals vary in the degrees to which they have the ability to do so.

Shapiro (1989) found that the "core beliefs" of his subjects could be investigated and analyzed along the four different dimensions which he describes below:

> (1) Is ultimate reality thought to be positive (benign), negative (malevolent), neutral (indifferent), or some combination thereof, and, within each of these views, how is the problem of evil addressed? (2) Does the belief reflect a theistic or nontheistic position? (3) How much of ultimate reality is (can be) due to human effort and free choice? (4) What claim, if any, does the belief make to universal applicability, and how evident is a particularistic path in the statement of the belief? (p. 16)

Shapiro's content analysis is informal and nonstatistical, but it is effective in subsuming the most salient characteristics of his subjects' belief systems. His approach and findings were especially validating in light of the thrust of this paper, since all four of his "core beliefs" already had been employed in the world view investigation which I had initiated.

Shapiro (1989) also addresses questions such as: How are these beliefs formed? What are the antecedents to the development of such beliefs? What are the consequences of holding such beliefs?

In an effort to understand how beliefs are formed, Shapiro asked: Are there "catalytic events" which cause one to change one's view of ultimate reality? "Do we voluntarily and consciously choose this belief, or does it seem as if we 'receive' it, almost as if it 'comes to us' and is beyond our control?" (p. 18). Shapiro also wonders about the role that mystical experiences and faith have in affecting the unfolding of individual belief systems. Finally, he speculates about the purposes that such beliefs and experiences serve in the meaning-making process of individual lives.

So, with some brief examples of what has been done in the past with this world view/frame of reference construct, and with a good example of a fairly current and somewhat analogous investigation at hand, I shall now describe a systematic attempt to develop a structured interview with which to probe this world view phenomenon. The classification system developed to categorize my respondents' world views will then be reviewed.

Construction of World View Interview

At the time the World View Interview was developed (Miller, 1982), the only similar study available was that of Holzner, Mitroff, and Fisher (1980). Their study offered a precedent, but it was not comprehensive enough. Also, its scope was not wide enough to fit the general population, nor deep enough to probe the concomitant epistemological and personality variables that seemed to merit investigation.

After an in-depth investigation of the literature in a variety of disciplines, a list of the most likely dimensions belonging to a comprehensive world view began to emerge. Significant variables and constructs were found in Pepper's (1970) book on *World Hypotheses*, in the anthropological-sociological research of Kluckhohn (1967), and in Churchman's (1971) text *The Design of Inquiring Systems*. From studies such as these, a list of variables or dimensions that—at least theoretically—belonged in a comprehensive world view was constructed. This list subsumed the content issues addressed by Holzner et al. (1980), Shapiro (1989), and others. In addition to the "value" and "content" variables included, a set of cognitive and personality variables was incorporated into the interview as well. Included in this list were items relating to the subject's degree of reflectivity (with respect to one's world view), the degree and kinds of commitments made, the degree of cognitive rigidity vs. flexibility, a locus of control estimate, an ego level estimate, a Perry (1970) epistemological position estimate, an estimate of the subject's ability to articulate his world view, and, finally, an estimate of the degree of the comprehensiveness of the subject's world view.

The above variables were then made part of an interview which gave the subjects the opportunity to talk about their world views in an open-ended manner. Questions probing for additional variables that the author deemed important were added, e.g., those which addressed the interplay between personality dynamics and the choice of/development of one's world view.

Some paraphrased and abbreviated sample World View Interview questions follow: Would you say that you have a world view or philosophical frame of reference? Could you talk in detail about it? When did you first develop one? How often—and under what circumstances—do you think of it? How do changes in your world view happen? Do you actively work to change and modify it? How might your world view affect your behavior?

The above examples do not capture the degree of intricacy or depth of the actual questions. Appendix A contains the complete World View Interview.

World View Classification System

Many of the notions of the theorists which were drawn upon in the process of developing the World View Interview were also used as the World View Classification Grid or categorization system was constructed. These theorists (Churchman, 1971; Pepper, 1970) have carefully analyzed world views which have appeared throughout history, and have summarized most of the basic presuppositions of the predominant world views. With their descriptions in mind, along with estimates of the personality and epistemological characteristics likely portrayed by adherents to such world views, I developed the World View Classification Grid (see Table 6.1). Brief descriptions of each of the nine world views posited are presented in Table 6.2. More detailed elaborations of each world view are discussed elsewhere (Miller, 1982).[1]

The actual structure and organization of the World View Classification Grid (Table 6.1) was determined by the postulated content and philosophical characteristics of the various world views. It had to be modified only slightly by the actual epistemological orientation and personality variables of the subjects. A grid of three tiers or rows—with three world views in each tier—was constructed. Following are some of the theoretical assumptions or hypotheses which informed the development of the World View Classification Grid:

1. Formal operations thinking is assumed to be the cognitive prerequisite for all nine of the world views, but postformal thinking is more likely to be found in World Views 4 through 9—with the greatest likelihood of its occurrence in World Views 7 through 9.

2. There are qualitative and measurable differences found among the world views of the different tiers. The three tiers or rows comprise what is called the Epistemological Dimension. An important question relating to one's placement in a particular row is: "Where is the individual's locus or

source of truth?" It is assumed to be "outside of self"—in events, objects, or authorities—for those in the first tier or Objective row-group. It is assumed to be "within self" for those in the Subjective row-group, and it is expected to be dialogical (Buber, 1969) or dialectical (Hegel, 1967; Riegel, 1978; Basseches, 1984) for those in the Dialogical row-group. (See World View Classification Grid, Table 6.1.)

3. The columns of the World View Classification Grid also depict substantive differences in the world views of the subjects. The columns help to differentiate among world views which are Teleological (belief in "ends," "ultimate designs," and "purposes"), Antiteleological (consciously opposed to a belief in ultimate designs, and purposes), and Ateleological (suspended or withheld belief about ultimate ends, designs, and purposes). Also addressed in this dimension are issues relating to the subject's perception of being and reality (ultimate reality), and thus this dimension is most appropriately called the Teleological-Metaphysical Dimension.

4. The interplay of the underlying epistemological and teleological variables forms the foundation for the nine different world views (see the World View Classification Grid, Table 6.1). General descriptions of each of the world views (Table 6.2 below) were developed with these underlying factors in mind, and are consistent with them.

5. Degrees of growth, development, and change in world views and related structures (e.g., cognitive and ego) are expected over the course of one's life. Horizontal or lateral changes can take place as well as vertical movement from one tier to the next. In order to accurately portray the multidirectional possibilities for change, the World View Classification Grid ideally would be presented in three dimensions or on a globe—with movement, transitions, or growth potentially occurring in any direction.

6. Those with world views on the first tier or Objective row-group seem to want or need a frame of reference which is fairly structured regardless of whether their particular world view is scientific or traditionally theistic. The degree of reflectivity or consciousness brought to the choice of world view will tend to be low. Moderate to high degrees of cognitive rigidity are expected from this group along with moderate levels of ego development (SCT scores in the I-3 to I-4 range)[2] and an external locus of control.

7. Those with world views in the Subjective row-group (second tier) are expected to be in a somewhat relativistic and "internal"—and perhaps even self-conscious—position. The degree of reflectivity and consciousness brought to this position is expected to be moderate to high, and these subjects are expected to be the most "open-minded" or cognitively flexible of those in the study. The locus of control is expected to be internal, and the ego levels are anticipated to range from moderate to high (SCT scores ranging from I-4 to I-5). Sometimes these individuals have a difficult time making commitments to causes, people, and events beyond themselves.

Table 6.1
World View (WV) Classification Grid

Epistemological Dimension (One's Source of Truth)	General Descriptors	The Teleological-Metaphysical Dimension (One's Relationship to Meanings, Goals, Nature, and God)		
		Antiteleological (Against Telos)	Ateleological (Without Telos)	Teleological (For Telos)
Objective	1-Reflectivity: Low–Mod.	WV#1	WV#2	WV#3
(Outside)	2-Commitment to: Law & Order, Church &/or Dogma, Scientific Paradigm, Experience Itself: Mod.–High	Atomism	Stoicism	Traditional Theism
"You: It"	3-Rigidity: Mod.–High	(Mechanistic-	(The Doer &	(Law & Order
"I-It"	4-Locus of Control: External	Reductionistic)	Experiencer)	Position)
	5-Ego Level: Moderate			
	6-Perry Positions 1–4	-Transition-	-Transition-	-Transition-

Subjective

(Within)

"Self; I"

1-Reflectivity: Mod.–High
2-Commitment to: Self & Self-Preoccupation: Low–Mod.
3-Rigidity: Low–Mod.
4-Locus of Control: Internal
5-Ego Level: Mod.–High
6-Perry Positions 4–6

	WV#4	WV#5	WV#6
	Nihilism	Skepticism-Agnosticism	Traditional Humanism
	(Nothing is Knowable)	(The Doubter & Questioner)	("Man is the Measure . . .")
	-Transition-	-Transition-	-Transition-

Dialogical

(In relationship)

"I-Thou"
"I-Other"
"Man-God"

1-Reflectivity: Mod.–High
2-Commitment to: Something Beyond Self, e.g., Social Projects & One's Own Life Project: High w/"Care"
3-Rigidity: Moderate
4-Locus of Control: Dialogical
5-Ego Level: Mod.–High
6-Perry Positions 7–9

	WV#7	WV#8	WV#9
	Pantheistic Monism	Integrated-Committed Existentialism	Integrated-Committed Theism & Humanism
	(Eastern Mysticism)	(A "Maker of Meaning")	(True Commitment Beyond Self)
	-Transition-	-Transition-	-Transition-

Note: From Miller & West (1993)[3]

Table 6.2
World View (Philosophical Frame of Reference) Listing

World View 1—Atomism

It makes the most sense to me to think of all reality as being comprised of small particles called atoms. And I believe that to make sense of things, we only need to break them down into their atomic parts and study the relationships that exist among them. Most often, these relationships are precise enough to formulate them with mathematical exactness. Phenomena as diverse as human relationships and events in the physical world all can be treated with equal precision. We need no gods nor a deity to give meaning to existence. Science can give us all the answers.

World View 2—Stoicism

I would say that there really is no rhyme or reason to events that occur, and that there are no fixed orders, purposes, or meanings in life. Given this state of affairs, it seems that the best thing for people to do is to keep busy. I may not be able to control things on a larger perspective, but I can control my attitude toward what happens and what I do with my life.

World View 3—Traditional Theism

It seems to me that there is a universal purpose and meaning to life. These purposes and meanings are most likely predetermined, and are likely determined by a deity or God or some "higher" form of intelligence. Our purpose in life is to understand these meanings and to live in accordance with them. The unhappiness that exists in the world is a result of people and nations not living in accordance with these realizations.

World View 4—Nihilism

I do not think that anything can be claimed to be true with any sense of certainty. There is no such thing as reliable knowledge, and no God or gods or moral order in the universe. Given these facts, people can do with their lives whatever they wish. Everything is entirely up to the individual, for in the long run, nothing really matters anyhow.

World View 5—Skepticism-Agnosticism

I do not know what—if anything—human beings can know for sure. I tend to doubt anybody or any system that says it has the ultimate truth about anything, and I am especially suspicious of any claims to "official" truths whether they come in the form of religion or science. At best, everything is relative. Despite this doubting position, I believe that I keep an open mind that receives new input and information.

World View 6—Traditional Humanism

I would say that we cannot be certain of any fixed purposes or predetermined meanings or "ends" toward which the universe and/or individual lives are moving. Despite this absence of certainty, things do matter and there is a general direction in which the world and human lives move. We are in charge of our own lives, and the community of the world is in charge of "Spaceship Earth." Both individuals and groups must endeavor to establish appropriate and positive meanings and goals. The ecology movement, the human potential movement, and the peace movement are considered important causes.

World View 7—Pantheistic Monism

Personal and/or spiritual awareness are the most important things to be worked at during this life, so that I can more greatly appreciate the specialness and uniqueness of each moment. Activities and aesthetic pursuits are valuable in and of themselves. I am not working toward ultimate goals that are predetermined, nor do I believe in a personal god who oversees everything. But I do commit myself to understanding myself and the world more completely, and to appreciating all of life.

World View 8—Integrated-Committed Existentialism

Nothing is intrinsically or ultimately meaningful. What is "right"—and the particular goals that are important to work toward—can best be arrived at through conversation and dialogue with concerned others. I am committed to care for people and the world despite the lack of a master plan or blueprint, and despite the apparent relativistic nature of things. I see my life as being comprised of a series of ongoing commitments to self-exploration and the world's needs.

World View 9—Integrated-Committed Theism & Humanism

I believe in a God or gods—or something greater than myself, but I do not see things as being predetermined or part of a preordained divine scheme. I think that one should remain in dialogue with that which is perceived as being divine or greater than the self. Through introspection, an exploration of values, and this dialogical relationship, one can orient oneself and commit oneself to worthwhile goals and projects. It seems that there is a general "direction" in which lives and worlds should move, but things are not fixed or etched in stone. Lives and events can change and improve through individual and collective human effort. Human relationships, social causes, ecology, and world peace are the kinds of commitments in which I might invest time and energy.

Note: From Miller & West (1993)[3]   This table includes only abbreviated descriptions of the nine world views included in the World View Classification Grid. See Miller (1982) for more detailed descriptions.

8. Those with world views on the third tier or the Dialogical row-group are assumed to think in a more dialectical (Hegel, 1967; Riegel, 1978; Basseches, 1984) or dialogical (Buber, 1969) manner. They arrive at "truth" in relationship with the other, regardless of whether the "other" is a person, event, or concept. Levels of reflectivity are assumed to be moderate to high. Their ego levels are anticipated to be in the moderate to very high range (SCT scores ranging from I-4 to I-6), and their locus of control is considered to be "dialogical." These individuals are also fairly open-minded. These subjects are committed to projects and events "beyond self," such as social projects, global issues, and environmental concerns. Their "projects" appear to be consistent with and consciously evolve from their world views.

Methodology

Subjects

Subjects were 40 adult males between the ages of 28 and 57 (mean age = 37). I set a minimum of 28 years, since it was assumed that an individual must live at least this long to arrive at a fairly crystallized and expressible life and world view. Subjects over 57 years were not used because of the projected 10-, 20-, and 30-year follow-up interviews.

To increase the sample's diversity in life and world views, the subjects were chosen from five vocational and professional areas (viz., physical scientists, social scientists, lawyers, military personnel [officers and non-commissioned officers], and ministers/priests).

Most of the subjects had advanced degrees, either academic or professional. Subjects averaged 19.2 years of formal education. There were 6 Ph.D.'s, 2 A.B.D.'s (all but dissertation), 7 J.D.'s (Juris Doctor), 2 M.B.A.'s, 6 with either an M.A. or M.S. degree, and 6 with a B.A. or B.S. degree. All the remaining subjects had some college coursework. At least ten subjects had more than one advanced degree. Hence, the sample was comprised of highly motivated and professionally oriented individuals of above-average intelligence.

Ten different religious affiliations were represented. There were 11 Catholics, 7 Anglicans, 5 Presbyterians, 2 Jews, 2 Baptists, 2 "other" Protestant, 1 Hindu, 1 Unitarian, 1 agnostic, and 8 who claimed to have no religious preference at all.

The sample was deliberately selective. Ideally, I wanted to obtain a fairly even distribution of subjects within the various world view categories outlined. The subjects were volunteers and were contacted through friends, colleagues, and various institutions (e.g., university and government offices).

Assessment

Each subject was administered the World View Interview (Appendix A) by the author. The questions from the interview protocol were read to the subjects at a pace which permitted comprehensive responses. Interviews were conducted during a four-month period in the fall of 1980. (Ten-year follow-up interviews began in the summer of 1990, and are still in progress.) Upon meeting with a subject, the investigator discussed briefly the purpose of the study and answered any questions that the subject may have had about the study. Before the interview began, the subject completed both the Dogmatism Scale and Loevinger's Washington University Sentence Completion Test (WUSCT)—two standardized instruments which assess personality and cognitive variables. After a brief rest, the interview process was started. Each interview took from three to five hours to complete, and all were finished on the same day they were initiated.

Interview protocols were scored according to the guidelines established (Miller, 1982).[4] Using these scores, I assigned each subject to one of the nine world view categories depicted on the World View Classification Grid (see Table 6.1). To check interrater reliability, protocols were analyzed independently by a second rater who had been trained in the use of the "General Instructions for Evaluating and Scoring the World View Interview."

The ego level test responses from the Washington University Sentence Completion Test (WUSCT) were scored by a trained WUSCT scorer according to Loevinger and Wessler (1970) guidelines. Each of the subject's responses to the 36 sentence stems was individually scored. Then the cumulative frequency distribution of the subject's scores was compared with what Loevinger calls an "automatic ogive" table, which permitted the derivation of a total protocol rating. This ogive score, converted to a 10-point scale, was used for comparative and statistical purposes.

The Dogmatism Scale, a self-report questionnaire designed by Rokeach (1960), was scored by the investigator since the scoring process is an objective one. This scale was used to determine the degree of "open- or closed-mindedness" (cognitive flexibility vs. cognitive rigidity) of the subjects. The Dogmatism Scale is comprised of 40 statements to which the subject expresses agreement or disagreement at various levels (e.g., +3: "I agree very much," to –3: "I disagree very much"). The responses were then converted to a 1 to 7 scale by adding a constant of 4 to each item score. The individual's total score is the sum of scores obtained on all 40 items on the test (Rokeach, 1960).

The subjects also were assigned to one of the Perry positions of "intellectual and ethical development" (Perry, 1970) on the basis of their responses to specific World View Interview questions (e.g., #1, #4, and

#6), as well as from an overall impressionistic rating of their responses throughout the interview. The Perry scheme was used to facilitate the process of making a "scaled judgment" concerning the subject's level and quality of commitments. The issue of commitment is especially critical in determining the assignment of a subject to the Dialogical row-group in the Epistemological Dimension of the World View Classification Grid.

Results

Large amounts of data have been generated by this study—especially by the World View Interviews. At this point, I shall present a few of the most important objective and statistical findings. A more qualitative analysis, including a review of representative responses to specific World View Interview questions, will follow in the next section.

I found that everyone interviewed had some version of a world view. The world views of the subjects, once analyzed and evaluated, could be classified according to the typology or grid defined above as the World View Classification Grid (see Table 6.1). Specific placements of the subjects in the respective world view categories can be observed in Table 6.3 below.

These placements were subjected to an interrater reliability check since the significance of other findings are, to some degree, contingent upon the reliability of these world view placements. The two raters achieved substantial agreement.[5] Subjects were fairly evenly distributed among the rows of

Table 6.3
World View Placements of Subjects

Epistemological Dimension	*Antiteleological*	*Ateleological*	*Teleological*
Objective	WV#1	WV#2	WV#3
$n=17$	$n=3$	$n=3$	$n=11$
Subjective	WV#4	WV#5	WV#6
$n=12$	$n=0$	$n=6$	$n=6$
Dialogical	WV#7	WV#8	WV#9
$n=11$	$n=1$	$n=2$	$n=8$
	col. $n=4$	col. $n=11$	col. $n=25$

Table 6.4
Comparisons of Critical Variables along Epistemological Rows

Epistemological Dimension	Ego vs. Dogmatism Correlations	Ego*# Levels Means	Dogmatism+ Score Means	Perry Position Means
Objective n=17	r=−.38	6.06	149.06	6.59
Subjective n=12	r=−.50; p<.10	6.83	121.50	6.75
Dialogical n=11	r=−.21	7.09	132.46	7.91
	Sample Correlation: r=−.48; p<.01	Sample Mean: 6.58	Sample Mean: 137.23	Sample Mean: 6.90
		Range: 5–8	Range: 94–221	Range: 5–9

*ANOVA indicates significant row-group differences in ego level scores, F(2,37) = 5.55, p<.01.
#All ego level (WUSCT) scores displayed have been converted to a 10-point scale.
+ANOVA indicates significant row-group differences in dogmatism scores, F(2,37) = 5.25, p<.01.

the World View Classification Grid, but not the columns, as illustrated in Table 6.3.

The relationship between ego level and dogmatism scores was inverse among each of the respective row-groups or Epistemological levels, as indicated in Table 6.4. Those with the higher levels of ego development in each of the three levels had the more flexible cognitive styles or modes, and those with the lower levels of ego development had more rigid cognitive styles. For the entire sample, a significant inverse correlation between ego level and dogmatism or cognitive rigidity was also found.

Subjects in the separate rows of the World View Classification Grid (Epistemological levels) differed significantly with regard to ego development scores. The average ego level score for subjects in the Dialogical row-group was 7.09 after conversion to the 10-point scale. This score is nearly equivalent to a score of I-4 on Loevinger's scheme; it is referred to as the Conscientious stage in Figure I.1. The average ego level score for subjects in the Subjective row-group was 6.83, and it was 6.06 (approximately I-

3/4; Self-conscious) for those in the Objective row-group (see Table 6.4). The range of ego level scores for the entire sample was 5 to 8 (10-point conversion scale) or I-3 to I-4/5 (Conformist to Individualistic in Figure I.1). The average ego level score for the entire sample of 40 subjects was 6.58—a score in the transition area between Self-conscious and Conscientious according to Figure I.1. Ego level scores along the Teleological-Metaphysical Dimension were not significantly different.

Row-groups along the Epistemological Dimension also differed significantly with regard to dogmatism. Average or mean scores for each row-group are indicated in Table 6.4.

Along the Teleological-Metaphysical Dimension or column-groups, the analysis of variance revealed no statistical differences. Nonetheless, the mean scores of each column-group merit examination. The Antiteleological column-group obtained the highest score (mean = 157.25) for dogmatism. The Teleological column-group achieved the second highest score (mean = 137.92), and the lowest dogmatism score was achieved by the Ateleological column-group (mean = 124.73). The range for dogmatism scores in this sample was 94 to 221, with a sample mean of 137.23.

Ego level scores and Perry positions were correlated positively, $r = .48$, $p < .01$. Dogmatism scores and Perry position scores were negatively related $r = -.26$, $p < .05$.

Discussion

The results indicate that the World View Classification system seems to work for the placement of the subjects into one of the nine world views or philosophical frames of reference. In general, the World View Classification Grid accommodates the existing world views fairly well. I found that some of the subjects were able to discuss their world views in a more articulate manner than others. It was as if the more verbal or eloquent subjects brought a personal, vigorous reflection and awareness to the thinking that they did around world view kinds of questions. In this context, it could even be said that one or two of the subjects had only vaguely defined world views, but they were close enough to ones described in this project that both raters were able to place them within world views contained on the World View Classification Grid.

In terms of the placement of the subjects among the nine different world views in the World View Classification Grid, I found the distribution to be varied and uneven (see Table 6.3). One world view, Nihilism (WV#4) had no subjects. World View 7 (Pantheistic Monism) had only 1 subject, and World View 8 (Integrated-Committed Existentialism) had only 2. The relatively small sample size involved in this research, and the degree to which my subjects were embedded in the cultural and philosophical traditions of the West, are offered as a partial explanation of this finding. For this reason, I cannot say that this presentation of the World View Classification Grid will be the definitive one. Nor can I say that it is sufficient to include the full range of possible world views. It is open to revision and transformation. One might wonder, as we ask questions about the comprehensiveness of the grid, if we are running up against the limitations of the hypothetico-deductive or empirical approach discussed in the introductory chapter. The empirical data and the test scores can only take us so far in envisaging theoretical models and schemes—especially those which point the way toward the further reaches of human development.

When the placements into the row- and column-groups were analyzed, a fairly even distribution of subjects among the row-groups of the Epistemological Dimension was noted. This finding seems to be consistent with some of the initial assumptions of this research, e.g., subjects would be found at each row, and fewer subjects would be found at the postformal and postconventional levels. Although abstract thinking in the subjects was taken as a given, the degree to which this thinking would be formal or postformal was assumed to vary among subjects. It was assumed that some subjects would display metasystematic or dialectical—or some other variation of postformal thinking. As it turned out, only 5 subjects received WUSCT scores at the I-4/5 level (conversion scale score of 8). If we refer to Table I.1, we see that SCT scores of I-4/5 are in the postformal-postconventional tier—albeit at a lower level in that tier. There were 11 subjects who received Perry position scores of 8 and 2 who received scores of 9. These findings offer further evidence to support the claim that higher levels of education, professional training, and background experiences do not, in themselves, guarantee movement into the postconventional tiers. They also seem to informally corroborate the estimated percentages of adults found in each tier as discussed in the Introduction, and as elaborated upon by Cook-Greuter in Chapter 5.

In terms of the column-groups, the Teleological-Metaphysical Dimension, 25 subjects were placed in the Teleological category. The second most common placement was the Ateleological group with 11 subjects, and only 4 subjects were found in the Antiteleological group (refer to Table 6.3). The large number of subjects placed in the Teleological column-group was expected given the popularity of Western philosophical and theological assumptions based largely on Aristotelian philosophy and Judeo-Christian beliefs. Both the Antiteleological and Ateleological positions can be considered philosophical stances in their own right, and they can also be thought of as reactions to the teleological preoccupation of our culture and society. When they are manifested as reactions against the predominate societal views, preliminary findings suggest that this is a difficult posture for one to sustain. These subjects will likely return to a Teleological position over time. If the Antiteleological stance is embedded in one's religion (Hinduism) or in a professional view (a strict reductionistic scientist), then the stance is less likely to be equivocal or temporary.

Within the above context, it is interesting to note that the Anti-teleological subjects had the highest dogmatism scores of any column-group (mean = 157.25). This finding supports Rokeach's (1960) notion that one can be dogmatic or an ideologue regardless of whether one leans to the right or the left, and despite whether the ideas in question are religious, political, or scientific. An oppositional stance is most often as strongly held and stated as that from which it is revolting.

The Ateleological group had the lowest dogmatism score (mean = 124.73)—a score well below the sample mean. Subjects in this group typically did not take strong ideological stances in any direction.

That subjects with higher ego scores (WUSCT scores) also had lower dogmatism scores was anticipated. Subjects who are cognitively flexible are more likely to demonstrate the ability to deal with ambiguity and cognitive uncertainty. Loevinger (1976) found that higher ego stage subjects were capable of experiencing and conveying feelings and discussing internal states, ambiguities, and conflicts. Cook-Greuter (1990, and Chapter 5) found this to be the case with those at higher ego levels as well. She also stresses the need for a theory of ego development that permits further differentiations of internal experience and ego states for those at the post-formal tier of development. The results of this study seem to support Cook-Greuter's position.

The statistical findings that reflect the significant differences among ego levels and dogmatism scores of the subjects in the various row-groups of the Epistemological Dimension (see Table 6.4) further substantiate the suggested interrelationship of personality and cognitive variables with world view types. More open-minded and cognitively flexible subjects—those who can deal with both internal or external ambiguities and conflicts and be more open and inclusive—seem to uphold world views which reflect such attributes. Those with higher ego levels and lower dogmatism scores also appear to reflect more about themselves, their lives, and their world views. Their personalities could be described as more self-accepting; they seemed to be more open to experience in general, and more open to the ideas and experiences of the other as well.

The positive correlation which was found between ego level scores and Perry positions may reflect similarities in the constructs under investigation. The negative correlation between dogmatism scores and Perry positions was anticipated, but the level of significance was less than expected. It turns out that the subjects placed in Epistemological row-group 3 (the Dialogical row-group) had slightly higher mean dogmatism scores than those placed in the Epistemological-Subjective row-group as illustrated in Table 6.4. It is conjectured that this higher "dogmatism" or cognitive inflexibility score comes with the increased level of commitments demonstrated by these subjects. They have lost or discarded the relativistic or temporizing quality which was manifested rather clearly by those in the Subjective row-group. This kind of cognitive transition had been predicted by Perry (1970), and it was demonstrated by my subjects in both the cognitive and emotional realms.

Overall, it appeared that those subjects who had world views in the Objective row-group had both cognitive styles and frames of reference which were rather rigidly constructed and relatively less open to the possibility of incorporating new data. It seemed that these individuals were less willing or able to deal with shades of gray or ambiguities; they attempted to force new data/experiences into existing cognitive structures. The thinking of these subjects appeared to be wedded to linear causality (Koplowitz, 1984). It seemed to force the comprehension and processing of new experiences into an "unchanging structured whole" or into a "closed system of lawful relationships" (Basseches, 1984). Their personalities could be described as less self-accepting, and they were generally less accepting of new experiences and the experiences of others.

An anecdotal example of the above was provided by one subject from the Objective row-group (WV#3) who said: "I learned what was right as a child from my parents and the church. They gave me all I needed to know; so why bother changing it." A brief summary of his position is found in the old saying "If it ain't broke, don't fix it."

Those subjects in the Subjective and Dialogical row-groups were found to be much more open to new information and new experience. Their analysis of new experience (new data) took a more dialectical form. Their thinking was less linear, and they were more able to deal with internal and external ambiguities, and to see/experience things within the context of interactive relationships and change. Their cognitive structures appeared to be open to change and transformation. Their personalities, in general, could be described as more open, more accommodating; these subjects were more accepting of others' experiences.

It might even be said that some of the subjects placed in the Subjective row-group were "too open" to new experiences in that they sometimes almost seemed stymied by their relativistic stances. It was as if they became overwhelmed by the options and possibilities available to them. One subject in the Subjective row-group (WV#5—Skepticism-Agnosticism) described his rather extreme relativistic stance as being "pathetic." He was bothered by the passive nature of his position, and how immobilized he was by it. Yet he believed that there was little he could do to change.

Another subject who had been classified in the Subjective row-group (WV#6—Traditional Humanism) exclaimed that one of his main objectives and delights in life was "learning something new everyday." He described his own thinking and development in terms almost classically Hegelian. He described moving from thesis to antithesis in both his thinking and in life experiences. This subject actively sought out novel experiences, i.e., experiences that "push your mind and challenge your thinking." He contended that "people are miserable because they haven't taken any interest in learning things."

Subjects in the Dialogical row-group seemed to be the ones most actively committed to continually changing and transforming their world views. Sometimes this commitment to change or transformation seemed tied into specific religious or theological beliefs, and at other times it seemed to stem from a secular and well-formulated philosophy of life. Some of those grouped in World Views 7 through 9 were seeking transcendent experiences of a mystical or spiritual nature such as those discussed by Alexander and Langer (1990), Nuernberger (Chapter 4), and Funk (Chapter 1). Again, the notion of "dialogue" seems to capture the essence of this world view. Many subjects in the Dialogical row-group talked as if they had an obligation to work on their world views. These subjects, in general, were the ones most committed to social reform, and were more likely to subscribe to a universal ethic and exhibit the caring nature described by Vasudev (Chapter 9) and Druker (Chapter 8).

One subject placed in WV#9 (Integrated-Committed Theism and Humanism) spoke stridently against those with "fixed systems" of beliefs and values. He talked about working hard at developing a world view or frame of reference. He mentioned specific occurrences and experiences that changed his way of thinking about events, phenomena, and relationships. For example, he believed that the unacceptable tenets of his fundamentalist religious background forced him to look for broader and more integrating ways of making sense of his world. This subject mentioned—as did many who worked at their world views—that much of the effort put into his world view thinking was due to a "reaction against" parental, societal, and/or religious values. Such forces and influences, he stated, made it imperative that he find better ways of interpreting events and experiences—ways that were not as static, dogmatic, or rigid.

It was experiences such as the above, or some personal crisis, death of a loved one, or loss of a job that often became the impetus or "trigger event" for transformations in the world views of our subjects. Such events often heightened their awareness or consciousness, and forced them to actively strive to resolve some personal dilemma or philosophical conundrum brought about by the crisis. Some subjects reported that these transformations in world views were preceded by a period of depression. It was as if the cognitive and affective uncertainty—before the transformation occurred—was unbearable. Resolving this discomfort through the search for a more comprehensive set of constructs or frame of reference became a singular concern for them during such a period. Then, finally, a new, often higher form of equilibrium was realized.

Ten-year Follow-up Study

In terms of the ten-year, longitudinal follow-up study, too few subjects have gone through the interview process for any substantive generalizations to be drawn from the results. Nonetheless, some initial impressions from the results currently on hand will be mentioned.[6]

Neither the dogmatism scores nor the WUSCT ego level scores of the subjects have changed remarkably during the ten-year period. For the most part, minor changes in both directions were noted on both the WUSCT and the Dogmatism scales, although it was found that the WUSCT ego level scores remained more constant than the dogmatism scores.

As mentioned above, one subject who was initially categorized in WV #5 (Skepticism-Agnosticism) was troubled by his temporizing and relativistic stance. He talked about consciously trying to change or transform his position. This man described an attempt to take on both a more positivistic *and* humanistic frame of reference. He also described increased commitments to self, others, and society. In the process of making these changes, his dogmatism score increased from a fairly low score of 116 to a slightly more mid-range score of 123. Perhaps both his increase on the Dogmatism Scale and his lowered ego level score (from I-4/5 to I-4) can be attributed to this effort. Although his Dogmatism Scale score remained below the sample mean, his positions on philosophical and value-oriented questions were certainly firmer during the second interview. And despite being categorized once again in WV#5 (Skepticism-Agnosticism), some of his responses sounded somewhat like those typical of a WV#1 (Atomism) position, and others had more of a WV#9 (Integrated-Committed Theism & Humanism) quality to them. He seemed to be "in transition"—perhaps to WV#9. It was only after lengthy deliberation that he was again placed in WV#5. It was as if this subject brought conscious attention to his meaning-making process, and began to change his world view through an effort of will.

Another subject placed in WV#6, Traditional Humanism, experienced a 12-point reduction in his dogmatism score (132 vs. 120). He spoke both directly and indirectly about the changes in his thinking, and a broadening of outlook which was precipitated by his relationship with a new spouse and a new job. At the same time he talked about increased commitments to family and children. He also mentioned decreased commitments to "idealistic" values and goals. This is also the subject who spoke so clearly about conflicts and changes in a dialectical manner. These expressed changes notwithstanding, the interview scoring process placed this subject in the same world view group (WV#6—Traditional Humanism) in which he was initially placed ten years ago. His ego level score remained unchanged.

In brief, it must be said that major or highly significant changes in world views or personality and cognitive styles have not been witnessed thus far in the second round of interviews and tests, although minor changes indeed have been noted. Structural changes seem to occur fairly slowly in adulthood. What has changed for all those interviewed is their capacity to talk about issues regarding world views. More recent follow-up results reveal even more subjects to be interested in growth and change. Additional subjects have begun to talk about spiritual issues and transcendent experiences (cf. Alexander et al., Chapter 2 & Introduction). We may wonder about the degree to which such findings are due to their participation in this project. In fact, one subject said very clearly that the initial interview had made a significant impact upon him over the past ten years. He said that during the ten-year interim he often thought about the interview and the kinds of questions posed. Near the beginning of the second interview he asked: "Are you aware of how this interview process itself can change people's lives?" Such an intervening variable was not anticipated at the beginning of this project, but is certainly understandable in retrospect.

With respect to the follow-up study, results obtained so far have not revealed quite what was projected in terms of world view, personality, ego development, and epistemological changes. It was anticipated that there would be more "mobility" or movement among world view positions; greater reductions in dogmatism scores; slight, but measurable increases in ego level scores; and more subjects seeking transcendent experiences. So far, these projected tendencies have not been manifested to the degree anticipated. Further quantitative and qualitative analyses must be conducted upon the completion of the follow-up study before these matters can be addressed in a more conclusive manner.

Summary

Overall, the findings supported many of the initial hypotheses. A method of investigating and classifying world views was constructed. The classification system developed held up well to tests of interrater reliability. I found that most people do have sets of usable constructs they live by which can be called world views, although the scope and breadth of their world views may vary considerably. The subjects' respective abilities to formulate and articulate their world views varied considerably as well.

It was noted that personality differences (e.g., self-acceptance and openness to self-exploration) and cognitive differences (open vs. closed-mindedness) seemed to relate to the kinds of world views the subjects held.

Those with the more cognitively flexible styles also were found to have higher ego levels. As a rule, these were the subjects who tended to be classified on the Subjective and Dialogical row-groups. These subjects also tended to be more dialectical in their thinking, and less "fixed-system" oriented. They brought a greater degree of awareness to processing information and to their world view choices. The world views chosen by these subjects were more expansive and less rigidly defined. These subjects were found to be in a kind of cognitive equilibrium which "welcomed" new data. In general, these people were highly motivated to change; they sought out change. Therefore, it was anticipated that they would be the ones who most likely would change—and evidence advances and transformations in world views, cognitive styles, and ego levels. This study confirmed this hypothesis as it highlighted the roles that motivation, intention, and openness play in both the lives *and* world view choices of those who seek further growth and continued development.

The results of this longitudinal study thus far suggest that an individual's world view or philosophical frame of reference may be one of the major factors to be considered in an analysis of adult ego, personality, and cognitive development. It appears that certain world views—with their concomitant ego levels and cognitive processing styles—may be more adaptive than others. Or, perhaps it should be said that certain world views are chosen by those who are more flexible and who are motivated to seek changes and transformations in their lives. Such world views may serve adult growth better because they provide an outlook on life which welcomes new data and information, thus contributing to the happiness and well-being of those who hold them.

The results also vividly portray the many ways in which individuals can engage in making sense of their experiences, and generally create meaning during the adulthood years. The differences in these ways are sometimes quite subtle. Through an analysis of the *content* component of postconventional thought and world views, coupled with the investigation of structural and process variables, these subtle differences among the variety of patterns in adult development and meaning making will continue to be elucidated.

Notes

1. Detailed descriptions of the nine world views discussed in this study and depicted on the World View Classification Grid can be obtained by contacting Melvin E. Miller, Department of Psychology, Norwich University, Northfield, Vermont 05663.

2. All WUSCT scores (ego level scores) were converted to a 10-point scale for comparison/statistical purposes.

3. This table was reprinted with permission from J. Demick and P. M. Miller (Eds.), *Development in the Workplace* (Hillsdale, NJ: Lawrence Erlbaum

Associates, Publishers, 1993), Chapter 1, by M. E. Miller and A. N. West, Influences of World View on Personality, Epistemology, and Choice of Profession.

4. To obtain the detailed scoring procedures for the World View Interviews, please contact the author at the above address.

5. In assigning subjects to the nine world view categories, the two raters achieved substantial agreement (Kappa = .70; see Elder et al., 1991). Raters agreed very well in placing subjects along the Teleological-Metaphysical Dimension (i.e., the columns of the WV Grid). Collapsing across the rows of the grid, the interrater reliability for assigning subjects to columns was k = .80. Conversely, raters also agreed well on assigning subjects to Epistemological categories (i.e., assigning subjects to rows of the WV Grid, collapsing across columns). For row placements, k = .66. Hence, raters' agreement in assigning subjects to the cells of the WV Grid was substantial.

6. At the time of this writing, the second wave of assessments and interviews was approximately two-thirds complete.

Acknowledgments

I would like to thank Susanne R. Cook-Greuter, Dina DuBois, J. Gregor Fetterman, and Alan N. West for their helpful comments and suggestions on earlier versions of this manuscript.

Appendix A

World View Interview

In this interview I am going to ask you a few questions dealing with your goals, philosophy of life, your views of things in general, and with what sort of person you think you are.

LEAD 1: It seems that most people have some kind of goals that they have set for themselves. I would like for you to tell me about some of your goals and ambitions.

Primers:
a) What may be some of the "specific goals" which you have established for yourself?
b) For your family?
c) How did you arrive at these goals?
d) Do you have goals which extend to your community? Nation? Or perhaps even the world?
e) Are the goals which you have established for yourself given priority over those you have mentioned for family, community, etc.?
f) Who are some of the people who may have influenced you as you formed or developed these goals? Would you talk about how they might have influenced you?

LEAD 2: Along the same lines as the first question, I have another which may actually be an extension of the first. As we think about our goals, thoughts of a philosophy of life or "guiding principles" often come to mind as well. I would now like you to describe your philosophy or your "view of the world" as clearly as you can. (Take some time to reflect upon or think about your position if that would be helpful.)

Primers:
a) How did you happen to arrive at such a philosophy or viewpoint?
b) What kinds of circumstances make you think of this philosophy or world view?
c) Do you think of it in times of "crises," at "critical moments," or at times of "big decisions," e.g., graduation, starting a new school, beginning a new job, etc.?
d) How would you say that this philosophy or viewpoint affects your behavior in general?
e) How might you say that your philosophy affects your thinking, perhaps even at times when you might not be aware of it (sort of unconsciously)?

f) How might your philosophy and the goals and ambitions that you previously mentioned be related to each other?

g) Who are some of the people that influenced the development of your philosophy? Can you think of specific events or occasions where these people influenced you? How did they influence you?

Be sure to get: a listing of "crises," "turning points," "milestones," or "hurdles."

NOTE: Does the philosophy affect the behavior? Does the philosophy affect the thinking? Did the philosophy help the individual "over the hurdles" or through the crises?

LEAD 3: In conjunction with the first two questions, I would like to know how much of an emphasis you place upon the need for personal discipline and hard work as requisites for your achieving these goals and objectives and for living in accordance with your philosophy. Or do you place more of an emphasis upon living life to its fullest, upon adventure, and upon experiencing a variety of things with little regard for the consequences (at least in terms of goal achievement and/or societal acceptance)?

Primers:
a) Do you believe that people should discipline themselves in order to keep their behaviors in line with societal and cultural expectations? Explain.
b) In general, would you say that you place a greater emphasis upon discipline and hard work than upon happiness and fulfillment? Please explain.
c) If you would happen to fail at some given endeavor or fail to achieve one of the goals which you mentioned above, would you believe that the failure was your own fault—the result of your own shortcomings, or a general lack of preparedness? Or would you see your failure as being the result of the situation or circumstances beyond your control? What about a combination of such factors? Please explain.

Be sure to get: their need for impulse control and their relative emphasis upon discipline vs. fulfillment.

LEAD 4: It is not uncommon to discover that one's philosophy changes to varying degrees throughout one's life. Since you were a child, how might your philosophy have changed?

Primers:
a) Under what circumstances have you experienced these changes?

b) Sometimes changes in one's philosophy just sort of happen. How about that? Has this been your experience? Explain. (Are some of the changes unconscious?)

c) At other times people actively change their philosophy. How much have you deliberately thought through the changes that have occurred in your philosophy?

d) We talked before about major "turning points" or "crises" and "challenges" that you have encountered. Would you add/detail any more at this point? (Please do so!) Did these experiences change how you thought about things?

e) Are there other significant people that influenced you or had an effect upon these changes? Explain.

Be sure to get: a description of general changes in philosophy and how they occurred. Are the changes unconscious or conscious? (Active or passive?) How much of each variable was conscious or unconscious? Did the crises affect the philosophy or vice versa?

LEAD 5:   Since we are talking about change, I also would like to know what future changes you anticipate in your philosophy of life and also in your goals and ambitions.

Primers:
a) What are your personal goals for five years from now (re: job and family and anything else)?

b) Have you thought about goals for 10 and 15 years in the future? What goals do you have in mind for these periods as well?

c) What goals do you hold for yourself for your "aging years"? Please explain!

d) What changes do you anticipate in your philosophy? (Cover the same time frame to include the aging years.)

e) Please attempt to elaborate on the philosophy or world view that you might subscribe to during the final years of your life.

Transition: Most of the questions concerning your philosophy of life have been rather general up to this point. Now I would like to move into some more specific questions concerning your philosophy.

LEAD 6:   We all differ in how we estimate or envisage what might be called the general "scheme of things." Would you say that things are sort of laid out in a specific kind of way (like an overall design or plan— something like "predestination"), or do you think things happen in sort of a haphazard way—by chance?

Primers:
a) Please explain in as much detail as you can how much of a design or order one can expect to find in life.
b) Does this order or design (or lack thereof) occur in human lives as well as in nature? Explain! Where does order or design come from?
c) Would you describe this order (or lack thereof) which you perceive, in terms of both nature itself and human nature, as being basically good or evil? Perhaps neutral? Please explain your position in considerable detail.
d) Do you conceive of yourself as having some place or position in this design, or in the overall scheme of things?
e) Would you have any obligations or responsibilities in this "scheme of things" which you have defined? To yourself, family, friends, community, and world at large?
f) How strongly do you feel obliged to be helpful or of service to other persons?

Be sure to get: a fairly precise delineation of subject's idiosyncratic estimation of the "scheme of things"—when possible. Do they have a well-defined position?

LEAD 7: Given your answers to the preceding question (determinism or indeterminism), would you say that the efforts and strivings of human beings make much of a difference in terms of what happens in their lives, and—in the overall order of things? In short, to what degree does human effort count? Or . . .

Primers:
a) How much control would you say that you have over your life—over what happens to you or what you become?
b) Do you see yourself as essentially being the "pilot of your own ship"? Or would you say that outside forces and circumstances are more powerful factors in dictating what happens to you?

LEAD 8: As you think about nature and human affairs, do you believe that it makes sense to attempt to arrive at general principles and theories which abstractly define and categorize them? Or do you believe that we should be more concerned with individual persons and particular events in all of their uniqueness?

Primers:
a) Should we emphasize the similarities in people, events, and nature, rather than the differences?

b) Do you believe that we can (ever) arrive at mathematical models which adequately capture the essence of human nature and nature at large? How precise can such models be?

c) And, finally, would you say that nature is divided into two or more distinct realms or spheres (e.g., physical-mental, energy-matter, mind-body, etc.), with each realm being governed by separate laws? Or would you say that nature (including human nature), should be conceived of as a single manifold or unitary system?

d) What is a "fact" for you? Do facts change? Can they ever conflict with each other?

e) How do you solve problems?

LEAD 9: Many people in our society subscribe to or hold some kind of religious belief or preference, although they differ in the degree to which they actually practice their religion. I would like to know if you have a particular religious preference or affiliation? If so, what is it? Would you describe the relationship that exists between your theological beliefs (or lack thereof) and your philosophy of life?

Primers:
a) How has this preference or affiliation (if any) affected your philosophy of life?

b) Was it instrumental or influential in helping you develop it?

c) Does the philosophy in turn affect your religion or theology?

d) Which one (religion or philosophy) is actually more influential in affecting your thinking and behavior?

Be sure to get: an exact description of the religious or theological position.

Transition: I would like to change the direction of our questions slightly, and ask you a few questions relating to the kind of person you are, and perhaps more precisely how you assess or judge your personal qualities.

LEAD 10: How would you, in general terms, describe your personality? (If their definition does not reflect a fairly sound understanding of the meaning of personality, then give them an operational one.) Many people feel that there is something like a "basic core" to the kind of person they are. Please explain or describe your "basic core" as you interpret it. Or, better yet, how would you describe yourself to yourself?

Primer:
Would you give me a term or brief phrase that best summarizes who you are?

LEAD 11: Do you ever reminisce, reflect upon, or think about your personality? If so, how often? Under what circumstances?

Primers:
a) Would you say that your personality remains basically the same from day to day?
b) Do you ever notice changes in your personality? When? Under what circumstances?
c) How satisfied are you with your present personality?
d) Do you ever feel a need or a desire to change any aspect of it—or to improve it or refine it?
e) Do you actively strive to change it or to improve it (refine it)?
f) Do you have any particular goals or objectives in mind for the development of your personality?
g) Tell me about your emotional life. How do you experience and/or express your emotions? Can you think of an example of an especially emotional experience that you have had? Please discuss this experience and your responses to it.
h) Were there any particular people who influenced the development of your emotions and personality? Who were/are these people? Please explain.

Be sure to get: Are the efforts at personality improvement or change active/conscious or more unconscious?

LEAD 12: You talked before about your "life goals" and philosophy. What connection, if any, might you see existing between them and your personality? Please explain.

Primers:
a) What kind of pressure might your philosophy exert upon you to change your personality or behavior?
b) What kinds of demands to change your personality might be made upon you by your goals and ambitions?
c) What kinds of demands to change your personality might have been made upon you by other people?
d) When you set goals like the ones you mentioned, did you ever question whether you had the necessary personality qualities to achieve them, or did you think that some kind of personality changes might be in order?

LEAD 13: Most people feel that they have some special talents, abilities, or qualities, and they can usually identify them. Please name and describe the special qualities and abilities that you have.

Primers:
a) How do you feel about how you have used your talents and abilities to this point in your life?
b) When you think about your talents and abilities, do you feel a need or desire to continually develop them?
c) Do you feel an urge to develop any other potential abilities that you think you might have?
d) Have you ever considered any actual steps that you might take to develop your abilities, talents, and potentials? (Latent abilities?)

LEAD 14:   In asking the above questions, I have been more or less directing the discussion. At this point, I would like to ask you about those "special aspects" of yourself that we have not touched upon. Just what exactly haven't we covered about you in connection with your philosophy of life, your goals and ambitions, and how they are related to your personality?

Primers:
a) What additional questions should I ask you? (What is *the* question that I haven't asked?)
b) Is there any special information about your life and development that you would like to tell me before we part today?
c) After I leave here today (or when you leave here), what is that one thing that you will wish that you would have told me?

References

Alexander, C. N. & Langer, E. J. (Eds.). (1990). *Higher stages of human development*. New York: Oxford University Press.

Basseches, M. A. (1984). Dialectical thinking as metasystematic forms of cognitive organization. In M. L. Commons, F. A. Richards & C. Armon (Eds.), *Beyond formal operations: Late adolescent and adult cognitive development* (pp. 216–238). New York: Praeger.

Buber, M. (1969). *Between man and man*. (M. Friedman, Ed. & R. G. Smith, Trans.). New York: Macmillan Co. Original work published 1947.

Churchman, C. W. (1971). *The design of inquiring systems: Basic concepts of systems and organization*. New York: Basic Books.

Commons, M.; Richards, F. & Armon, C. (Eds.) (1984). *Beyond formal operations: Late adolescent and adult cognitive development*. New York: Praeger.

Cook-Greuter, S. (1990). Maps for living: Ego development stages from symbiosis to conscious universal embeddedness. In M. Commons, T. Grotzer & J. Sinnott (Eds.), *Adult development, models and methods in the study of adolescent and adult thought,* 2 (pp. 79–104). New York: Praeger.

Elder, G. H.; Pavalko, E. & Clipp, E. C. (1991). *Working with archival data*. Beverly Hills, CA: Sage Publications.

Gibbs, J. (1979). Kohlberg's moral stage theory: A Piagetian revision. *Human Development* 22: 89–112.

Hegel, G. W. F. (1967). *The phenomenology of mind*. New York: Harper.

Holzner, B.; Mitroff, I. & Fisher, E. (1980). *An empirical investigation of frames of reference: Case studies in the sociology of inquiry*. Unpublished manuscript. University of Pittsburgh.

Kaufman, G. D. (1981). *The theological imagination: Constructing the concept of God*. Philadelphia: The Westminster Press.

Kegan, R. (1982). *The evolving self: Problems and process in human development*. Cambridge, MA: Harvard University Press.

Kluckhohn, C. (1967). The study of values. In D. Barrett (Ed.), *Values in America*. Notre Dame, IN: University of Notre Dame Press.

Kohlberg, L. (1983). *Essays in moral development: The psychology of moral development,* vol. 2. New York: Harper & Row.

Kohlberg, L. & Armon, C. (1984). Three types of stage models used in the study of adult development. In M. L. Commons, F. A. Richards & C. Armon (Eds.), *Beyond formal operations: Late adolescent and cognitive development* (pp. 383–394). New York: Praeger.

Koplowitz, H. (1984). A projection beyond Piaget's formal operations stage: A general system stage and a unitary stage. In M. L. Commons,

F. A. Richards & C. Armon (Eds.), *Beyond formal operations: Late adolescent and adult cognitive development* (pp. 272–295). New York: Praeger.

Loevinger, J. (1976). *Ego development: Conceptions and theories.* San Francisco: Jossey-Bass.

Loevinger, J. & Wessler, R. (1970). *Measuring ego development,* vol. 1: *Construction and use of a sentence completion test.* San Francisco: Jossey-Bass.

Loevinger, J.; Wessler, R. & Redmore, C. (1970). *Measuring ego development,* vol. 2: *Scoring manual for women and girls.* San Francisco: Jossey-Bass.

Miller, M. E. (1982). World views and ego development in adulthood. *Dissertation Abstracts International* 42: 3459–3460.

Miller, M. E. (1988). Developing a world view: The universal and the particular. *The New England Psychological Association Newsletter* 5: 3–4.

Miller, M. E. & West, A. N. (1993). Influences of world view on personality, epistemology, and choice of profession. In J. Demick & P. M. Miller (Eds.), *Development in the workplace* (pp. 3–19). Hillsdale, NJ: Lawrence Erlbaum Associates, Publishers.

Pepper, S. (1970). *World hypotheses.* Berkeley: University of California Press. Original work published 1942.

Perry, W. G. (1970). *Forms of intellectual and ethical development in the college years.* New York: Holt, Rinehart & Winston.

Riegel, K. F. (1978). *Psychology mon amour: A countertext.* Boston: Houghton Mifflin.

Rokeach, M. (1960). *The open and closed mind.* New York: Basic Books.

Shapiro, D. (1989). Exploring our most deeply held belief about ultimate reality. *ReVision* 12 (1): 15–28.

CHAPTER SEVEN

Cultivating Postformal Adult Development: Higher Stages and Contrasting Interventions

William R. Torbert
Wallace E. Carroll School of Management, Boston College

For the last several years, the senior management at Pilgrim Health Care—the most rapidly growing Massachusetts health management organization in the early 1990s, ranked first nationally in customer satisfaction by the August 1992 *Consumer Reports*—has been engaging, as a team, in early episodes of *action inquiry* (an approach to organizational change, scientific research, and personal transformation described in this chapter, as well as in Torbert, 1987a, 1991, 1992a). The best articulated motive for this practice on the part of Pilgrim's senior management is its commitment to engage in continual quality improvement in terms of its own practice, as it simultaneously implements an organization-wide quality improvement program.

During the same time period, the senior management of ABB—the highly successful Swedish-Swiss conglomerate that employs some 200,000—has been, as a team, practicing Vedic Transcendental Meditation (see Chapter 2 in this volume). As with any significant organizational initiative, many motives fuel this practice; one motive is to appreciate more deeply what ABB's espoused corporate commitment to "Life-Long Learning" for all employees means (Gustavsson, 1991; Philipson, 1992).

As this chapter will discuss, the practice of action inquiry and the Vedic/TM method are the only two educational interventions that have empirically been shown to facilitate adult developmental transformation beyond formal operations. The primary concern of this chapter is to present experiential tastes, theoretical outlines, and empirical findings of the action inquiry approach to adult learning, adult development, and leadership. The

Vedic/TM approach and the empirical research relating to it is well discussed in Alexander's chapter in this volume and will be reviewed only briefly later in this chapter in order to compare its educational process and documented outcomes to the action inquiry approach.

The Action Inquiry Approach

The action inquiry approach to adult learning, development, and leadership is to integrate inquiry into action, rather than separating them into reflection, on the one hand, and action, on the other hand—into "ivory tower" vs. "real world." On a personal scale, this implies an attempt to widen and deepen one's awareness meditatively in the very midst of one's workaday action (Torbert, 1992b, 1992c, 1994). On an interpersonal scale, integrating action and inquiry implies speaking in ways that simultaneously assert, illustrate, and inquire into others' responses (Argyris et al., 1985; Torbert, 1981a, 1987a). On an organizational scale, integrating action with inquiry results in the creation and re-creation of liberating structures that simultaneously increase participants' awareness, empowerment, and productivity (Torbert, 1991). On all three scales, the action inquiry approach is intended to invite reframing of assumptions and developmental transformation at appropriate moments.

The action inquiry approach is based on a model of experiential reality that posits (and shows how to test for) four qualitatively distinct, yet simultaneously present "territories of experience" (Torbert, 1973, 1991):
1) the outside world (e.g., empirical data, organizational outcomes);
2) one's own behavior as self-apprehended (e.g., one's own organizational action as it occurs);
3) one's own and others' feelings and thoughts (e.g., organizational norms and strategies); and
4) transcognitive consciousness, or attention, which can potentially embrace all four territories at once.

The model of four "territories of experience" draws attention to the possibility that one's attention may focus:
1) predominantly, or alternatively, on any one of the other three territories of experience; or
2) on analogies or incongruities among any two of the above territories; or
3) unitively on the simultaneous coexistence and interplay among all four territories of experience.

This theory of learning from experience addresses the current concern in the field of postformal adult development (Marcus & Wurf, 1987; Alexander, Druker et al. 1990) for learning theory that embraces the capacities for empirical, operational knowing, for abstract, hypothetical reasoning, and for subjective self-knowing. This theory also provides a viable substructure for early-stage developmental theory through formal operations: developmental progression can be understood to involve successive concentration on developing reliable operational awareness of an additional territory of experience, or on the interplay among several. More specifically:

1. Knowledge and behavioral control of one territory of experience—the outside world (as in learning to ride a bike)—are the primary objectives during the Imperial or Opportunist stage of development (stage names taken from Kegan [1982] and Torbert [1987a]—see Table 7.1 below).

2. Knowledge and cognitive-emotional control of a second territory of experience—one's own behavior (in relation to subsidiarily inferred group norms)—are the main objectives of the Interpersonal or Diplomat stage.

3. Knowledge and logical control of a third territory of experience—thought itself—are the primary objectives of the Technician stage.

4. Hypothetical reasoning that coordinates these three territories of experience—thought, action, and outcomes—is the primary objective of the Institutional or Achiever stage.

5. Explicit concern with the fourth territory of experience—transcognitive awareness—and with the actual, existential interplay among all four territories of experience in the midst of one's daily actions commences only at the postformal stages of development, particularly the Magician and Ironist stages. (Approaches such as phenomenology, symbolic interactionism, and postmodernism, with their analytic acknowledgment of the role of perspectival awareness, are characteristic of the Strategist stage.)

Western scientific thought over the past five centuries is itself a creature of the formal operations stage of development. It has generally assumed that only two of the four layers discussed here exist: 1) the outside world or "territory," which is assumed to include one's own behavior since that is externally visible; and 2) the thinking process or map, which is assumed to include consciousness as some form of self-reflective representation.

Beyond Formal Operations

According to the theory of learning from the four territories of experience, adult development beyond formal operations, when it occurs at all, is catalyzed by the interplay of existential awareness and unique historical circumstance. "Existential awareness" means awareness of the consciousness territory, not as a hypothetical possibility in the thinking territory, but as a vivifying reality in the present moment.

The content of any moment of such existential awareness may be primarily "positive," primarily "negative," or it may be primarily "reconciling." "Positive" moments of existential awareness include the

Table 7.1
Stages of Development according to Different Theories

Stage	Torbert	Kegan	Loevinger	Vedic
1	**Impulsive** *Impulse rules reflexes*	Impulsive	Impulsive	Early represen- tations
2	**Opportunist** *Needs rule impulses*	Imperial	Opportunist	Concrete thinking
3	**Diplomat** *Norms rule interests*	Interpersonal	Conformist	
4	**Technician** *Craft logic overrules group norms*	(transition)	(transition)	Abstract reasoning
5	**Achiever** *System effectiveness rules logic*	Institutional	Conscientious	
6	**Strategist** *Principle rules system*	(transition)	Autonomous	Advanced development of affect and ego
7	**Magician/ Clown** *Process rules principle*	Interindividual	Universal (Cook- Greuter, 1990)	Cosmic consciousness
8	**Ironist** *Intersystemic development rules process*	—	—	Refined cosmic consciousness

meditative contemplation of the consciousness territory, or a sense of alignment and congruity across several territories (e.g., saying what one means and doing what one says). "Negative" moments include moments of conscience when one recognizes an incongruity between two or more territories (e.g., hearing oneself espouse one value, while enacting another). "Reconciling" moments occur when the very act of reframing one's own awareness from immersion in one territory to a more inclusive awareness of multiple territories itself transforms a sense of stuckness into a nonproblematic flow of experiencing.

The immediate effect of such a moment of existential awareness—whether positive, negative, or reconciling—may be either to motivate and facilitate further such moments (further ongoing learning from experience) or to accelerate action in the other three territories and disengagement from the consciousness territory, thus discontinuing the process of learning from experience.

The long-term effects of repeated moments of such existential awareness include recognition of:

1) the uniqueness of relationships and contexts (Gilligan et al., 1990);
2) the importance of timing (e.g., finding teachable moments) and placing (e.g., creating unique market niches) in relational, organizational, and social initiatives;
3) the multiplicity and relativity of different frames or paradigms (Perry, 1970);
4) the dilemmic (rather than problematic) and paradoxical (rather than well-defined) nature of social life (Basseches, 1984);
5) the primacy of integrative, analogical, or metaphorical thinking (over analytical, deductive thinking) in comparisons across territories of experience (Torbert, 1989); and
6) inquiry as a primary life-value—as a political type of action, a spiritual type of search, and an aesthetic taste—not just as a scientific, intellectual value secondary to some answer; inquiry as primarily action inquiry and only secondarily as reflective inquiry (Torbert, 1991).

The Strategist Stage

In the first postformal stage of development (subjects in action inquiry research measured at Loevinger's [1978] stage 4/5 transition and stage 5 Autonomous), the person is inspired by moments of existential awareness to construct an explicit and distinctive integrative theory of self and world that recognizes development (e.g., theories such as those of Hegel, Marx, Freud, or Kohlberg). The value of existential awareness, or the integration of principle and practice, may (or may not) be the primary espoused value; but the dominant enacted value will be the imposition of a (sophisticated) language on experience, not the simultaneous tasting of preconceptual, conceptual, and postconceptual experience. This stage corresponds closely to Richards and Commons's (1990) "metasystematic" stage and to the stage called "dialectical operations" (Fowler, 1981; Basseches, 1985). Torbert (1987a) offers the following summary characterization of this Strategist stage:

> Aware of paradox; Process oriented as well as goal oriented; Enjoys variety of roles; Relativistic; Witty; Values individuality, unique niches, historical context; Recognizes importance of principle, contract, theory, judgment for making good decisions, not just rules and customs; Fascinated by complex interweaving of emotional dependence and independence in relationships; Creative conflict resolution; Aware of dark side, of profundity of evil, and tempted by its power. (p. 149)

The Magician/Clown Stage

The second postformal stage of development is most closely approximated by Kegan's Interindividual stage and by Loevinger's 5/6 transition and Loevinger's stage 6 (especially as reconceptualized by Cook-Greuter in Chapter 5 as the Universal stage). In this stage, the person moves from being in the "right" frame of mind to having a reframing mind that repeatedly subordinates itself to the existential awareness of this moment, divesting itself of its presuppositions. Allegiance to the consciousness territory and to awareness of the actual interplay in real time among the four territories becomes primary. A journal excerpt of a person measured at the Magician stage appears below, by way of illustration.

If one thinks of each territory as a system, then this stage is consistent with Richards and Commons's (1990) next postformal stage, which they call "paradigmatic," where the relations between systems come to be recognized as a unified paradigm. The Richards and Commons language has a predominantly "metasystematic" tone, however, and is at some distance from the existential "feel" of this next stage—a feel that perhaps may be conveyed by the phrase "indomitable vulnerability."

This vulnerability to constant self-transformation generates a capacity to meet others of any station in life in their full height and depth—to meet others as evolving selves preeminently and as inhabitants of a particular role or stage logic only secondarily. Such true mutuality in meeting is key to the very possibility of exercising developmentally transforming power (which is never unilateral, always mutual [Torbert, 1991]). Such is the power of the court jester, the clown, the Trickster God, the consummate consultant, the wounded healer, the true magician. Torbert (1987a) aptly characterizes this Magician/Clown stage of development in the following summary phrases:

> Ego-identity disintegrates, near-death experience; Impression of spirit rising from ashes; Participates in historical/spiritual transformations; Creates

mythical events that reframe situations; Exercises attention, researching thought, feeling, action, and effects; Anchors in inclusive present, seeing light and dark, order and mess; Blends opposites; Shamanistic body-mind integration; Treats time and events as kairatic, symbolic, analogical, metaphorical. (p. 214)

The Magician recognizes that the polarization between good and evil—between victory and defeat, between the sacred and the profane, between classes, races, or sexes, between I and Thou—is recreated in each moment by our relatively fixed and one-sided perspectives on the world. Evil emanates from the character of our fallen, passive attention; it cannot be permanently defeated. Indeed, to fight against it as though it were only outside ourselves reinforces it. Action inquiry becomes, for the Magician, not so much a theory of managing as an ongoing jousting, at one and the same time, with one's own attention and with the outside world. (p. 213)

These relatively abstract ways of describing Magician/Clown-stage experiencing can be complemented by the following illustration from the journal of a person measured at the Magician/Clown stage by the Loevinger sentence completion form:

Some days he would pick up a book by one of the great philosophers—it might be Hegel talking about our upside down world or Wittgenstein demonstrating how much more subtle and complex our everyday language is than our attempts abstractly to "understand it all"—and the book would come alive to him. He would turn the pages as though reading an adventure story, stirred to see these philosophers struggling with the same questions he felt. But other days he'd open the same book and see an impenetrable haze of gobbledygook.

What really began to confuse him, though, was the thought that occurred to him as he was accelerating for the second time during his jog—that second acceleration after the initial stiffness loosens and after the first breath deepens, then rasps, and after the ensuing surrender to a slower pace brings that delicious sense of liquefaction—that second acceleration when one is momentarily running so strongly that one believes one could go on forever and effortlessly turns one's attention away from the running which is taking care of itself, to "eternal" questions. The thought that occurred to him then and that very quickly demonstrated itself as his chest filled with pain (and thus began to remind him again of what he was actually doing) was that he was only interested in the eternal questions at rare moments.

Others thought of him as of an unusually philosophical turn of mind and this may indeed have been true, but the fact remained that however much more than "the man in the street" he may have mused on the eternal questions (he *was* "the man [running] in the street" now, he mused, the car exhaust beginning to penetrate unpleasantly to the pit of his stomach, distracting him from his pleasure in the river flowing past on the other side), he did not think of them often. He sometimes went for four or five hours wholly immersed in whatever he was doing without wondering about the meaning of it all— sometimes, in fact, for days at a time (although it was difficult to remember such times when he *was* thinking about the eternal questions since the questions seemed so inescapable and all-embracing when they did manage to attract his attention at all).

Now the pain in his chest led him to sight a bench two hundred yards ahead and aim resolutely to maintain his pace till he reached it—which resolution led him to wonder whether he was being lazy to stop so soon or masochistic to press himself so hard—which led him to concentrate on breathing more intentionally rather than letting his breath tear at him involuntarily. At any rate, he managed to forget his perplexities of the moment before as effortlessly as he had encountered them.

Later that day, though, he was reminded of the episode when he picked up Bergson's *The Creative Mind* and discovered with mounting excitement that it began:

> What philosophy has lacked most of all is precision. Philosophical systems are not cut to the measure of the reality in which we live; they are too wide for reality. Examine any one of them, chosen as you see fit, and you will see that it could apply equally well to a world in which neither plants nor animals have existence, only men [sic], and in which men would quite possibly do without eating and drinking, where they would neither sleep nor dream nor let their minds wander.

The further he read into the book, however, the more disappointed he became, for he found no more references to eating or drinking, or to the different ways of going to sleep, dreaming, and waking, or to the purposes and effects of jogging or chanting, or to going to the bathroom, or to the fundamental fickleness of attention as it ranges among these concerns, and so he began to wonder whether he had missed the point, which made him wonder, a bit more urgently than before, what the point of this story, as a whole, is. . . .

The Ironist Stage

In the third postformal stage (not represented in the Loevinger and Kegan schemes, but parallel to the Vedic refined cosmic consciousness stage), the person learns to clothe (to mask, to shield) his or her transformational vulnerability and charisma and to create institutional vehicles for encouraging development whenever another is ready for and seeking transformation. The person comes to value the distances and incongruities among the territories of experience, and the contingent validity of the earlier developmental crystalizations, as much as the moments of alignment and congruity among the territories and the moments of transformation. In Richards and Commons's (1990) terms, this is the "cross-paradigmatic" stage, when different paradigms are comprehended and related. But where their language stresses unification (as does Loevinger's Integrated stage), this theory highlights the values of stress and contrast, calling this the Ironist stage:

> The belief that all distances and tensions could be permanently obliterated in an effortless, classless utopia strikes the active attention as mere passive lunacy. Quite the contrary, the Ironic leader cultivates a quality of awareness and action that highlights the dynamic tensions of the whole enterprise—not so starkly as to engender terror and hopelessness—but rather in just the tones that can make their significance visible to other members and challenge them to higher performance and further development.
>
> To help achieve this kind of super-vision, the Ironic leader often takes on an outer role as a mask—does the opposite of what would be "natural" for him or her—just as the monkish Dag Hammarskjöld did in becoming the world's first global politician. In this way, the executive is exposed at every moment to just those realities to which, by inclination, he or she would remain blind.
>
> Thus, Jean Riboud—long an avowed socialist and supporter of the Mitterrand government in France—served as CEO of Schlumberger, Ltd., by several measures the best-managed capitalist company in the world. Thus, the debonair Gandhi doffed his three-piece lawyer's suit and donned a primitive loin cloth, taking a lead role in transforming India from colony to nation.
>
> Thus, a saint at the Ironic stage of development could be expected to take the role of a devil in public. Among several of the Middle and Far Eastern religious traditions, this process of masking one's charisma—one's sacred caring—has a name: "the Path of Blame." As a way of combating the dependence of the student and encouraging independence, the spiritual teacher who chooses this path acts in precisely ambiguous ways—in ways of questionable taste, devilishly—and attracts either questions or blame. (Torbert, 1987a, pp. 218–219)

Comparison to Vedic Postformal Stages

The action inquiry approach of learning from four territories of experience, along with the three postformal stages of development outlined above, is structurally consistent with recent research on the Vedic Psychology of human development, though they appear to be processually and descriptively different (see Alexander's chapter in this volume, as well as Alexander, Davies et al., 1990). Both approaches posit a transcognitive consciousness as different from the ordinary daytime waking state as that is from nighttime sleep. Both also posit three postformal stages based on an increasing apprehension and appropriation of the omnipresence of such a consciousness (the three Vedic stages are named cosmic consciousness, refined cosmic consciousness, and unity consciousness). Here, however, the similarity between the two approaches ends.

Each approach offers a very different sense of how transcognitive consciousness may be approached. Consequently, it is not surprising that the descriptions of the three stages along the path of approach also differ. Some of this difference in description of the three stages may be due to the fact that the Strategist stage described above seems to correspond best to a stage that Alexander, Davies et al. (1990) briefly allude to as preceding the three Vedic postformal stages. If so, then the Magician stage may correspond most closely to the Vedic cosmic consciousness stage and the Ironist stage may correspond most closely to refined cosmic consciousness. Even with this adjustment, however, a major difference in flavor between the two approaches remains. This difference may be the basis for a fruitful complementarity between the two in future work.

The Vedic theory and Transcendental Meditation procedures are first accepted on priestly authority (whether that authority be conceived of as the millennial Vedic tradition, as the personal authority of the Maharishi, or the scientific authority of the hundreds of TM studies). The theory claims that there is a "natural," "spontaneous," "effortless" tendency for consciousness to evolve that is usually blocked by psychobiological stress. The Vedic theory and the efficacy of Transcendental Meditation are then tested in terms of self-reports by those engaging in TM and the consequences that follow from engaging in TM. The consequences—in terms of enhanced development, lowered recidivism in prison studies, enhanced longevity in elderly studies, etc.—are most impressive (see Chapter 2 this volume; Alexander, Dixon et al., 1989; Alexander, Langer et al., 1989; Alexander, Davies et al., 1990).

The self-reports highlight the calm, relaxed, unitive nature of the awareness attained during the practice of TM, but these reports are less persuasive than the experimental studies for two reasons. First, TM practitioners may be learning this language for describing their meditative experience from books and TM teachers as much or more than from the meditative experiences themselves and may therefore be unintentionally suppressing other elements of their experience. Second, the self-reports are predominantly about "relaxing" meditative experiences rather than experiences when the person is under greater stress. (This critique of the possible incompleteness of the self-reports does not, of course, in any way vitiate the impressive findings about the outcomes of Transcendental Meditation practice.)

By contrast to the Vedic approach, in the theory of learning from four territories of experience through action inquiry, the primary emphasis falls not on the spontaneous, effortless, and dogmatic nature of postformal development, but rather on its voluntary, intentional, and idiosyncratic nature. Postformal development is seen as occurring through a process of action inquiry in everyday life. As such, action inquiry can include, but is not limited to, forms of solitary or group meditation; more generally, it involves meditation-in-action that embraces stress and contradiction as well as relaxation and unity. Of course, there may be other efficacious approaches to postformal development besides these two; in this early period of exploration of the phenomenon of postformal development, it will advance the field to articulate each.

Let us characterize the action inquiry approach a little more and indicate some of the empirical findings of action inquiry research, before comparing the effects of the Vedic approach and the action inquiry approach to cultivating postformal development.

Testing the "Four Territories" Paradigm and the Postformal Stage Characterizations through Action Inquiry Research

Action inquiry research, or collaborative inquiry (Reason & Rowan, 1981), is a form of research that persons, groups, or organizations undertake with others and in relation to their social and natural environments. Action inquiry studies the interplay among one's own internal practice of attention, one's thinking/feeling, and one's own action and outcomes in everyday life; analogously, at the organizational scale, action inquiry studies the interplay among mission, strategy, operations, and outcomes (Torbert, 1976, 1981b, 1983a, 1987a, 1991). It is *not*, in other words, primarily an academic form of research, nor primarily a spiritual belief system. The researchers are themselves also subjects and practitioners; the subjects are also researchers; and the aim is to create communities of inquiry within communities of social practice (Argyris et al., 1985). Insofar as external empirical research instruments are used, they are developed with or agreed to by the subjects. The subjects also are offered feedback on their own performance on measures, as well as on the general results of the study. Because the initiators of empirical research are also practitioner-colleagues of the other subjects, they have access to observations of the subjects that range far beyond the formal empirical measures.

The theory of learning from four territories of experience invites each potential participant to begin by an action inquiry process of testing in any one or any combination of the four territories whether and how action inquiry works. For example, in the "consciousness" territory, the individual may test the intuitive plausibility for himself or herself of the primitive, paradigmatic claim that four such territories exist (directions for such testing are offered in Torbert, 1991). For example, let us follow Descartes's test for the existence of the thinking territory.

In his *Discourses on Method and Meditations* (1637/1960) Descartes develops confidence (indeed, certainty) about the proposition "I think:

therefore, I am." He demonstrates that in attempting to doubt that one is doubting, one can "see" with ineradicable certainty that one is doubting (i.e., thinking). This effort served *for him* as a test of the intuitive plausibility of the thinking territory and of his existence in this territory.

His own writing about this test, however, is not very clear and does not explicitly invite his readers to conduct the same test for themselves. Others conducting Descartes's test may agree with the result without finding it of great significance (not serving either to shake or to construct the foundations of their personal paradigm because they are not at a developmental point where their current paradigm is at risk for them). Yet others conducting Descartes's test may recognize that it, in fact, confirms the intuitive plausibility of *two* territories of experience:

1) the thinking territory (since the attempt to doubt one's doubting is undeniably [in that moment] thinking); and
2) the consciousness territory (since the "seeing" of one's doubting is not the same quality of experience as the doubting itself) (Torbert, 1991).

Does the reader follow this demonstration, not merely in terms of its logic, but by actually trying to doubt that one is thinking, thereby "seeing" one's doubting (one's thinking)?

Empirical Findings about the Effects of Postformal Development

Let us now examine empirical tests of how managers measured at postformal stages actually perform, in order to see whether there is evidence that late-stage managers integrate action and inquiry rather than splitting them. Table 7.2 offers an overview of developmental distributions of managers and professionals at different hierarchical levels in organizations in six different studies (Study 1—Smith, 1980; Study 2—Davidson, 1984; Study 3—Torbert, 1983a; Study 4—Gratch, 1985; Study 5—Quinn & Torbert, 1987; Study 6—Hirsch, 1988). The findings are generally consistent with other "ego demographic" studies. In every sample except the small sample of entrepreneurial professionals, the modal category is the Technician stage (Loevinger's 3/4 transition). Also, managers at postformal stages are rare in every sample: only 8% of all those tested measured at the Strategist stage; and only one Magician/Clown-stage score was found in all the samples (see Torbert, 1994, for a study of six executives at the Magician/Clown stage). At lower levels of organizational hierarchies there is a high proportion of early-stage (Diplomat and Technician) managers and a low proportion of later-stage (Achiever and Strategist) managers (Studies 1, 2, 3). These proportions gradually reverse themselves as the study samples reflect the upper levels of organizational hierarchies (Studies 4, 5, 6). However, even at the senior-most organizational levels only 15% of those sampled are at the Strategist stage (on the other hand, 78% of those

Table 7.2

Percent Distribution of Managers by Developmental Position in Six Studies

N=497	Impulsive	Opportunist	Diplomat	Technician	Achiever	Strategist	Magician	Ironist
Study 1: First Line Supervisors (n=37)	0	0	24	68	8	0	0	0
Study 2: Nurses (n=100)	0	2	9	54	31	4	0	0
Study 3: Jr./Middle Managers (n=177)	0	5	9	43.5	40	2.5	0	0
Study 4: Senior Managers (n=66)	0	0	6	47	33	14	0	0
Study 5: Sr. Mgrs. & Top Executives (n=104)	0	0	3	43.5	39.5	14	0	0
Study 6: Entrepreneurial Ophthalmologists (n=13)	0	0	0	38.5	38.5	23	0	0

measured as Strategists are in the three senior manager samples). There is no significant correlation between age and stage of development; for example, most of the subjects over 60 are found in the supervisory sample where the modal stage is Diplomat.

A natural question is whether and how managerial behavior and outcomes differ by stage of development. A number of studies have now addressed this question and have yielded the following findings:

1. At each successive stage of development, a higher proportion of managers ask for a personal feedback session on their Loevinger sentence completion form (n=281) (Torbert, 1987a; Quinn & Torbert, 1987).

2. On a 34-item in-basket test, early-stage managers tend to handle items one at a time, whereas later-stage managers are more likely to organize the items strategically, are less likely to take the presented framing of problems for granted as correct, and are more likely to delegate in a collaborative and inquiring fashion (n=49) (Merron et al., 1987).

3. When managerial project groups include one or more managers measured at the Strategist stage, group task performance is more effective, group time-use is more efficient, and members perceive greater group support for their own learning (n=16 groups) (Torbert, 1987b).

4. In a regulated, stable-frame industry (public utilities), executives measured at the Strategist stage report feeling isolated and ineffective at persuading others to take their business concerns seriously. At the same time, on a battery of physical health questions, those measured at the Strategist stage rank as being in the best health (n=104) (Quinn & Torbert, 1987).

5. In a small (n=13), intensively studied sample of entrepreneurial ophthalmologists, those measured as Technicians, Achievers, and Strategists exercised significantly different business strategies from one another, with widely different results in terms of gross annual revenues. (There was a small negative correlation between revenues and both age and years in practice.)

For the Technicians (n=5), technological expertise was the key to success in their practice. Since they insisted on hands-on participation in every technical phase of their operations, they saw essentially one patient at a time; their average gross annual revenues were about $330K.

The Achievers (n=5) focused on their office staff as the essential ingredient to a successful practice. These doctors knew how to involve their staff, and delegated responsibility to them. Thus they could see approximately three patients at a time; on average their practice grossed $1,300K in annual revenues.

Finally, the Strategists (n=3) concentrated on broader strategic issues, such as overall patient satisfaction, critical service gaps, unoccupied niches, and partnership contracts with fellow professionals. In so doing they could create multisite practices, which served approximately three times again as many patients as the Achievers. Their gross annual revenues were again three times that of the previous stage, averaging $4,200K. Furthermore, the lowest revenue for an entrepreneur at each stage was at least twice as large as the highest revenue for an entrepreneur at an earlier stage, and the smallest practice at each stage was more than twice as large as the largest practice at the prior stage (Hirsch, 1988; Torbert, 1991).

6. In another small, intensively studied sample (n=17), deliberately structured to include managers who had or had not evolved from the Achiever stage to the Strategist stage over the prior five years, systematic differences were found in the way that managers at the two different stages a) managed subordinates, b) related to superiors, and c) took action initiatives. Although all the managers in the study were conscientious, effective, and upwardly mobile, Strategists were more likely to:

a) articulate principles for their own leadership practice and notice and learn from discrepancies;
b) seek to understand subordinates' frames and work toward new shared meanings;
c) create new spheres of action for subordinates and themselves by testing their superiors' and organizations' constraints;
d) negotiate differences in frame and/or perception explicitly with superiors;
e) base their actions on principles rather than rules, if the two are at odds, even when the rule is established by their superiors;
f) view their own action processes as uniquely crafted rather than as generalizable and rule governed; and
g) define effectiveness in terms of setting a stage on which multiple aims can be achieved through an iterative process of reframing and creating new shared meanings, rather than in terms of getting their own initial processes and solutions adopted (Fisher & Torbert, 1991).

7. In the smallest sample of all (n=6), the researcher deliberately sought out subjects at the rare Magician stage and found that:

a) all were key players in multiple organizations simultaneously;
b) all varied their pace between urgency and leisureliness within each workday;
c) all monitored the analogical alignment or incongruity among activities of the self, the group, the organization, and the larger social system; and
d) all were viewed as charismatic, but exercised this quality not to generate worshipful subservience, but rather to challenge others and support their initiatives (Torbert, 1994).

Given the small sample sizes of most of the eight different sets of findings on the practical effects of postformal development just summarized, each study can be considered as no more than suggestive. The consistency of the findings across all eight studies and across a variety of methods is, however, quite striking. In a number of ways, these findings reflect increasing integration of action and inquiry at the later stages of development. These practical findings, along with whatever spiritual or theoretical interests one has in postformal development, raise the question of what sorts of educational interventions/institutions cultivate postformal development.

Two Approaches to Cultivating Postformal Development

The question of what sort of educational interventions cultivate postformal development has been addressed both by the Vedic/TM approach and by the action inquiry approach. Both approaches to encouraging postformal development are effective (though differently so) in terms of measurable outcomes. By contrast, developmental studies at other institutions of higher education show little or no change for the sample as a whole between pre- and posttesting (Chandler, 1991; Miller, Chapter 6 this volume).

In the case of the Vedic approach, recent studies show that only graduates of Maharishi International University (MIU) show significant positive development beyond the Institutional or Achiever stage (as measured by the Loevinger [1978] Sentence Completion Form), as compared to graduates of three other universities (Chandler, 1991). Overall, alumni from the three other universities showed no change at all, and the alumni from the other university who showed the most change showed less than half as much change on average as the MIU alumni. The positive findings from Maharishi International University alumni represent an average .31 stage progression over a ten-year period from pretest to posttest.

The findings to date in regard to the action inquiry approach are interestingly different. One finding shows that, after the Wallace E. Carroll School of Management at Boston College restructured its MBA program to invite students to participate in improving not just their analytic competence, but also their managerial competence through action inquiry, it attracted a developmentally different student population from before the restructuring. Prior to restructuring at graduation only 2.5% of the MBA students scored beyond the Institutional or Achiever stage (on the Loevinger test); by contrast, after restructuring a full 25% scored at postformal stages *at entry*. Thus, a different group, with a much higher proportion of persons at a postformal stage of development, volunteered to enter the program once it restructured (see Torbert, 1981a, 1987a, 1987b, for descriptions of the restructured program).

Once in the program, 10% (18 of 180 in two different cohorts) showed a full stage change beyond the Achiever stage during its 20-month duration (that is, either from 3/4 to 4/5 or from 4 to 5 on the Loevinger measure). Half-stage regressions and progressions balanced one another, so the average movement was a .1 stage progression. Given the relative brevity of the program and the rarity of any postformal development in most settings, it is difficult to determine just how positive a finding this is. The reader may compare it to the .3 stage progression found in MIU alumni. This comparison is complicated by two differences: 1) the large difference in elapsed time between pre- and posttests for the two samples; and 2) the fact that the pretest baseline for the MIU sample was higher (just above the Achiever stage on average) than for the BC sample (just above the Technician stage on average). The first difference may act to exaggerate the MIU effect. The second difference may act to exaggerate the BC effect. On average, it appears that the Vedic/TM approach practiced at Maharishi International University had a stronger effect on cultivating students' development.

A second finding from the action inquiry MBA program is easier to interpret: 84% (15 of 18) of those who showed a full stage change voluntarily sought and won a (nonremunerative) consulting role during the second year of the program (and 94% [15 of 16] of those who participated in the consulting role showed a full stage change) (Torbert, 1991). This role, gained through a competitive application process, exposes students to a summer consulting course, to consulting to four first-year project groups, and to a weekly clinic session, all of which encourage them to engage in action inquiry research in the midst of professional practice, much as the first-year activities themselves also do. What causes the near-unanimity of stage change among the consultants by contrast to the near-nonexistence of stage change among the remainder of the class? Two factors appear to contribute: 1) the additional exposure to action inquiry; and 2) the voluntary commitment by the consultants to continue to explore the action inquiry approach.

Upon graduation from the restructured program, a few graduates initiated an action inquiry group of 15 to 20 persons that met regularly for five years, with a few membership changes each year. The group met once every three weeks without formal leadership to reflect together on their ongoing experiences at work and in other parts of their lives; in addition, subgroups of 3 met once between meetings to provide one another with ongoing consulting. In a later intensive study of 15 graduates, of whom 6 had participated in the action inquiry alumni group, those who participated in voluntary action inquiry showed significantly more developmental change over the six-year (on average) period between tests than those who did not. The 6 action inquiry participants showed a total of 12 steps of developmental progression (a "step" representing half a stage) and no regression—an average of one full stage of progression—whereas the 9 nonparticipants in action inquiry showed three progressive steps and two regressive steps—an average of one-eighteenth of a stage of progression) (Fisher & Torbert, 1991; Torbert & Fisher, 1992c). The chi square statistic shows this difference to be significant beyond the .05 level. Thus, again, voluntary participation in action inquiry is associated with postformal developmental progression.

One Practice Context that Cultivates Postformal Development

The unique, interrelated elements of the Wallace E. Carroll School of Management MBA program that are intended to encourage action inquiry and cultivate postformal development have several qualities in common:
1) they highlight each participant's potential for initiative and do not require adherence to any particular theory;
2) they provide each participant with performance feedback on his or her initiatives across all four territories of experience on tasks of practical significance;
3) they offer on-the-job training in giving, receiving, digesting, and responding with new initiatives to such performance feedback; and
4) they encourage the cycle of offering feedback and developing new initiatives to occur as close in time as possible to perceptions of error, incongruity, or conflict.

In all these respects, these systems represent a kind of Continual Quality Improvement program focused on all organizational levels (not just production) that is more sophisticated than any CQI program in operation in industry today, and which is relevant to schools and other organizations as well as to industry (Torbert, 1991).

Detailed descriptions of these systems are offered elsewhere (Torbert, 1981a, 1987a, 1987b, 1991), but several examples can help the reader gain a concrete sense of what is meant. In terms of highlighting initiative, all students belong to action-project groups and each student plays a leadership role (i.e., every member of each group is a leader—project leader, meeting leader, process leader, evaluation leader, etc.). In terms of providing feedback, each group works with a second-year consultant whose primary role is to offer such feedback when requested; also, every group (and every faculty-run class) engages in a feedback process in the middle of the semester with discussion of the results and adjustments, as well as at the end of the project or semester.

All of the foregoing represents on-the-job training, but one further example is a weekly two-hour clinic session held for the consultants during which they both discuss and role-play their current group intervention dilemmas.

Much of the foregoing also indicates the effort to encourage feedback and new initiative as close to the original action as possible. The most dramatic example of this is an end-of-the-year event involving all 16 student teams that have consulted to live businesses and agencies, with responsibility for documenting the efficacy of their work in terms of changes that their clients have already implemented. On this day, all the student teams make professional oral presentations of their work to their peers, the school's faculty, and several local area CEO's. Each presentation is judged on 12 different criteria as soon as it is completed, and every team receives 45 minutes of quantitative and qualitative feedback at the close of the day, including its relative standing among all the presentations.

In the decade since these systems were originally implemented at the school, they have generated both considerable pride and considerable controversy. During that time, the school has moved from being unranked among the top 100 schools of management to being ranked in the top 25, to serving as the single concrete model for the discussions of a national commission on what twenty-first-century schools of management should look like (Hennessy & Rosenblum, 1990).

Conclusion

The theory of learning from four territories of experience through action inquiry leads toward a distinctive approach both to scientific research and to postformal adult development. This theory is structurally consistent with several other conceptualizations of postformal development—notably the Vedic/TM approach—but significantly different in process.

Empirical findings showing the actions and outcomes of managers at the first postformal stage of development offer additional practical reasons for individuals and institutions to become interested in cultivating postformal development.

The organizational conditions for cultivating postformal development under the action inquiry approach are shown to include unusual degrees of voluntariness, initiative, and feedback. These organizational conditions are also shown to be consistent with contemporary managerial concerns for Continual Quality Improvement.

At present, the Vedic/TM approach is being used at Maharishi International University and at the Swedish-Swiss conglomerate ABB. The action inquiry approach is being used at the Carroll School of Management, Boston College, and at Pilgrim Health Care. Since both the Vedic/TM approach and the action inquiry approach have been shown to effect postformal adult development, perhaps the two approaches can be tried together in a future field experiment.

Acknowledgments

I would like to thank Howard Chandler and Susanne Cook-Greuter for their helpful comments on an earlier version of this chapter.

References

Alexander, C.; Dixon, C.; Chandler, H. & Davies, J. (1989). The Vedic psychology of higher stages of development. Paper presented at the fourth Adult Development Symposium. Cambridge, MA: Harvard Medical School Department of Psychiatry.

Alexander, C.; Langer, E.; Newman, R.; Chandler, H. & Davies, J. (1989). Transcendental meditation, mindfulness, and longevity: An experimental study with the elderly. *Journal of Personality and Social Psychology* 57 (6): 950–964.

Alexander, C.; Davies, J.; Dixon, C.; Dillbeck, M.; Drucker, S.; Oetzel, R.; Muehlman, J. M. & Orme-Johnson, D. (1990). Growth of higher stages of consciousness: Maharishi's Vedic Psychology of human development. In C. Alexander & E. Langer (Eds.), *Higher stages of human development: Perspectives on adult growth* (pp. 286–341). New York: Oxford University Press.

Alexander, C.; Drucker, S. & Langer, E. (1990). Major issues in the exploration of adult growth. In C. Alexander & E. Langer (Eds.), *Higher stages of human development: Perspectives on adult growth* (pp. 3–32). New York: Oxford University Press.

Argyris, C.; Putnam, R. & Smith, D. (1985). *Action science: Concepts, methods, and skills for research and intervention.* San Francisco: Jossey-Bass.

Basseches, M. A. (1985). *Dialectical thinking and adult development.* Norwood, NJ: Ablex.

Chandler, H. (1991). Transcendental Meditation and awakening wisdom: A ten-year longitudinal study of self-development. Unpublished doctoral dissertation. Maharishi International University, Fairfield, IA.

Cook-Greuter, S. (1990). Maps for living: Ego development stages from symbiosis to conscious universal embeddedness. In Commons, M., et al. (Eds.) *Adult development, models and methods in the study of adolescent and adult thought, 2* (pp. 79–104). New York: Praeger.

Davidson, J. (1984). The effects of organizational culture on the development of nurses. Unpublished doctoral dissertation. Boston College School of Education, Chestnut Hill, MA.

Descartes, R. (1637/1960). *Discourse on method and meditations.* New York: Macmillan.

Fisher, D. & Torbert, W. (1991). Transforming managerial practice: Beyond the achiever stage. In R. Woodman & W. Pasmore (Eds.), *Research in organizational change and development* (vol. 5). Greenwich, CT: JAI Press.

Fowler, J. (1981). *Stages of faith: The psychology of human development and the quest for meaning.* New York: Harper & Row.

Gilligan, C.; Murphy, J. M. & Tappan, M. (1990). Moral development beyond adolescence. In C. Alexander & E. Langer (Eds.), *Higher stages of human development: Perspectives on adult growth* (pp. 208–225). NY: Oxford University Press.

Gratch, A. (1985). Managers' prescriptions of decision-making processes as a function of ego development and of the situation. Unpublished paper. Columbia University Teachers College, New York.

Gustavsson, B. (1991). *The transcendent organization.* Edsbruk, Sweden: Akadewitryck AB.

Hennessy, J. & Rosenblum, J. (1990). *Leadership for a changing world: The future role of graduate management education.* Los Angeles: Graduate Management Admissions Council.

Hirsch, J. (1988). *Toward a cognitive-developmental theory of strategy formulation among practicing physicians.* Ann Arbor, MI: University Microfilms International.

Kegan, R. (1982). *The evolving self.* Cambridge, MA: Harvard University Press.

Kegan, R. (1994). *In over our heads: The mental demands of modern life.* Cambridge, MA: Harvard University Press.

Loevinger, J. & Wessler, E. (1978). *Measuring ego development,* vols. 1 & 2. San Francisco: Jossey-Bass.

Marcus, H. & Wurf, E. (1987). The dynamic self-concept: A social psychological perspective. *Annual Review of Psychology* 38: 299–337.

Merron, K.; Fisher, D. & Torbert, W. (1987). Meaning-making and management action. *Group & Organization Studies* 12: 274–286.

Perry, W. (1970). *Forms of intellectual and ethical development in the college years: A scheme.* New York: Holt, Rinehart & Winston.

Philipson, J. (1992). Maharishi corporate development. Personal communication during executive visit at Boston College, Chestnut Hill, MA.

Quinn, R. & Torbert, W. (1987). Who is an effective, transforming leader? Unpublished paper. University of Michigan School of Business, Ann Arbor, MI.

Reason, R. & Rowan, J. (1981). *Human inquiry: A sourcebook of new paradigm research.* London: Wiley.

Richards, F. & Commons, M. (1990). Postformal cognitive-developmental theory and research: A review of its current status. In C. Alexander & E. Langer (Eds.), *Higher stages of human development: Perspectives on adult growth* (pp. 139–161). New York: Oxford University Press.

Smith, S. (1980). Ego development and the problem of power and agreement in organizations. Unpublished Doctoral Dissertation. George Washington University School of Business and Public Administration, Washington, DC.

Torbert, W. (1973). *Learning from experience: Toward consciousness.*

New York: Columbia University Press.

Torbert, W. (1976). *Creating a community of inquiry*. London: Wiley.

Torbert, W. (1981a). The role of self-study in improving managerial and institutional effectiveness. *Human Systems Management* 2 (2): 72–82.

Torbert, W. (1981b). Three chapters in P. Reason & J. Rowan, *Human inquiry: A sourcebook of new paradigm research* (chapter 11, pp.141–152; chapter 29, pp. 333–348; chapter 37, pp. 437–446). London: Wiley.

Torbert, W. (1981c). Interpersonal competence. In A. Chickering (Ed.), *The modern American college* (pp. 172–190). San Francisco: Jossey-Bass.

Torbert, W. (1983a). Executive mind, timely action. *ReVision* 4 (1): 1–23.

Torbert, W. (1983b). Identifying and cultivating professional effectiveness: "Bureaucratic action" at one professional school. Paper presented at American Society for Public Administration, New York.

Torbert, W. (1987a). *Managing the corporate dream: Restructuring for long-term success*. Homewood, IL: Dow Jones-Irwin.

Torbert, W. (1987b). Education for organizational and community self-management. In S. Bruyn & J. Meehan (Eds.), *Beyond the market and the state* (pp. 171–184). Philadelphia: Temple University Press.

Torbert, W. (1987c). Management education for the twenty-first century. *Selections,* 3 (3): 31–36.

Torbert, W. (1989). Leading organizational transformation. In R. Woodman & W. Pasmore (Eds.), *Research in organizational change and development,* vol. 3 (pp. 83–116). Greenwich, CT: JAI Press.

Torbert, W. (1991). *The power of balance: Transforming self, society, and scientific inquiry*. Newbury Park, CA: Sage Publications, Inc.

Torbert, W. (1992a). The true challenge of generating continual quality improvement. *Journal of Management Inquiry* 1 (4): 331–336.

Torbert, W. (1992b). Finding the chaos in a developmental model and in the action awareness of late-stage executives. Paper presented as part of a symposium on "Modeling the Dynamics of Transformation" at the Academy of Management Meeting, Las Vegas, NV.

Torbert, W. & Fisher, D. (1992c). Autobiographical awareness as a catalyst for managerial and organizational development. *Management Education and Development*, 23 (3): 184–198.

Torbert, W. (1994). The "chaotic" action awareness of transformational leaders. *International Journal of Public Administration*, forthcoming.

PART IV

Postconventional Ethical and
Moral Development

CHAPTER EIGHT

The Ethics of Enlightenment: An Expanded Perspective on the Highest Stage of Moral Development

Steven M. Druker

The Need to Understand the Fullest Potential of Ethical Development

A truly adequate theory of moral development should include knowledge of the highest level of ethical life and also knowledge of how to cultivate it. A clear concept of the highest ethical stage is essential, since, as Piaget (1970) has noted, a developmental theory does not rest on its rudimentary stage but rather hangs from its postulated highest one. Any theory based on an inadequate understanding of the highest level of ethical life would most likely focus at best on only a partial aspect of the ethical dimension—and view it as unrelated to the whole.

A recurrent theme in ethical thought, sounded by thinkers from Plato (1945) to the contemporary developmental psychologist Jane Loevinger (1976), is that the level of one's ethical life is an expression of the level of one's overall development as a human being. If this is so, it is reasonable to expect that the fullest understanding of moral development would arise only in conjunction with the fullest understanding of human development in general. Yet, as Plato, Spinoza (1930), and several others who express the above theme emphasize, the developmental levels which are ordinarily observed do not reveal the full ethical potential of human life: a potential for living in harmony with the universe as a whole.

In this vein, there seems to be substantial evidence that individuals throughout history have attained higher levels of human development which, compared to the ordinary, more commonly understood planes of life, represent an ethical phase transition. Aldous Huxley (1945) points out that recognition of these higher levels of human development is integral to what Leibniz termed the "Perennial Philosophy," a philosophy expressed within traditions found in virtually every culture and voiced by individuals throughout the ages. In this philosophy, everything and every self in the universe has the same unmanifest, unified ground level, and one can gain transcendental experience in which this unified level is an immediate reality. Further, one can develop the capacity to expand one's limited self to this cosmic level and live in attunement with the universe as a whole, spontaneously performing action which is right in the fullest, most all-encompassing sense.

There are many accounts of individuals who have had experiences which are transcendental and nondualistic in character (e.g., Bucke, 1969; Maslow, 1971). Lawrence Kohlberg (1981) notes that experiences of this sort often do stimulate a significant transformation of ethical life—a transformation to a "cosmic perspective" which goes beyond the perspectives ordinarily associated with even the highest levels of human reasoning. In fact, he concludes that some type of trans-reasoning, unitive experience is an essential factor in the development of this highest ethical orientation. In Kohlberg's view, if we identify the value premises and thought processes which are minimally sufficient to generate the fullest, most universal level of moral reasoning, we find that they are insufficient to generate the "cosmic" ethical orientation. This means that even when considering solely the cognitive level, the fullest expression of ethical life transcends the fullest function of formal operational thought.

In Kohlberg's view, moving to the cosmic ethical level involves a distinct shift in ego alignment. He emphasizes that although the ego standpoint associated with the highest conceivable stage of principled moral reasoning is that of individual mind abstracted from its localized particularities and functioning in its most universal mode of conceptual reasoning, it remains the perspective of a particularized, individual awareness. He postulates that the subjective standpoint of the next higher level transcends the perspective of an individual, even when reasoning in a fully universal mode. Rather, it is more a perspective which would be associated with a nonlimited awareness—a perspective that represents the standpoint of the universe as a whole.

If such a highest ethical stage does exist, gaining a thorough understanding of it should shed important new light on ethics and ethical development. Yet scientific study of such a cosmic stage has, to most researchers, appeared problematical. A major reason is that the primary source of data has seemed limited to subjective reports of individuals who, for the most part, are unavailable for detailed investigation. Further, most of the subjective descriptions do not readily relate to modes of experience with which the researchers themselves are familiar; and it has seemed difficult to understand them in terms of the parameters through which human development is ordinarily studied. For instance, although Huxley (1945) states it is an empirical fact that these higher-level experiences only arise through the development of specific internal conditions, he can say little more about these conditions than that they apparently involve factors such as being loving and pure in heart. In consequence, transcendental experiences and the cognitive perspectives based upon them are commonly categorized as "mystical."

Because scientific knowledge of the cosmic stage of ethical development has appeared limited, most Western scientists have tended to give a limited interpretation of its significance. For example, Kohlberg (1981) interprets the cosmic perspective as cosmic in flavor but not in fact. He appears to view transcendental experience as subjectively meaningful but not as genuinely veridical—not as the true experience of a more basic and comprehensive level of reality in which self and universe are in actuality united. Further, he describes the cosmic perspective as merely a conceptual construction. In Kohlberg's view, the perspective is still that of an individual ego, an ego attempting to project itself towards its conception of the cosmic.

During recent years, major advances have occurred within both the most modern and the most ancient systems of knowledge which suggest the appropriateness of taking an expanded view on the cosmic perspective. The world's oldest continuous tradition of knowledge, the Vedic tradition, has always been recognized as providing one of the most comprehensive descriptions of a cosmic level of human development; but, for the reasons outlined above, Western thinkers have interpreted it in a limited way. However, over the last 35 years, Maharishi Mahesh Yogi, a leading representative of and authority on the Vedic tradition, has demonstrated it can be viewed as scientific and that its concepts can be understood in relation to the concepts of modern science. Maharishi's explanation of Vedic thought sets forth a systematic, detailed theory of a) the characteristics and ontological status of the transcendental level, b) the process through which it is experienced, c) how such experience facilitates human development to stages based in a level of mind beyond conceptual reasoning, and d) how these stages are higher developmental levels in terms of both cognitive and ethical dimensions.

This theory proposes that the individual psyche can expand to genuinely cosmic proportion, becoming coextensive with a transcendental level of consciousness which is the ground state of existence, the unified field of natural law, described by Maharishi as the "cosmic psyche" (Orme-Johnson, 1988). Further, it states that action at the cosmic level represents a distinctly new and fuller style of ethical functioning. Maharishi frames these various ideas as scientific hypotheses predicting specific kinds of subjective experiences as well as measurable physiological, psychological, and behavioral changes. Moreover, the predictions can be tested through utilization of a set of simple, natural mental techniques which are said to enable any individual to regularly experience transcendental consciousness. These techniques—taught as the Transcendental Meditation and TM-Sidhi program—have been derived by Maharishi from the Vedic tradition, and he describes them as the applied, practical aspect of Vedic theory (Maharishi, 1972). The availability of these techniques (which Maharishi refers to as a technology of consciousness) makes possible 1) widespread direct investigation into the nature of the transcendental level and the perspectives which develop through experiencing it, and 2) standard research into the physiological, psychological, and behavioral correlates of the regular experience of transcendental consciousness.

Concomitant with the revival of a procedure for systematic experience of the deepest levels of reality as described by Vedic theory, modern physical science has been developing a picture of the universe which is similar in many respects to key aspects of the Vedic picture. Consequently, many important Vedic concepts have become increasingly understandable in terms of modern science. Moreover, an extensive and growing body of research on the effects of the Transcendental Meditation and TM-Sidhi program is providing increasing support to major aspects of the Vedic theory of human development.

This chapter will examine 1) the Vedic theory of the cosmic level of human ethical development; 2) how it appears to fulfill the various characteristics and criteria of right action and ethical maturity identified by leading thinkers in ethics; and 3) how this provides a ground for the integration of features which have always seemed to some significant degree incommensurable—such as the features of universality and autonomy (usually associated with the activity of reason) with those of love, care, and responsiveness (commonly associated with the function of feelings). Because Maharishi's exposition of Vedic theory a) brings to light several basic points which have apparently been overlooked for many centuries, and b) is presented in the form of a science and in terms understandable by contemporary Western minds, this chapter discusses Vedic theory as interpreted by him. Accordingly, Maharishi's theory will frequently be referred to as "Vedic Science." Further, as Orme-Johnson, (1988) has done, his exposition of the Vedic theory of human development will frequently be referred to as "Vedic Psychology." Through this examination it can be seen how the cosmic level of ethical life, as described by Maharishi, meets the criteria of a structural developmental stage and satisfies the recognized requirements for a highest and most complete level of ethical development.

Vedic Psychology: On Development of a Genuinely Cosmic Level of Life

In Maharishi's Vedic Psychology, human beings can live their full potential by developing higher states of consciousness. There are three such states: cosmic consciousness, refined cosmic consciousness, and unity consciousness (Maharishi, 1972). They develop sequentially, each succeeding state a fuller expression of life than its predecessor. Although they differ from each other in some respects, they share basic features which set them apart from all previous developmental levels; and they can be considered three stages of the genuinely cosmic level of human life, the level known as "enlightenment" (Maharishi, 1972). Alexander, Heaton, and Chandler (Chapter 2, this volume) discuss Vedic Psychology's theory of the basic features of enlightenment, how it develops, and its relationship to previous developmental stages. Therefore, this section only briefly summarizes these topics and primarily focuses on the cosmic status of enlightenment. The following sections discuss the ethical features of enlightenment and how it suggests new perspectives on theories of ethics and moral development.

According to Vedic Psychology, enlightenment is a distinct developmental level based in a nonconceptual, transcendental mode of experience. In transcendental consciousness, awareness is solely aware of itself. It is a state of "pure consciousness" devoid of all thoughts and other objects of consciousness. This is the deepest, most basic level of consciousness and underlies all other levels of mind. Whereas the other levels are active and differentiated, transcendental consciousness is nonactive, silent, and unified. It is the "simplest state of awareness," and it is unbounded and infinite.

In Vedic Psychology, unbounded pure consciousness is the source of thought, and the active states of consciousness are its localized fluctuations. Further, not only is pure consciousness the source of the mental, subjective aspect of existence, it is also the source of the objective aspects as well. In Vedic Psychology, mind and matter are ultimately not two separate realms of reality. Both mental phenomena (thoughts and feelings) and physical phenomena (matter and energy) are fluctuations of one fundamental field— unbounded pure consciousness. The mental fluctuations differ from the physical in that they are finer (subtler). Physical bodies are the more precipitated expressions of the unbounded field of pure consciousness.

In the standard view of Western psychology, consciousness is a product of the nervous system, while in Vedic Psychology the nervous system is an expression of consciousness. In the Vedic view, it is more natural to explain matter as a particulate derivation from consciousness than the emergence of something as subtle and lively as consciousness from matter.

Parallels between Vedic Science and Modern Science

Although Vedic Psychology's theory of consciousness differs from the standard position of modern Western psychology, it has many parallels to modern physics. According to relativistic quantum field theory—the most successful and comprehensive theory of physics—the universe is composed of certain basic nonlocalized fields, and all forms of matter and energy are fluctuations (excitations) of these fields (Pagels, 1982). The ground state of a field is its state of least excitation. This spatially unbounded ground state is the stable basis for all active states while in itself remaining unmanifest, nonchanging, and perfectly orderly (Itzykson & Zuber, 1980).

Within the last few years, physics has developed a comprehensive picture of the unification of these matter and force fields at the level of an underlying unified field. Theories of the superstring (Antoniadis et al., 1987; Schwarz, 1985; Waldrop, 1985) describe a unified field in which all forms of matter and energy coexist in a state of perfect balance known as "super symmetry." This unified field gives rise to the vast diversity of the universe through "spontaneous dynamical symmetry breaking," a process in which the field interacts with itself (Hagelin, 1987).

It is interesting that while ancient Vedic Science is based in a subjective approach centered in the experience of the unified field of consciousness and modern science is based in an objective approach which starts investigation with the field of differences, the latter has also arrived at an underlying field of unity. Further, the attributes physics ascribes to the unified field are experienced as attributes of pure consciousness: unbounded, unmanifest, perfectly orderly, infinitely dynamic, etc. The major difference is that Vedic Science ascribes consciousness to the unified level. Maharishi (1982) states that by approaching the unified field from the side of physical objects, the mode of knowledge remains indirect and theoretical, and only a glimpse is provided. He explains that because the unified field transcends the level of physical expression, it can only be fully known through a subjective approach which is nonphysical and involves expansion of consciousness.

Pure Consciousness as the Basis for a Genuinely Cosmic Perspective

According to Vedic Psychology, pure consciousness is experienced through expansion of awareness, which corresponds with a settling down and refinement of both mental and physical activity. Because pure consciousness is the simplest, most natural state of awareness, experiencing it is effortless. Many people have spontaneous (though sporadic) experiences of transcendental consciousness. The Transcendental Meditation technique is a simple mental technique which enables such experiences to occur on a regular basis.

Although transcendental consciousness is most natural, ordinarily the nervous system and physiology do not function with the degree of coherence necessary to support its experience. Stress is the limiting factor. Maharishi (1972) employs the term "stress" quite broadly to denote the result of any overload or strain on the nervous system (which manifests as a chemical or structural abnormality). The lower the general level of stress in the nervous system, the more stable, adaptable, and integrated it is. This supports expansion of one's ordinary level of awareness.

The deep rest and refinement gained through experience of transcendental consciousness release stress, allowing the system to develop progressively greater coherence. Eventually, the physiology undergoes a thorough structural and chemical transformation to a stress-free level of maximal coherence. Such a physiology supports greatest expansion of awareness, enabling spontaneous experience of the transcendental level of pure consciousness along with all other active states of mind and at all times, even while sleeping. This is the state of enlightenment.

Thus, according to Vedic Psychology, enlightenment is neither generated through nor characterized by conceptual thinking; rather, it is characterized by a specific type of spontaneous direct experience (continuous unbounded awareness) based in neurophysiological transformation. Once attained, it is irreversible.

In Vedic theory, the perspective of an enlightened person is genuinely cosmic. The self is identified not with one's individuated personality, thoughts, and feelings but with unbounded pure consciousness. In the fullest stage of enlightenment ("unity consciousness") one directly experiences pure consciousness as the unified field of natural law and perceives every object as an expression of unmanifest, unbounded consciousness—one's own Self (Maharishi, 1972).

The Ethical Features of Enlightenment: Action in Harmony with Natural Law

Just as the perspective in the state of enlightenment is uniquely different than at any lower stage of development, so are its ethical features.

Maharishi's Theory of Right Action: The Close Connection Between Consciousness and the Effects of Behavior

Maharishi's theory of ethics differs in key respects from the major approaches in Western thought, particularly in its understanding of the relation between quality of mental state and the results of action. One of these approaches focuses on the inner state of the actor and does not give much relevance to the actual consequences of the ensuing action, while the other emphasizes outer results over inner virtues. For the inner-oriented approach, there is no necessary connection between the ethical quality of an action and the quality of its results because a) the actor's underlying state of mind is the source of the ethical quality of action, and b) even highly moral motivations can fail to produce significant beneficial results. Immanuel Kant is one of the most important philosophers associated with this viewpoint. In his theory, acting ethically is a twofold process. First, one's reason derives particular conceptions of duty in line with the highest moral principles, and then one wills to act in line with duty. The ethically relevant analysis ends at the point where mental activity begins to evoke physical activity. As long as the reasoning is ethically right and the willing is aligned with reason, the ensuing action is ethically right, whatever the concrete particulars of the attendant behavior and its effects might be.

Utilitarianism exemplifies another main approach. It judges the rightness of thought and action by how much actual benefit they produce, the optimal situation being the greatest good to the greatest number. In this view, the actions of one who is high-minded and scrupulous yet ineffective are of less moral value than those of a person who through mixed motives and devious means generates widespread benefit.

Compared with Kant and the Utilitarians, Maharishi's theory is unique: it acknowledges the importance of inner state as well as outer results while recognizing a basic link between them. This is because he identifies an expanded range of ethically relevant mental life and a more intimate connection between mental activity and the physical environment.

In the view of most Western thinkers, mental activity produces socio-environmental effects only indirectly through consequent physical activity. For Kant, there is inconsistent translation of the moral quality of thought into actual influence because the chain of physical causality is contingent on factors other than mental intention. Through innocent miscalculation of cause and effect, or through intervention of unforeseen events, good intentions can create harmful results. Therefore, the result of action is not a valid indicator of the actor's mind nor of the action's moral worth. Because Utilitarians also recognize a gap in the influence of the mental realm upon the physical, they feel justified in adopting a similarly one-sided, albeit opposite, approach.

For Maharishi, mental activity has direct socioenvironmental effects, resulting in direct translation of the quality of inner state into the quality of external influence. As a prelude to examining this concept, it is helpful to note that we commonly acknowledge the power of subtle inner conditions to radiate outer influence. For instance, two people could both attempt to follow the principle of speaking truth in a constructive manner and could use the same words, and yet the effects could be dramatically different. If one speaker harbored a grudge against his listener, it would negatively flavor the communication through tone of voice, facial expression, etc. Yet, Maharishi's analysis goes even deeper than this. The quality of consciousness generates significant influence on others which transcends the level of effects directly associated with commonly observable modes of interaction such as word-meaning, tone of voice, etc. This is because he views individuals as intimately interconnected through the nonlocalized field of consciousness. In his theory, excitations generated within the field at one location propagate throughout and spread either orderly, coherent influence or disorderly, entropic influence, in a manner parallel to the wave phenomena described in quantum physics (Maharishi, 1976). Coherent fluctuations in the field of consciousness have constructive, life-supportive influence on other people, while incoherent excitations have negative, life-damaging influence. Maharishi states that although one may through deliberation override ethically negative impulses in choosing a basic course of action, one cannot thereby fully eradicate them or their influence (Maharishi, 1966).

It is evident that the Vedic perspective greatly expands the sphere of ethics, to the extent that it becomes all-encompassing. In this theory, one is ever affecting others, even if there is no outwardly apparent interaction, because the quality of the style of functioning of one's nervous system generates substantial effects throughout the immediate surroundings, and to a significant degree, throughout the entire universe.

The ethically significant factor is not fully reducible to the forms of logical operations and role-taking utilized in moral reasoning; rather, it is the degree of orderliness and coherence of consciousness, which is a function of the degree to which the nervous system has progressed toward its state of maximum stability and adaptability. Individuals who have not reached enlightenment vary in their degree of development of consciousness according to their degree of neurophysiological coherence.

Therefore, in this theory, it would be more ethically relevant to know what degree of pure consciousness has been stabilized than in what form someone articulates moral reasoning. While the theory recognizes a significant role for reasoning, it holds that reason's importance is subordinate to a more comprehensive factor—the level of coherence in the consciousness which is generating the reasoning.

In Maharishi's understanding there is good reason for reason's subordinate status. First, making a fully satisfactory determination of the optimal course of action is quite difficult through reason alone, because real life situations are usually complex, with a large number of relevant factors. Yet, in the view of many moral philosophers (e.g., Hare, 1981), correct moral decisions must take account of all possible relevant information.

From Maharishi's perspective, because of the varied and often subtle field effects of consciousness, many of the relevant factors cannot be consciously known, and even in the case of those which are, adequately weighing their possible permutations is beyond the ordinary capacity of reasoning. Moreover, due to the all-pervasive nature of the field effects, the range of involved parties includes all of humankind. Therefore, the exact influence which any given action will have on the extended social environment is incalculable: "[T]he influence of one thing on all other things is so universal that nothing can be considered in isolation. . . . [T]he question of right and wrong is a highly complicated problem . . . because reason is limited and the vision of the human mind is minute when compared to the vast and unlimited field of influence produced by an action in the whole universe" (Maharishi, 1966). Finally, even to the extent that reason can determine the correct course of action, whether this knowledge is in fact acted upon (and, if so, in what manner) is dependent on factors beyond reasoning, such as feelings and dispositions, which are intimately related to the degree of coherence of consciousness. Accordingly, Maharishi (1966) states that the key determinant of the ethical quality of action is one's level of consciousness.

Stabilization of Enlightenment as an Ethical Phase Transition

Given the above perspective on morality, one might wonder whether Vedic Psychology conceives of consistent and correct ethical action as a genuine possibility. In fact, it does recognize such a possibility, and it holds that the very interconnectedness of things which makes fully adequate action impossible on the basis of reason alone makes ethical mastery a spontaneous reality at a level beyond reason.

The Vedic theory may be summarized as follows:

A. The cosmos is a highly integrated system, and the laws of nature as a whole function to sustain and promote integration, orderliness, and growth. The total potential of natural law is fully available at the level of pure consciousness (the unified field)—a level at which the entire cosmos exists in a state of perfect balance, harmony, and infinite correlation.

B. When a person's awareness is fully established at this level of harmony and infinite correlation, these values become automatically and completely expressed in thought and action. For the enlightened individual, "every impulse of consciousness is the impulse of natural law. Thoughts and actions . . . are always in full accord with all the laws of nature" (Maharishi, 1982). Such a person is spontaneously in harmony with everybody and everything. Thus, the key ethical feature of enlightenment is "spontaneous right action" in harmony with natural law (Maharishi, 1972).

C. When there is stress in the nervous system, individual awareness cannot remain settled in its least excited state of pure consciousness. Whereas the enlightened individual is attuned to the holistic value of natural law and thus expresses the balance and the harmonizing influence of the constructive power of nature, the individual whose awareness is not fully expanded does not draw on as comprehensive a level of intelligence. He/she thus operates on a plane where there is greater apparent division between things and harmonizing principles are not as active. In these circumstances, life is based on *partial* values of natural law. The greater the degree of stress, the less the individual can express the completely harmonizing tendency of the holistic value of natural law and the more he/she can be said to be out of harmony with nature as a whole.

D. The major watershed in ethical development is represented by the transition to enlightenment. Although growth toward enlightenment is a progressive development of greater capacity for right action, as long as behavior is influenced by some degree of stress, it cannot be fully right and life-supportive on all levels of existence. Only when the last stresses are gone does individual psyche fully expand to identify with the level of cosmic psyche and spontaneously function from that level at all times. The enlightened individual acts with the full support of nature. Thus, actions are maximally efficient and successful. The coherent quality of consciousness spontaneously translates into life-supporting effects, transcending the limitations acknowledged within the Kantian and Utilitarian perspectives.

In Maharishi's description of spontaneous right action, intuition is highly developed and one generally responds to situations with little or no deliberation (Maharishi, 1972). However, it would be incorrect to label such action "irrational," with all its negative connotations. Rather, such action is metarational. Although moral theorists often classify desire and feeling as irrational, inconsistent, and unreliable, desire and feelings at the fully developed stage of life are impulses embodying the total potential of natural law and are therefore unwaveringly consistent in their orderliness, harmony, and life-supporting character. They fully express the intelligence and universality which are aimed at by reason in its highest form while going beyond the limits of reasoning.

Prior to enlightenment, impulses and desires are products of a limited perspective and have the potential to be disorderly and antisocial. Therefore, they must frequently be intercepted and scrutinized from the more orderly and unbiased perspective associated with reason. In such a case, deliberative reason functions to filter out the undesirable effects of impulse and to impose order and universality on impulses which are deficient in them. In enlightenment, on the other hand, reason does not function to check and reorganize morally unreliable desires; rather, it serves (when appropriate) to implement desires which are already ethically correct.

Reason here functions as the handmaiden of virtuous feelings rather than as the policeman over unsocialized ones.

The concept that a fully developed person can spontaneously act in an ethically correct way with little need for deliberation is shared by many major traditions in the East and West (Fingarette, 1977). Fingarette states that in this conception, one "does the right and the good . . . as the issue of his spontaneous response to the situation and the moment." Moreover, he notes that "even such a ceremonial and self-discipline oriented teacher as Confucius could be quoted by his disciples as saying: 'At seventy I could follow the dictates of my own heart; for what I desired no longer overstepped the boundaries of right.'" Such a progression toward spontaneously right feelings and desires is, in Maharishi's understanding, the result of increased refinement of consciousness associated with increased refinement and integration of the nervous system.

Evidence Supporting Maharishi's Theory

It has been stated that one of Maharishi's unique accomplishments is the formulation of the essence of the Vedic tradition of knowledge in terms of a science. Obviously, to fully verify every aspect of his ethical theory (such as spontaneous right action in harmony with natural law) through standard empirical means would be difficult. However, the theory predicts several phenomena which should be observable as individuals regularly experience pure consciousness (and thus theoretically progress toward enlightenment); and many of these phenomena are not expected to occur in other models of psychology and physical nature. In recent years, a large body of scientific research on individuals practicing the TM and TM-Sidhi program has consistently yielded results in line with the various predictions of Maharishi's theory, revealing it to have exceptional predictive power.

Because Chapter 2 in this volume reviews a large part of the research, this section will only briefly summarize some of the major findings.

Higher States of Consciousness as Involving Higher
Levels of Physiological and Mental Coherence

Extensive research confirms that the TM technique induces a fourth major state of consciousness, different from sleep, dreaming, and ordinary waking state (e.g., Wallace, 1972). It also demonstrates that this experience of higher consciousness is associated with a broad range of physiological changes indicative of lowered stress and increased coherence measured in terms of numerous standard parameters, including coherence between different areas of the brain as measured by EEG (Badawi et al., 1984). The evidence further indicates the orderliness achieved during practice of the

TM technique is progressively stabilized outside of meditation (e.g., Levine, 1976). All the observed physiological changes are in the direction of increased integration and normalized function of the biological system.

Coherence of Consciousness as Correlated with Positive Social Attitudes and Behavior

Several studies support the major prediction that as one develops toward enlightenment and consciousness becomes more coherent, thoughts, feelings, and behavior become progressively more positive and socially constructive. For example, Nidich et al. (1983) found a significant relationship between high frontal EEG alpha coherence—which correlates with subjective experience of pure consciousness (Orme-Johnson & Haynes, 1981)—and prosocial behavior contributing to the cohesion and harmonious functioning of a social group. Frew (1974) found greater cooperation between coworkers and also between workers and supervisors after they began the TM program. Further, in prison populations, TM program participants have shown significant reductions in anxiety and negativity (Abrams & Siegel, 1978; Alexander, 1982), and also in recidivism (Bleick & Abrams, 1987; Dillbeck & Abrams, 1987).

Consciousness as a Field

Several well-designed studies support the theory that consciousness is a field and that an individual's coherence spreads through the field to positively affect others. For example, even as few as 1% of an urban area practicing the TM technique correlates with significant reduction in crime rate (e.g., Dillbeck et al., 1981). The hypothesis that coherence of consciousness is the key factor underlying the crime rate reduction is strengthened by further studies which measured greater effects when meditators are participants in the TM-Sidhi program, an advanced phase of the practice through which greater levels of mental coherence are subjectively experienced and increased neurophysiological coherence is typically measured (Orme-Johnson & Haynes, 1981). For instance, far fewer TM-Sidhi program participants seem to be required to reduce crime. When the meditators are only practicing the TM technique, they must amount to 1% of the population; but if they also practice the TM-Sidhi program, significant crime reductions occur when they account for only the square root of 1% (Dillbeck et al., 1987; Orme-Johnson et al., 1988). (Time series analysis has ruled out cyclical variations and factors such as changes in police procedures.) Depending on the size of the coherence-creating group, these apparent field effects can be quite extensive. They have been measured throughout a large region (Dillbeck et al., 1987), an entire nation (Orme-Johnson et al., 1988), and even worldwide (Dillbeck, 1987).

Enlightenment as the Most Integrated Stage of Ethical Behavior

Important thinkers have identified various characteristics and criteria of right action and ethical maturity, several of which are ordinarily considered to be incommensurable—and often incompatible or even irreconcilable. Enlightenment appears to fulfill all these criteria in the highest degree and to provide the ground for thorough integration of *all* aspects of ethical life.

One of the most influential concepts in moral philosophy is that ethical action is action in a universal mode, a mode in which one responds to a particular situation not from the biases of one's localized perspective but on the basis of principles which could be agreed upon and followed by everyone—principles which would be consistently followed by anyone with a nonbiased and objective perspective. Kant (1975) holds that only through the universal style of functioning can there be adequate expression of the highest aspect of human nature. According to his theory: a) It is logically demonstrable that the essential level of human life is a transcendental ego or self: a "unity of consciousness" which is "pure, original and unchangeable" (Kant, 1963); b) we can never directly experience this deepest level of our nature but we can know the character of its fullest expression—our rationality, which operates through principles and rules that are universal; c) on the practical level of ethics, one is acting in accord with the law of one's own nature (which is rational) only when action willfully conforms with rules which can hold universally; d) therefore, action can be autonomous only when directed by universal reason, since otherwise it is determined by forces not expressive of one's essential self; and e) accordingly, autonomous self-governance can be sustained by following one basic principle: the "categorical imperative"—the noncontingent rule that one should always act so that the underlying maxim (principle) of the action could be universalized (Kant, 1975).

Lawrence Kohlberg (1971) interprets his extensive research on the development of moral reasoning as in many ways supportive of Kant, indicating that the growth of moral maturity is *in fact* characterized by progressive growth in the qualities of universality, autonomy, and objectivity. Kohlberg holds that as one grows in autonomy, judgment becomes less conditioned by morally irrelevant external factors and increasingly influenced by the intrinsic "oughtness" or rightness of universal principles. He theorizes that the fullest expression of universality, autonomy, and objectivity corresponds to a social cognitive perspective which: a) can view all particular interactions in relation to everyone else who could be affected and to society as a whole, and b) can appreciate the individuals involved not only in terms of situation-specific and culturally relative factors but also in terms of universal abstract considerations about human beings *qua* human beings (e.g., fairness and respect for persons). Operationally, such a perspective displays complete reversibility, since starting from any individual's position, the final decisional outcome will be the same. For Kohlberg, moral decisions at this level are made through "ideal role-taking," a "moral musical chairs" played on the mental level (Kohlberg, 1979). In this procedure, one first takes the role of every individual involved in the situation and appreciates the situation from his/her point of view. Then, through a higher-order abstraction, one appreciates how each particular role would itself role-play, which involves seeing how each individual would view things as he/she were inserted in the different vantage points of the social situation. By assessing whether each of the various initial claims would be modified (and if so, how) as the original claimant changed places with everyone else, one could reach a decision which would be maximally "equilibrated" in that it would be judged best by an outside observer who had equal probability of playing any role. Obviously, in order to rearrange all of the roles and evaluate the effects, this highest perspective must be the perspective that is most abstracted from the social situation. Yet, while being most abstracted from the particular relations, it must be extremely sensitive to them, since it is abstracted from them only so it may have the flexibility a) to become each of them, then b) to become *all* of them as an interactive system, and then c) through a process of self-referral, to resolve all possible interactions into one optimal system of interactions reflecting the greatest degree of equilibrium. Thus, in Kohlberg's theory, the ideal level of moral development entails development of an awareness which can, in one sense, "be" every possible human role and which, in any specific situation, can compute the possible permutations of the various roles and arrive at the most equilibrated, harmonious arrangement.

The state of enlightenment as described by Maharishi represents a maximization of the characteristics and capacities which Kant and Kohlberg associate with moral development, fulfilling them to a greater degree than these thinkers have considered possible. In Maharishi's account, the enlightened individual's actions are always autonomous expressions of his or her highest nature, which is the most universal value of intelligence. Accordingly, the principles underlying the actions are fully universal (they are the laws of nature). Further, action is always guided by the universal perspective, never by limited, bounded considerations aimed at benefiting solely oneself or a few others in ways not harmonized with universal requirements.

Moreover, enlightenment presents a model of a stage which can continually sustain the fullest expression of equilibrated operations (as discussed by Kohlberg). In Kohlberg's understanding, the broader the awareness and the more abstract the perspective, the greater the capacity for universal and reversible ethical behavior. Maharishi describes enlightenment as based on the level of awareness which is completely unbounded: the level of pure consciousness, which is unqualified consciousness transcendental to all relative contexts. Thus, it is a perspective which is maximally abstracted from particular contexts and relations. Further, just as Kohlberg's most abstract perspective (taken as an ideal type) is able to assume all possible localized perspectives and all their possible interactions, so the pure consciousness state displays this capacity—and in the fullest degree. This is so because pure consciousness is the unified field, the nonlocalized common basis of every differentiated psyche. It is the matrix of every localized perspective and contains within its structure the organizing intelligence for the cosmos as a whole. It is the level at which the potential interactions between localized perspectives are constantly being gauged and balanced. Maharishi (1972) says the cosmic psyche is like a gigantic computer which accesses all relevant information about the myriad possible influences of everything on everything else and automatically determines the most balanced system of interrelations. In this theory, an individual whose awareness has opened to the cosmic level functions with his mind connected to this cosmic computing process. When awareness assumes the most abstract and comprehensive perspective—that of cosmic psyche—then one's thought and action are *automatically* supportive of optimally equilibrated social relations. According to this theory, in taking the fullest perspective, one is in essence taking the perspective of all possible perspectives. Of course, one is not consciously aware of all of the possibilities and their permutations (this would be impossible, owing to the infinitely complex causative interactions). Yet, the theory holds that one's actions are those which would result from having consciously gone through such a computing process, and that they *are* the result of such a process actually occurring (automatically and silently) within the deepest structure of one's consciousness.

The concept that nature operates through a continuous unmanifest process of equilibrating all possibilities is important in modern physics as well as in Vedic Science. According to the law of least action, any natural process always takes the path in which the quantity known as the "action" is minimal (Feynman et al., 1965). Yet, in the theory of quantum mechanics, nature can be said to recognize more than a single possible path for any given situation. In fact, the theory holds that all possible paths are in some sense present on the level of the quantum wave function, which underlies the level of discrete, observable phenomena. Although this underlying level is unmanifest, the theory recognizes it as a level which structures the manifest level; and the interactions of the unmanifest wave functions actually generate measurable effects. In the case of a particle in motion, while all possible paths are present on the quantum mechanical level, most cancel through destructive interference, with the result that the remaining possible paths fall along the path an observer sees taken. Further, the other possibilities are not completely canceled but just reduced to levels of probability so low that they cannot manifest. Consequently, because they are still present on the unmanifest level, when considered from this basic level it is as if the particle "looks at all the other possible trajectories" as it proceeds (Feynman et al., 1965).

In Vedic theory, at the most basic level of existence all possibilities for everything in the cosmos are lively and are continuously interacting, automatically equilibrating to the optimal arrangement of cosmic balance. When consciousness expands to this level, thought and action become direct expressions of the laws of nature supporting the most balanced cosmic arrangement, and they arise as pure expressions of the law of least action (Maharishi, 1982). According to Maharishi, in enlightenment the mind functions most naturally and most in tune with the way nature as a whole functions. This results in the full operation of the law of least action on the mental level, which corresponds with the complete spontaneity and effort-lessness of thinking and acting which the enlightened individual experiences.

From Universality to the Truly Cosmic

Not only does enlightenment represent the fullest realization of univer-sality, but, as noted earlier, it represents the expansion of universality to embrace the genuinely cosmic. For Kant and Kohlberg, thinking in a universal mode means merely that one is thinking in a mode appropriate for all other rational minds. Further, they do not view the principles and rules which guide action in the universal mode as the laws of nature themselves. They believe these rules could *in principle* serve as laws of nature because they a) are regular and uniform, and b) could be prescribed for anyone in the same circumstances. However, they believe that *in fact* there is no necessary connection between moral rules and the laws of nature. In Maharishi's theory, the enlightened individual operates at the level of the unified field. Thus, whether consciously following rules or not, all thought and action of such an individual are ultimately structured by the constructive power of natural law, and he or she verily acts *as* the laws of nature.

In light of the above, there is a great difference between reaching equilibrated decisions through a merely universal mode rather than a cosmic one. In the universal perspective as described by Kohlberg, although the subject imaginatively puts himself into other perspectives, there is no necessary congruence between his "playing" of that role and the realities of that particular role. The difficulty in achieving sufficient correspondence increases with increase in the relevant factors which must be considered.

Similarly, properly assessing the possible relations between roles is also very complex. As an ideal, any rational individual would be able to take perspectives and equilibrate them in the same way; in actuality, the individual can only approximate the ideal to the best of his abilities (especially his sensitivities). Thus, even assuming there are individuals who habitually function at Kohlberg's proposed highest stage of moral reasoning, it would be dubious any could actually operate as a fully universal subject at all times.

In contrast, the individual at the cosmic level (as described by Maharishi) participates in a direct and intimate way in all other perspectives and responds to the actual complex forces involved in the interactions between all people. Further, although it is reasonable to assume that no individual could, relying primarily upon reasoning, *always* operate at the fully universal level, Vedic Psychology holds that once the cosmic level is stabilized, there is no regression—one *always* spontaneously acts as a cosmic psyche. Consequently, one's actions would always be right in a universal and objective sense, since they would always be in harmony with the constructive power of natural law.

From a theoretical viewpoint based in a level other than transcendental consciousness, not only does the universal fail to reflect the cosmic, but the cosmic even fails to encompass the universal. For example, in Kohlberg's (1984) theory, a key characteristic of a universal mode of cognitive function is that while the *content* of thought varies from individual to individual, the underlying *form* of thought does not. This means that a universal cognitive mode is based in universal mental structures and operations. Kohlberg believes that such universal structures and operations develop automatically and unconsciously through direct interaction with the environment. He refers to this spontaneous, nondeliberative processing of experience as a "first-order mode" of cognitive activity. Kohlberg believes these unconsciously structured forms of mental operation can be attributed to the impersonal, universal aspect of self (ego purely in its aspect of the rational knower), and that this aspect of the self can be theoretically abstracted from all particularities. In the case of the logical operations described by Piaget, this aspect is the "epistemic ego," the abstracted knower. In Kohlberg's moral judgment stages, it is the "rational moral subject." Because Kohlberg views the first-order modes of thinking and their associated stages as independent of the particularistic, personal aspects of self, he terms them "universal."

However, Kohlberg (1990) regards the cosmic orientation which develops from transcendental experience to be a product of self-conscious, self-reflective conceptual thought and thus based on "second-order" or "meta-modes" of cognition rather than on first-order modes. In such "second-order" modes, the self generates meanings by consciously reflecting upon its concrete, particularistic, and nonuniversal aspects (such as personality) and its particular life experiences. This process involves a particular philosophy of life. Thus, on the level of its content, Kohlberg recognizes the cosmic stage as the fullest, most mature stage of ethical thought, surpassing even his proposed highest stage of moral reasoning in ethical-ontological integration. Yet, on the level of structure, he holds that this stage is not even universal and is in fact *less* universal and also *less* based in immediate experience than are any of the lesser integrated moral stages which precede it.

In contrast, cosmic perspective as described by Maharishi does not arise on the basis of reflective thinking or specific experiences in the ordinary waking state of consciousness. It arises through and is structured upon experience of unbounded pure consciousness which is transcendental to external experience and is universally available. Such experience is even *more* primary than are the first-order modes of thinking, since it is not generated at the level of thinking but exists at a more basic level, the level of immediate awareness which is the background for all thoughts and feelings. In fact, the level of ego associated with the basic forms of awareness described by Maharishi is even more abstract than the "epistemic" ego discussed by Piaget; it is the level of experiencer per se, which necessarily underlies the capacity for operational reasoning. This ego, as pure experiencer (pure knower), is present in the same form within everyone.

In light of the above, growth to enlightenment represents the case in which a universal level of self is most fully abstracted from all particularized levels. Further, such abstraction is not merely a logical possibility appreciated solely on the level of theory, as is the case with reasoning stages. According to Vedic Psychology, in the first stage of enlightenment (cosmic consciousness) one directly and concretely experiences one's abstract Self completely separate from all active aspects of the psyche. It exists solely as the knower—the silent, nonactive witness of all one's thought and activity. Further, when the fullest level of enlightenment (unity consciousness) is gained, this most abstract level of self is experienced in its full value as cosmic psyche, the unified field of natural law present at the basis of every individual mind and every object. Thus, rather than rendering the cosmic as structurally less than universal, this theory describes how the universal perspective associated with reasoning can expand to and be integrated within a perspective which is cosmic in every respect.

The Role of Feelings

Another consequence of generating ethical theory primarily from the perspective of universal reason adopted by Kant and Kohlberg rather than from a unified field-based perspective is that not only does the universal fail to fully exemplify the cosmic and vice versa, but the level of universality identified is not sufficiently universal to adequately include the level of desire and feeling. For instance, Kant states that the transcendental self is the precondition for free will and morality but that it always remains transcendental to experience. Accordingly, he believes that the full intelligence, autonomy, and freedom of the transcendental level will never be completely expressed within human life. Kant (1975) says that if we were perfectly rational, all desires would naturally and spontaneously conform with the standards of reason. However, he states that because human life also belongs to the phenomenal world, the world of causal contingency, it is continually subject to desires which arise from this nonautonomous level—desires which are localized, contingent, and reflect forces other than the imperatives of universal reason. Consequently, Kant holds that a) there is an ever-present conflict between our duty to follow rational rules and our desires, and b) morally right behavior cannot be based in following natural inclinations, since these are primarily rooted in the phenomenal realm, a realm not expressive of our fuller nature. Thus, Kant sees morality as a constant struggle between the highest (yet incomplete) expression of the transcendental self—rational will—and the inclinations born of the nonautonomous side of human nature: a struggle between the universal and the local (and limited). In Kohlberg's theory as well, ethical universality is expressed through reason, not through emotions and feeling, and he similarly subordinates their role.

Other theorists such as Lawrence Blum (1982) and Carol Gilligan (1982) emphasize that the type and quality of one's feelings are highly important factors in the quality of moral behavior and that moral development involves much more than the capacity and tendency to govern one's actions through specific styles of reasoning. Gilligan has sought to describe how feelings such as love, care, and concern can expand on a morality which is primarily oriented toward calculation of rights and duties in the abstract. She theorizes there are two basic orientations toward moral issues: one focusing on rights and justice and the other grounded in care and responsiveness (Gilligan, 1982). She describes the former as largely based in capacity for abstract perspective-taking and the latter in sensitivity to the particular and concrete. From a rights orientation, one primarily views interpersonal dilemmas in the abstract by approaching them as competing claims to be balanced through formal reasoning. From the responsiveness orientation, one primarily views such situations in terms of a living network of relationships to be sustained through the activity of caring. In Gilligan's view, the tendency to perspective-take in the abstract, impersonal mode correlates with a conception of the self as somewhat separate from surroundings, as objectifiable, and as objective in operation. In contrast, Gilligan associates the tendency to have care and concern for particular needs of others with a conception of self as inherently connected with the social surroundings, and she feels that one with such a self-conception does not tend to objectify the self nor focus on the maintenance of objectivity. In Nona Lyons's (1983) description, one who functions as a "separate/objective self" talks about moral actions from a perspective toward others that seems grounded in a concept of duties which apply to oneself and all others abstractly considered as human beings. On the other hand, those people identified as "connected" seem to act more predominantly from a perspective toward others concerned with the interdependence of people. An aspect of this perspective is responsiveness to the needs of others.

Although Gilligan emphasizes the importance of the orientation based in feelings of care and concern and believes that it surpasses the orientation of abstract formal reasoning in its capacity for sensitive response to the particulars of concrete life situations, she yet is in agreement with Kant and Kohlberg that such a perspective does not exemplify the objectivity and universality characteristic of principled reasoning (Murphy & Gilligan, 1980). In fact, she states that as people become more sensitive to the realities of context, methodical application of principles becomes more difficult, and they often experience morality as somewhat relativistic and find that their principles as well as they themselves have become less "absolute" (Gilligan & Murphy, 1979).

It would seem that a complete morality should integrate both of the above perspectives, expressing the qualities of universality, objectivity, and consistency along with caring and a refined responsiveness to the particularities of context. Gilligan appears to believe that such integration can occur, and she and Murphy report that their recent research was guided by the idea that "[t]he balancing of these two points of view . . . [is] the key to understanding adult moral development" (Murphy & Gilligan, 1980). In their conception, the highest stage of moral thought comprehends the objective, principled approach and yet is also highly sensitive to the particularities of context, thus being the most adaptive and inclusive level (Murphy & Gilligan, 1980).

Gilligan's *In a Different Voice* (1982) continues the theme that fullest moral development involves an "integration" of the two perspectives. She states that the two orientations should be viewed neither as sequential stages, with one replacing the other, nor as alternative perspectives which are in opposition. Rather, she argues that they are "complementary" perspectives and can enrich and balance one another.

Yet her discussion does not appear to develop a detailed model of a fully integrated perspective. Further, it seems that in her view, integration of the two perspectives is often a situation in which distinct, incongruent forces temper one another to yield a behavior which represents a sum of vectors, moving along different lines than would have been determined by either contributing force acting alone. In such a situation, the integration is a matter of balanced participation by two different modes; however, the modes themselves remain at basis largely nonintegrated. For instance, the impulse of care is not viewed as thoroughly embodying the absolute, universal quality of principled reasoning.

Kohlberg's view also acknowledges that the two perspectives are integral to full ethical life; and he states they are aspects of one morality (Kohlberg, 1984). Yet he appears to conceive of feeling and caring as somewhat ancillary, stating that there are certain situations (involving conflicting claims) which can be adequately met only by the justice/rights perspective and another class (involving personal relations and special obligations) in which care and concern are most appropriate. Thus, although he feels that full justice incorporates care, he still separates the ranges of the two perspectives and conceives of them as often functioning separately. Even when care operates along with justice principles, Kohlberg holds that it does not improve on the quality of justice but rather supplements it in other moral dimensions. Consequently, he appears to maintain that it is often possible to do adequate justice to the needs of a situation without the influence of caring.

The above discussion indicates that even if one accepts the importance of integrating feeling and responsiveness with universal principledness, understanding exactly how a thorough integration would exist and operate has been difficult. On this question, Vedic Psychology again provides a viewpoint which appears to be more holistic. Maharishi (1972) states that as one evolves toward enlightenment, the field of thinking and the field of feeling are both progressively developed, and the relation between them is increasingly more balanced. As the mind develops, thinking becomes clearer and more comprehensive. As the feelings develop, one's actions increasingly express love, tenderness, and warmth and become more nurturing and life-supportive on all levels. In the state of full enlightenment, the fullest value of each is expressed, as well as the fullest integration between them. At this level, all thoughts and feelings are spontaneously in harmony with natural law, and thus a conflict between the dictates of reason and the impetus of desire could not arise.

However, although this theory postulates that action will generally become more adequate as the capacities of both thought and feeling expand, it holds that the fullest development of thinking and feeling, and of their integration, cannot be achieved solely on the levels of thought and feeling. Maharishi (1969) cites the Bhagavad-Gita as providing a case study which clearly illustrates this point. In his interpretation, the hero, Arjuna, is initially represented as an individual who is at a very high level of development but not yet enlightened. His mind and heart (thinking and feeling) are both functioning with great refinement, and yet he is placed in a dilemma in which they cannot be reconciled with one another. Arjuna is a warrior responsible for protecting society, and a great battle is about to begin between his army and forces representing injustice. As he surveys the battlefield, he sees that many of his beloved kinsmen are with the opposing army. His alert and purposeful mind clearly discerns the path of duty (to fight), but his loving heart cannot bear the thought of killing his kinsmen, and so it resists this course of action. Arjuna thus falls into a state of complete suspension. In Maharishi's view, this suspension is a sign not of weakness but of the strength of Arjuna's mind and heart. He states that the capacities of thinking and feeling may each be highly developed, and yet there can still be situations in which their responses will be in such opposition that agonizing suspension is the result. For Maharishi, this indicates that, on their own level, these two fields of life cannot be completely integrated. The solution to this problem is revealed to Arjuna by Krishna (who represents full knowledge). It lies in transcending thinking and feeling and experiencing pure consciousness. Maharishi states that because this least excited state of awareness is the ground state of consciousness and the common basis of both thinking and feeling, it is the level at which they are fully integrated. In his understanding, when the nervous system refines so that one naturally maintains awareness of pure consciousness while in activity, action will be in harmony with natural law and will represent a harmonization of the requirements of principled duty with the impulses of refined feeling. Krishna encapsulates this knowledge in saying to Arjuna, *"Yogastah kuru karmani"*—"Established in the state of yoga [experience of transcendental consciousness], perform action." Only by applying this knowledge is Arjuna able to dissolve his suspension and act in a way which fully reconciles duty and love. He valiantly engages in battle, upholding his responsibility to resist the forces of injustice, while his mind and heart remain balanced in the state of yoga. Accordingly, he is removed from impulses of violence and hostility. Freed from duality and divisiveness, he can fight forcefully while yet expressing the harmonizing influence of natural law.

Viewed in the above way, the essential relation between thinking and feeling is akin to relations between forces of nature in the physical world. Although forces such as electromagnetism and gravity are symmetric only at the level of the unified field and are distinct and functionally differentiated at all manifest levels, these different functions are themselves integrated and harmonious considered in terms of the total system of nature. In Vedic theory, thinking and feeling, when most natural, have a similar relationship. In this view, it is only when human life is stressed and therefore unnatural that thought and feeling function in opposition. As life becomes more natural, thought and feeling spontaneously become more integrated; and when life is fully normal and natural (in enlightenment) pure consciousness is so fully enlivened within individual awareness that thinking and feeling, although differentiated at the functional level, function in a manner fully expressive of the unity between them at their unmanifest common source.

There has recently been heightened interest in the question of whether women and men differ in capacity and propensity to function in the orientations of reason and care. Gilligan believes her research in the United States indicates that although most people do not exclusively function within either the justice or the care orientation, women generally function within the caring mode more of the time while the reverse is true for men (Gilligan, 1982). (Lyons's [1983] further research appears to support this position.) However, Gilligan explicitly refrains from positing either that such a difference is genetically based or that it is typical of all contemporary cultures or of times past. Kohlberg (1984) interprets extensive research employing his moral judgment instrument to indicate that any differences between males and females on capacity for moral reasoning are based in sociological factors and that when social circumstances are similar, competence is similar for both sexes.

In Maharishi's theory, prior to enlightenment individuals vary in the extent to which they are guided by thinking and feeling. However, as one develops toward enlightenment, one's mind and heart become increasingly developed and harmonized with one another, regardless of gender. In his theory, every fully developed individual will radiate fullness of both mind and heart and will exemplify an integration of intellect and tender feeling (Maharishi, 1972).

Maharishi's theory represents a perspective in which the limitations of other theories are transcended. For instance, as Shear (1973) notes, it accounts for the gap between reason and desire recognized by Kant while transcending Kant's position and identifying a level at which they become unified. Kant holds that the gap is insurmountable because it results from a fundamental division in human nature: a division between an aspect which expresses the autonomy and universality of a transcendental level and an aspect expressing the causal contingencies of the phenomenal world. Because of this division, Kant holds that the fullness of our transcendental level of being can never be fully expressed (nor even experienced) and that most of our natural inclinations will always be opposed to the highest aspect of our nature. In contrast, Maharishi's theory is based on direct experience of the transcendental fullness of life and recognizes this level of human nature as the source of *all* nature: of all thought and desire, and all physical phenomena. In this account, all desires arise from the unified field of pure consciousness, and when they appear to be in opposition to universal intelligence, it is only because they have become misaligned during the process of manifestation due to stress in the nervous system. The theory holds that when stress is completely removed and life is most natural, individual inclinations are spontaneously in harmony with the most universal level of intelligence.

Moreover, from the Vedic perspective it is understandable why thinkers who recognize that rational principledness and feeling-based care are both integral to a complete morality would yet have difficulty in understanding just how these two features can themselves be integrated. This is because any theory based solely on experiences of thinking and feeling will only perceive the levels at which they are not fully commensurable. According to Vedic Psychology, only by transcending both thinking and feeling and experiencing their unified source (pure consciousness) can one appreciate their fundamental harmony and allow that harmony to be progressively expressed on all levels.

It is important to note that this discussion is not intended as a criticism of Kohlberg and Gilligan—they provide astute descriptions of important aspects of ethical life. It is to point out that knowledge is always a function of the observational level through which it is gained. Accordingly, within any relative perspective (one not based within the transcendental unified field) the available knowledge of a phenomenon, while valid at that particular level, is yet partial. At each successively more comprehensive level of observation, new properties and dynamics come into play. For instance, Newton's laws, while a valid description at the macroscopic level, do not adequately describe the microscopic dimension. Further, while gravity always appears distinct from the other three forces at manifest time/distance scales, at the finest scale, there is unification. Similarly, one observer can provide a rich account of the formal, principled side of morality and another can provide a rich account of its feeling and care-based side; and yet only when observation encompasses the level of transcendental consciousness can the fullest possibilities of principledness and of feeling be comprehended, and only at that level can they be seen as thoroughly integrated.

The state of enlightenment as described by Maharishi provides the ground for full integration of those qualities of morality which are in seeming opposition. It represents a model in which awareness functions from a level which is fully universal (in fact, cosmic) and is yet infinitely responsive to the smallest particularity. In Kohlberg's view, the limited, "personal" actor must expand to an impersonal level in order to maintain universal principles. The movement is from where one is—individuality—toward where one ideally and normatively should be—universality. In the model of enlightenment, one always *is* at the universal level already and is not overshadowed by any influences born of individual limitations. In this state, one can freely move into *all* situations with love and care without losing the universal bearing. One is automatically universal in situations which are primarily personal (while one actually enriches the personal aspect) and more personal in situations which ordinarily call for the universality born of impersonality (while expanding the universal aspect). In the Vedic model of enlightenment, thinking occurs on the basis of a sensitivity (albeit largely tacit) to all relevant particularities; and choice is implemented in a manner which nurtures each individual. On the other hand, love, care, and all feelings are *absolutely* principled, since they function on the basis of and in full harmony with the most universal principles—the laws of nature.

In enlightenment, spontaneous responsiveness to the total situation is more salient in directing action than are deliberations about responsibility; and yet one responds in a manner which automatically fulfills all responsibilities that a universal, rational observer would identify. Interestingly, Gilligan and Lyons believe that to be fully responsive to individual needs, one must function through the orientation of a "connected self," the aspect of self experienced as tangibly linked with particular, localized relationships and surroundings; and they state that responsiveness diminishes as the "separate self" orientation becomes salient. However, by "connected self" and "separate self" they are referring to specific modes of conceptualizing oneself in relation to the social environment. From Maharishi's perspective, there is a much deeper level of self—a level at which separateness is maximum and yet coexists with the maximum value of connectedness. In this understanding, the deepest level of self is pure consciousness, the unified field. In cosmic consciousness, the first stage of enlightenment, this level is directly experienced as being separate from everything else (including all active states of one's mind). Because the field of pure consciousness transcends everything but is also the level at which everything is infinitely correlated, it is only when one fully acts from this level that one can be fully responsive; and in first reaching this stage, one experiences the complete separateness of Self from the manifest world. Maharishi (1969) emphasizes that this separateness is not detachment and does not result in aloofness; instead, he says it is the basis for a) infinite freedom, and b) the capacity to dynamically live in the world free from narrowness and limitation, expressing the creative intelligence of natural law with a full mind and heart. In the most advanced stage of enlightenment (unity consciousness) this experience of separation is said to dissolve as everything comes to be experienced in terms of and as an expression of the unmanifest Self (Maharishi, 1972). Yet it is only by first experiencing pure consciousness as Self, and experiencing its distinctness from manifest activity, that enlightenment dawns and one can perform spontaneous right action in which one is infinitely responsive on the basis of infinite connectedness. From Maharishi's perspective, if the self is a connected self only to the extent of being the limited individual ego ever caught up in the multiplicity of particularities, then care and concern, although meaning well, will not be able to give everyone what he or she truly needs from the standpoint of natural law. In this view, only through expanding awareness and experiencing the unbounded Self can one be fully connected with the total potential of natural law and thereby so intimately connected with all other people as to be spontaneously life-supporting in all relationships.

Conclusion

Maharishi Mahesh Yogi's modern reformulation of the developmental and ethical theory of Vedic Psychology suggests a new basis for the clarification and fuller resolution of the major theoretical issues of ethics and ethical development. Further, because Maharishi has formulated his theory of Vedic Psychology in terms of a science and has reintroduced the applied, practical aspect of Vedic Science (a simple technology of consciousness through which regular experience of transcendental consciousness is universally available), it is now possible for a thorough research program to test age-old theories that have been commonly regarded as unscientific and mystical. Consequently, even the hypothesis that human beings are intimately interconnected through field effects of consciousness is being extensively tested, and there are already promising signs that the dynamics of human interaction at a more subtle and pervasive level than sensory interaction can be learned with great precision and their ethical implications more fully understood. Therefore, through Vedic Psychology, the possibility exists for scientifically expanding our knowledge of ethical development to the cosmic dimension while actually achieving substantial acceleration in the ethical development of individuals and, through the influence of their coherence on collective consciousness, in the development of society's moral atmosphere and corresponding quality of life.

Acknowledgments

I gratefully acknowledge the extensive assistance and many editorial suggestions of Robert Ryncarz. I also wish to thank Sanford Nidich for providing insight and assistance; and to thank Geoffrey Golner, John Hagelin, and Robert Rabinoff for valuable suggestions on the discussion of physics; and Dennis Heaton and Charles N. Alexander for their helpful comments.

References

Abrams, A. I. & Siegel, L. M. (1978). The Transcendental Meditation program and rehabilitation at Folsom State Prison: A cross-validation study. *Criminal Justice and Behavior* 5: 3–20.

Alexander, C. N. (1982). Ego development, personality, and behavioral change in inmates practicing the Transcendental Meditation technique or participating in other programs: A cross-sectional and longitudinal study. Doctoral dissertation, Harvard University. *Dissertation Abstracts International* 43 (2): 530–B.

Antoniadis, I.; Ellis, J.; Hagelin, J. S. & Nanopoulos, D. V. (1987). Supersymmetric flipped SU[5] revitalized. *Physics Letters* 194B: 231.

Badawi, K.; Wallace, R. K.; Orme-Johnson, D. W. & Rouzere, A. M. (1984). Electrophysiologic characteristics of respiratory suspension periods occurring during the practice of the Transcendental Meditation program. *Psychosomatic Medicine* 46 (3): 267–276.

Bleick, C. R. & Abrams, A. I. (1987). The Transcendental Meditation program and criminal recidivism in California. *Journal of Criminal Justice* 15 (3): 211–230.

Blum, L. (1982). *Friendship, altruism and morality*. Boston: Routledge & Kegan Paul.

Bucke, R. (1969). *Cosmic consciousness: A study in the evolution of the human mind*. New York: Dutton.

Dillbeck, M. C. (1987). Intervention studies on reduction of domestic and international violence through collective consciousness. *Abstracts and summaries of contributed papers, Third Midwest Conference for the United States Institute of Peace*. Minneapolis: University of Minnesota.

Dillbeck, M. C.; Landrith, G. & Orme-Johnson, D. W. (1981). The Transcendental Meditation program and crime rate changes in a sample of cities. *Journal of Crime and Justice, 4,* 25–45.

Dillbeck, M. C. & Abrams, A. I. (1987). The application of the Transcendental Meditation program in corrections. *International Journal of Comparative and Applied Criminal Justice* 11: 111–132.

Dillbeck, M. C.; Cavanaugh, K. L.; Glenn, T.; Orme-Johnson, D. W. & Mittlefehldt, V. (1987). Consciousness as a field: The Transcendental Meditation and TM-Sidhi program and changes in social indicators. *The Journal of Mind and Behavior* 8: 67–104.

Feynman, R.; Leighton, R. & Sands, M. (1965). *The Feynman lectures on physics,* vol. 3. Reading, MA: Addison-Wesley.

Fingarette, H. (1977). *Self-deception*. New York: Humanities Press.

Frew, D. R. (1974). Transcendental Meditation and productivity. *Academy of Management Journal* 17: 362–368.

Gilligan, C. & Murphy, J. M. (1979). Development from adolescence to adulthood: The philosopher and the dilemma of fact. In D. Kuhn (Ed.), *Intellectual development beyond childhood*. San Francisco: Jossey-Bass.

Gilligan, C. (1982). *In a different voice: Psychological theory and women's development*. Cambridge, MA: Harvard University Press.

Hagelin, J. (1987). Is consciousness the unified field? A field theorist's perspective. *Modern Science and Vedic Science,* 1: 29–87.

Hare, R. M. (1981). *Moral thinking: Its levels, method and point*. New York: Oxford University Press.

Huxley, A. (1945). *The perennial philosophy*. New York: Harper.

Itzykson, C. & Zuber, J. B. (1980). *Quantum field theory*. New York: McGraw-Hill.

Kant, I. (1963). *Critique of pure reason* (N. Kemp Smith, Trans.). London: Macmillan. Original work published 1781.

Kant, I. (1975). *Foundations of the metaphysics of morals*. Indianapolis: Bobbs-Merrill. Original work published 1785.

Kohlberg, L. (1971). From is to ought. In T. Mishel (Ed.), *Cognitive development and epistemology*. New York: Academic Press.

Kohlberg, L. (1979). Justice as reversibility. In P. Laslett & J. Fishkin (Eds.), *Philosophy, politics and society,* fifth series (pp. 257–272). Oxford: Blackwell.

Kohlberg, L. & Powers, C. (1981). Moral development, religious thinking, and the question of a seventh stage. In L. Kohlberg (Ed.), *Essays in moral development*. San Francisco: Harper & Row.

Kohlberg, L.; Levine, C. & Hewer, A. (1983). Moral stages: A current formulation and a response to critics. *Contributions to human development,* 10. Basel: Karger.

Kohlberg, L. & Ryncarz, R. A. (1990). Beyond justice reasoning: Moral development and consideration of a seventh stage. In C. N. Alexander & E. J. Langer (Eds.), *Higher stages of human development*. New York: Oxford University Press.

Levine, P. (1976). The coherence spectral array (COSPAR) and its application to the study of the spatial ordering in the EEG. *Proceedings of the San Diego Medical Symposium* 15.

Loevinger, J. (1976). *Ego development: Conceptions and theories*. San Francisco: Jossey-Bass.

Lyons, N. (1983). Two perspectives: On self, relationships and morality. *Harvard Educational Review* 53: 125–145.

Maharishi Mahesh Yogi (1966). *The science of being and art of living*. Los Angeles: International SRM.

Maharishi Mahesh Yogi (1969). *On the Bhagavad-Gita: A new translation and commentary*. Harmondsworth, Middlesex, England: Penguin.

Maharishi Mahesh Yogi (1972). *The science of creative intelligence*. Los Angeles: Maharishi International University Press.

Maharishi Mahesh Yogi (1976). *Creating an ideal society: A global undertaking.* Rheinweiler, Germany: MERU Press.

Maharishi Mahesh Yogi (1982). Inaugural address. *International symposium: The applications of modern science and natural law.* Luxembourg.

Maslow, A. (1971). *The farther reaches of human nature.* New York: Viking.

Murphy, J. M. & Gilligan, C. (1980). Moral development in late adolescence and adulthood: A critique and reconstruction of Kohlberg's theory. *Human Development,* 23: 77–104.

Nidich, S. I.; Ryncarz, R.; Abrams, A.; Orme-Johnson, D. & Wallace, R. K. (1983). Kohlbergian cosmic perspective responses, EEG coherence, and the Transcendental Meditation and TM-Sidhi program. *Journal of Moral Education* 26: 166–173.

Orme-Johnson, D. W. (1988). The cosmic psyche—an introduction to Maharishi's Vedic Psychology: The fulfillment of modern psychology. *Modern Science and Vedic Science* 2: 113–163.

Orme-Johnson, D. W. & Haynes, C. T. (1981). EEG phase coherence, pure consciousness, creativity, and TM-Sidhi experiences. *International Journal of Neuroscience* 13: 211–217.

Orme-Johnson, D. W.; Alexander, C. N.; Davies, J.L.; Chandler, H.M. & Larimore, W.E. (1988). Effects of the Maharishi Technology of the Unified Field on conflict and quality of life in Israel and Lebanon. *Journal of Conflict Resolution* 32: 776.

Pagels, H. (1982). *The cosmic code.* New York: Simon & Schuster.

Piaget, J. (1970). *Structuralism.* New York: Basic Books.

Plato (1945). *The republic* (F. Cornford, Trans.). New York: Oxford University Press.

Schwarz, J. (1985). Completing Einstein. *Science* 85 (Nov.): 60–64.

Shear, Jonathan. (1973). *Western philosophy and the science of creative intelligence.* Unpublished lectures. Maharishi International University, Fairfield, IA.

Spinoza, B. (1930). Ethics. In J. Wild (Ed.), *Spinoza selections.* New York: Scribners.

Waldrop, M. (1985). String as a theory of everything. *Science* 229: 1251–1253.

Wallace, R. K. (1972). The physiology of meditation. *Scientific American* 226: 84–90.

CHAPTER NINE

Ahimsa, Justice, and the Unity of Life: Postconventional Morality from an Indian Perspective

Jyotsna Vasudev
Staunton Clinic, Sewickley Valley Hospital

Kohlberg's theory of moral development provides a rich format for investigating the dimensions of mature moral reasoning. As a developmental theory, it also allows us to explore moral development across cultures. The goal of this paper is to discuss postconventional morality from an Indian perspective. This paper is divided into three sections: The first section is a review of Kohlberg's theory, its criticisms, and its reformulation in view of its cross-cultural applicability. The second section introduces two moral concepts, *Ahimsa* and the unity of all life, which are rooted in the Indian tradition and figure prominently in a mature moral perspective. These concepts are elucidated through excerpts from a moral judgment interview with an Indian respondent. The third section discusses the challenge such data pose for Kohlberg's conception of morality, especially at higher stages of development.

Theory of Moral Development

Kohlberg's theory of moral reasoning is a significant departure from behavioristic, psychoanalytic, and social learning explanations of moral development. Following Piaget's model of cognitive development, Kohlberg has described stages of moral development which traverse childhood, adolescence, and adulthood; these stages represent transformations in conceptions of self, society, and justice. These developmental transformations hinge on an ongoing interaction between an individual's capacity to construe meaning and the structure of the social environment. In line with

Piaget, Kohlberg also has argued that this model meets criteria of cognitive development: a) Each stage represents a holistic structure of reasoning which implies that reasoning at a given stage is relatively consistent across different content areas. b) These stages represent an invariant universal sequence of development; this implies that an individual moves through the sequence in a manner where no stages are skipped and, once consolidated, there are no significant regressions in development. This model does not require a rate or ceiling for development; individuals may progress through the sequence at different rates and reach different end points in their development. c) Stages of development are hierarchical integrations; each successively higher stage includes the lower stages reintegrated at a higher level. Thus, individuals comprehend all stages below their own and not more than one above their own stage of reasoning. They also prefer the highest stage they can comprehend. More than three decades of investigation have produced empirical support for these developmental criteria (Kohlberg, 1981; Kohlberg et al., 1983).

Similar to Piaget's view of the child as a scientist, Kohlberg sees the child as a moral philosopher, as an interactive and proactive moral agent who constructs increasingly complex, more differentiated and better equilibrated structures of moral reasoning. In brief, the stages of moral reasoning represent structural transformations from a primitive notion of justice based on power and punishment to a principled form distinguished by rational, autonomous, and universalizable principles. The stage or structure of an individual's reasoning is derived by posing hypothetical dilemmas in a semi-structured interview. Each of Kohlberg's dilemmas involves a central value conflict in which a protagonist must choose a course of action. In the famous Heinz dilemma for example, Heinz has to choose between stealing or not stealing a life-saving drug for his ill wife, which he cannot afford. The structure of a respondent's reasoning is determined not simply by choosing a value, but by justifying, elaborating, and clarifying his or her moral point of view. In Kohlberg's research methodology, moral judgment interviews are scored by trained scorers using a standardized scoring manual. The Kohlberg scoring manual has undergone revisions over three decades to improve its reliability and validity.

In brief, Kohlberg's scheme comprises three levels of moral development which delineate three basic social perspectives an individual may adopt in relation to society: Preconventional, Conventional, and Postconventional. These levels are then further subdivided with two stages under each level. Stage 1, the punishment and obedience orientation, represents an egocentric and most primitive form of justice that is determined by concrete physical consequences and the dictates of authority. Stage 2, the instrumental relativist orientation, is still guided by self-centered interests, but these are framed by a concrete sense of fairness and reciprocity, i.e., a tit-for-tat morality.

Stage 3, the interpersonal concordance orientation, marks an important shift from the preconventional to conventional level of morality. The sociomoral perspective of this stage reflects the primacy of relationships with significant others; morality is identified with conformance to stereo-typical images of "good boy" or "nice girl" and maintaining loyalty and trust in close interpersonal relationships. Stage 4, the law and order orientation, begins to differentiate social perspective from a generalized social perspective. The individual uses the system to derive both sanctioned roles and rules of morality. A sense of justice dictates respect for and allegiance to the social order and its maintenance.

Stage 5, the social-contract legalistic orientation, represents a prior-to-society perspective; this implies that one attempts to define basic values and rights irrespective of social relationships or contracts. The notion of social contracts does not prescribe specific obligations for specific relations; "rather, legal or social commitments are viewed as something to which each partner to the contract freely obligates himself knowing that the others have equally and freely obligated themselves" (Reimer et al., 1983, p. 78). The U.S. Constitution, Kohlberg suggests, exemplifies Stage 5 reasoning about society and basic individual rights within any social system.

Stage 6, the universal ethical principle orientation, represents the highest moral point of view. Morality is defined in terms of autonomous ethical principles which are comprehensive, universal, consistent, and reversible. As general principles of justice, they underscore human rights, dignity, and freedom. Philosophically, Stage 6 is grounded in Kant's notion of categorical imperative and Rawls's (1971) view of justice as a rational choice when a moral agent operates from an "original position" under a "veil of ignorance" as to one's role or identity. These principles are universal and consistent in the Kantian sense, i.e., principles of justice are realized as universalizable principles which are not relative to specific moral agents and situations.

A noteworthy feature of Kohlberg's theory is the bridge it provides between psychology and philosophy; Kohlberg maintains that a psychological theory of moral reasoning remains inadequate if its philosophical underpinnings are not explained. Thus, in addition to specifying cognitive-developmental criteria, Kohlberg also has described the metaethical assumptions of his theory. This stance, however, has generated political, empirical, and philosophical controversies.

Gilligan (1982) argued that Kohlberg's model, derived from an all-male sample, was biased against women. Gilligan suggests that, compared to the proclivity of men to think formally and autonomously, women's thinking is contextual and embedded in relationships with others. By confining the criteria of principled morality to a deontological principle of justice, Kohlberg's theory ignores moral concerns central to women. Further, this emphasis on rights, autonomy, and rationality skews our understanding of adulthood in favor of separateness over connection with others. Gilligan (1982) proposed an alternative scheme which articulates a morality of care and responsibility.

Extreme cultural relativists maintain that Kohlberg's claim to the universality of this scheme of moral reasoning blatantly disregards irreconcilable cultural differences (Shweder, 1982). Further, given the infrequency of higher stages in non-Western cultures, others have criticized the elitist, ethnocentric, and socioeconomic bias in his theory (Buck-Morss, 1975; Edwards, 1975; Simpson, 1974; Sullivan, 1977). Given the roots of Kohlberg's theory in the Western tradition, Sullivan (1977) argues Kohlberg's penchant for liberal ideology and structuralism is a product of twentieth-century historical demands. Sullivan questions Kohlberg's "model of man" inherent in the Stage 6 orientation and its representation as the most ideal and equilibrated form of justice; he argues "because of the universality that he attributes to the stages of morality, his Stage 6 becomes *the* model of a moral man rather than *a* model of a moral man" (Sullivan 1977, pp. 6-7, emphasis in original). Simpson (1974) also comments on Kohlberg's partiality to Western philosophy and notes "surely an adequate explanation of the concept of morality throughout humanity implies the examination of its meaning in the non-Western world" (Simpson 1974, p. 89).

Given the philosophically stringent criteria and rarity of Stage 6 reasoning, some critics have questioned if Stage 6 represents a legitimate stage of development (Gibbs, 1977). Philosophers like Habermas (1983) find some of Kohlberg's claims problematic. Kohlberg (1971), noting the isomorphism between developmental psychology and moral philosophy, had claimed that "the scientific theory as to why people factually *do* move upward from stage to stage, and why they factually *do* prefer a higher stage to a lower, is broadly the same as a moral theory as to why people *should* prefer a higher stage to a lower" (Kohlberg, 1971, p. 223, emphasis in original). Habermas (1983) reproves Kohlberg for this identity thesis and its inherent naturalistic fallacy. Specifically, he finds it problematical that Kohlberg has maneuvered this fallacy to lend empirical support for his normative ethical stance.

Kohlberg's response to such diverse criticisms was shaped gradually by ongoing research and reformulations of his theory. Stage 6, for example, now is viewed as a necessary theoretical end point rather than an achievable stage in development. As a repository of pretheoretic assumptions, Stage 6 supports an attempt "to rationally reconstruct the ontogensis of justice reasoning, an enterprise which requires a terminal stage to define the nature and end point of the kind of development we are studying" (Kohlberg et al., 1983, p. 61). Furthermore, Kohlberg has rejected the "identity thesis" for a "complementarity thesis" and notes his empirical enterprise cannot validate the primacy of a justice-based ethic. Rather, it represents an orienting framework for interpreting and rationally reconstructing moral statements.

Gilligan's (1982) criticisms led to a reexamination of data for sex bias. In brief, with revisions in the scoring manual, there was support for Kohlberg's contention that when samples are controlled for education, socioeconomic status, and occupation, there are no differences between males and females (Gibbs et al., 1984; Vasudev & Hummel, 1987; Walker, 1984, 1986). Gilligan's criticisms did, however, prompt Kohlberg and his colleagues to incorporate considerations of care and responsibility in their view of morality. Although Gilligan's ideas are crucial and have received wide publicity, there continues to be a hiatus between these ideas and theory-driven research to explicate the relationships between moral orientation, age, stage, and sex (Vasudev, 1988).

Kohlberg's response to critics who had questioned the cross-cultural generality of his model has been informed by methodological refinements and ongoing research. First, as noted, the paucity of postconventional reasoning in non-Western cultures had prompted criticisms of ethnocentrism and Western bias. Regarding this, it should again be noted that Stage 6 currently exists as a conceptual rather than scorable entity and Stage 5, given revisions in the scoring manual, is infrequent even in the United States samples. Second, an increasing variety of cross-cultural studies have reported some postconventional thinking in diverse cultural settings. Third, comprehensive reviews of cross-cultural studies (Boyes & Walker, 1988; Snarey, 1985) suggest that Kohlberg's theory and method are reasonably culture-fair and do reflect moral issues, norms, and values relevant in other cultural settings. Further, these data also support the developmental criteria implied by this stage model. Despite this impressive support for his developmental theory and nonrelativistic stance, some cross-cultural studies also report that Kohlberg's model misconstrues or fails to appreciate some moral principles and concepts integral to other cultures.

Kohlberg's response to this challenge was understandably mixed. He continued to defend his justice-based ethic on empirical and philosophical grounds but seemed to be open in his general stance. Nisan and Kohlberg (1982) conceded that a claim to universality does not imply that Kohlberg's theory is a comprehensive representation of the whole moral domain in every culture. Thus, "it is possible that in other cultures, principles are held which are distinct from ours, and moral reasoning is used that does not fit the structure described by Kohlberg" (Nisan & Kohlberg, 1982, p. 874). Further, rather than asserting the primacy of justice as *the* principle, he stressed the empirical value of his orienting framework which is informed by this principle. He notes: "Personal endorsement of the philosophical adequacy claims of higher stages is a matter of choice, and one's personal stand may simply be that using the moral stage framework is a fruitful tool for scientific research" (Kohlberg et al., 1983, p. 65). This de-emphasis on justice is paralleled by his attempts to incorporate other universalizable principles such as agape, utilitarianism, benevolence, and care.

Ahimsa and Unity of Life: Theory and Research

After reviewing Kohlberg's theory of moral development and issues regarding its cross-cultural application, this section initiates a discussion of postconventional morality to expand Kohlberg's conception and introduce other moral principles that are not anticipated in his theory. This continues the discussion of issues which had emerged in my doctoral research (Vasudev, 1985). In brief, using a cross-sectional design, the generality of Kohlberg's stages was investigated in a well-educated, middle- to upper-middle-class sample of children, adolescents, and adults in India. Results of this study provided substantial support for Kohlberg's theory. First, all the stages of reasoning, i.e., preconventional, conventional, and postconventional, were found in the Indian sample. Second, there were no sex differences in any of the age groups. Third, a qualitative analysis of the interview revealed that some respondents spontaneously introduced Indian philosophical ideas in their moral reasoning. Although these ideas were central to their moral point of view, they were not comprehensible in terms of Kohlberg's moral development scheme and scoring system (Vasudev & Hummel, 1987).

To examine such indigenous values in moral reasoning, four respondents were interviewed in India. In addition to using Kohlberg's method and dilemmas, these respondents were encouraged to discuss morality from an Indian perspective to the extent that it was relevant to their moral point of view. This section introduces moral concepts integral to Indian thought, along with excerpts from an interview which exemplifies how a philosophical tradition becomes integrated and personalized in a mature moral view. Such data reassert the necessity to consider universal and culture-specific forms of postconventional morality.

In various Hindu religions and philosophical treatises, it is noted that *Ahimsa paramo dharma.* That is, *Ahimsa*, which translates as nonviolence or harmlessness, is the highest virtue and ultimate law of our being. According to the Mahabharata, *Ahimsa* is the highest religion, the highest penance, the highest truth from which all other virtues proceed. From Upanishadic and Vedic thought to modern philosophies and traditions, this concept occupies a central position in ethical discourse. As an axiomatic moral and spiritual principle, it prescribes a fundamental obligation not to inflict harm and to uphold the sanctity of life. In Buddhism, nonviolence is related to *Karuna*, which implies sympathy and compassion for the real and metaphysical suffering of other beings. In Jainism, it is framed as an absolute law of life which governs mundane behaviors like sleeping, eating, and walking. It is an elementary recognition that knowing one's own pain, one ought not to augment or perpetuate it on another living being. Thus, Mahavir, the founder of Jainism, placed *Ahimsa* above truth and stated, "I renounce all killing of living beings, whether subtle or gross, whether movable or immovable. Neither shall I myself kill living beings, nor cause others to do it, nor consent to it." The Jain scriptures introduced a hierarchical order of life based on the number of senses living organisms possess; the rule of *Ahimsa* is to sustain one's own life through foods with a minimum number of senses like plants, fruits, and nuts.

In the ancient scriptures, and among modern Indian philosophers, the issue of absolute nonviolence and *Aanrishan*, i.e., unnecessary killing, is often debated. The Mahabharata, for example, asks who there is who does not inflict violence? Even ascetics devoted to nonviolence somtimes commit violence but, by great effort, reduce it to a minimum. Similarly, Radhakrishnan (1926, 1958) argues that the ideal of absolute nonviolence is not practical as some violence is justified in an imperfect world, especially when its aim is human welfare; one is obligated to protect innocent lives, and not to do so is to acquiesce to evil. He suggests a modified principle of least violence that enjoins one not to cause harm beyond what is absolutely necessary.

Ahimsa is not restricted to tangible living organisms. One is enjoined not to harm "by mind, word or deed." In the twentieth century, Mahatma Gandhi promulgated "militant nonviolence" as a political and spiritual method of gaining India's freedom from British rule. For Gandhi, *Ahimsa* is synonymous with *Satyagraha*, i.e., truth-force or soul-force; he writes, "In the application of Satyagraha, I discovered . . . that pursuit of truth did not admit of violence being inflicted on one's opponent . . . for what appears to be truth to one may appear to be error to the other . . . so the doctrine came to mean vindication of truth, not by infliction of suffering on the opponent, but on one's own self" (Gandhi, 1951, p. 6).

In his psychohistorical study of Gandhi, Erikson (1969) insightfully comments that the "true method" guided by nonviolence is common to both Gandhi's political struggle to obtain freedom for India and to Freud's therapeutic endeavors. He notes that the practice of *Ahimsa* also implies a determination not to violate the essence of another person even if it is the enemy and to respect the truth in him or her (Erikson, 1969). Thus, "the concept of nonviolence is not, therefore, a rigid, religious dogma, nor is it simply an abstract metaphysical supposition. It is a principle that can be applied to all forms of life and can regulate interactions among people in keeping with compassion, justice and truth. Similar to Kohlberg's view of justice at Stage 6, nonviolence also may be viewed as a comprehensive, universalizable, reversible and prescriptive principle" (Vasudev & Hummel, 1987, p. 116).

To summarize, in the Indian tradition, *Ahimsa* has acquired broad social, political, and spiritual significance; its meaning is not restricted to human life, but is universalized to all forms of life as an injunction not to hurt and to avoid injury to all living beings. "It finds expression, for instance, in the vegetarian diet, which so many Hindus have always favored, and in the policy of pacifism and 'passive resistance' which, while never adopted universally, has probably had more followers at every period in India than in most other lands" (Edgerton, 1972, p. 185).

The vow and application of *Ahimsa* to regulate connections with all forms of life is related to a salient characteristic of Indian thought to regard reality as an integral whole which is represented in terms of gradations rather than dualities (Bishop, 1975). This allows for a flexible stance for appreciating both differences and connectedness. Diversity is not denied, but understood within a metacontext of reality in which there is unity in diversity. Another variation of this posture is that reality is characterized by diversity at the relative level and by unity at the absolute universal level. Spiritual progress is the gradual recognition that plurality is a manifestation of the "One," which is the ground of all beings. The "One" translates as God, Paramatma, or Brahman, i.e., universal soul or the ultimate reality. Hindu philosophers speak of Brahman in its paradoxical aspects as cosmic and acosmic and as relative and transcendental. In the Shvetashvatara Upanishad, the diversity of Brahman is captured as follows: "May the Lord of Love, who projects himself into this universe of myriad forms, from whom all beings came and to whom all return, grant us the grace of wisdom [for] He is fire and the sun, and the moon and the stars. He is the air and the sea . . . He is this man, He is that woman . . . his face is everywhere. He is the bluebird, he is the green bird with red eyes; he is the thundercloud, and he is the seasons and the seas" (Easwaran, 1987, Trans., p. 225).

This metaphysical doctrine promotes a spontaneous solidarity with all creatures and entails a moral obligation to treat other beings as one's own self. In his commentary on the Bhagavad-Gita, Edgerton (1972, p. 185) notes that:

> [O]ne of the most striking and emphatic of the ethical doctrines of the Gita is substantially the Golden Rule. Man must treat all creatures alike, from the highest to the lowest, namely, like himself. The perfect man delights in the welfare of all beings.

Here are two translated verses from the Bhagavad-Gita that correspond to the above:

In a knowledge-and-cultivation-perfected
Brahman, a cow, an elephant,
and in a mere dog, and an outcaste,
The wise see the same thing. (V. 18)

Himself as in all beings,
And all beings in himself,
Sees he whose self is disciplined in discipline,
Who sees the same in all things. (VI. 29)
(Edgerton, 1972, Trans.)

With this introduction to Kohlberg's theory and some fundamental notions in Indian philosophy, let us turn to an interview with a 50-year-old woman (S. J.) who is well versed in Indian and Western philosophies. In her discussion of justice and morality, she draws from her tradition to develop her point of view. In brief, she argues for universalizable values of life: equality, freedom, and dignity commensurate with Kohlberg's description of postconventional prior-to-society perspective. But the rich meanings, complexity, and grounding of her utterances are best understood by recognizing the linkage between her discourse and the tradition she inherited. Specifically, her justification interweaves justice with nonviolence, rationality with sacredness, and the personal with the universal.

In her response to the Heinz dilemma, S. J. asserted that she gave more weight to saving a life over property, regardless of who the person was. When asked to elaborate her position, she said:

The question why I should give life more weightage takes me to some deeper concerns and it links up with issues of what is the ground from which I decide what I ought to do and what I ought not to do. I used to believe that most of these grounds are very rational. But now my arguments stem from a deeper recognition of certain things which are considered sacred. I very self-consciously bring in the word sanctity, which is a non-causal word. In this framework, some things are sacred and because they are sacred, therefore, to violate that sanctity would violate my sense of being and I ought not to do it. My entire sense of values gets its meaning and its legitimacy by my recognition of that sanctity. These words are not easily intelligible unless you move into the framework of sanctity. Considering anything sacred means if I didn't do something at that end, I wouldn't be able to live as a full human being. For example, destruction to me is repulsive because it violates sanctity of life. Therefore, the framework in which I operate is not only sanctity of human life, but sanctity of all life.

When asked why she considered human life to be sacred, S. J. explained:

> I consider every human being, I say every with a capital E, as a set of infinite
> potentials. If you say why, have you *proved* it, [I would have to say] no. But
> I have ample evidence to say that I am justified in making that claim. I have
> probably inherited it in my tradition as an intuitive principle that it is easy for
> me to accept it. In the Indian tradition, we say, *har atma paramatma hai*, i.e.,
> every soul is an infinite soul. Thus, one may be a stranger, but not a stranger
> inasmuch as it is a soul. Therefore, my affinity for the infinite possibilities it
> has [leads me to see] that it is absolutely necessary that the body which is the
> manifest version of the soul should also be protected.

When asked what morality meant to her, she addressed her view of
justice using her experience with women's studies as follows:

> An issue in women's studies arose from a felt sense of injustice. The ethical
> issue was what kind of power relationships exist and whether they are just or
> unjust. From there, we went into the logic of why and on what grounds
> [injustice] has been sustained. . . . This involved a theory of equality. That is,
> what kind of just society will give some sense of equality and stature to
> women's lives. . . . If you talk of cooperation with men, cooperation is almost
> always among equals, never among unequals; otherwise, it is a relationship of
> either being exploited or exploiting others. I think the issue of justice really
> brought in the issue of what is fair and what [confirms] equality. . . . A
> relationship of dignity is one in which you can stand as an equal.

She then provided an expanded view which encompassed justice and
nonviolence. She said:

> The context of morality is how human beings should relate to one another
> . . . should there be certain kinds of principles which will give you guidelines
> for the kinds of relationships we should have. The most central issues in
> morality are justice and non-violence. For me, non-violence is the only way
> in which you can sustain the notion of justice . . . I think a non-violent
> relationship is a just relationship. By non-violence, I mean the recognition of
> the sanctity of a being with whom I relate. If I violate that sanctity, then it is
> an immoral situation . . . In all injustice, I am stepping on your being in some
> form or another. If I take something from you, if I use you, then it is a kind
> of violence against you as I am not giving you the stature, the equality, the
> kind of continuum with myself which gives a legitimacy to my saying that you
> are sacred.

When asked to discuss the place of nonviolence in the Indian tradition, she
explained:

> In the Indian tradition, at no point has non-violence needed to be proved. One

would have to justify violence, but never non-violence. In most Indian traditions like the Yoga Sutra, Jainism, Buddhism, etc., this is *the* central principle, and it has been metaphysically and pragmatically sustained. Metaphysically it relates to the continuity of life or unity of life, or to the notion of the soul. On pragmatic grounds, even if you want to go on a moral journey to evolve higher self-realization, what gives you support structures are things like Satya, *Ahimsa*, Aparigraha, i.e., truth, nonviolence, non-acquisition.

When asked to explain the connection and similarities between justice and nonviolence, she said:

I don't think that these terms are interchangeable or different. They sort of complete each other. I cannot understand the notion of justice unless I have some notion of non-violence, and I cannot understand the notion of non-violence unless I have some notion of justice. If I am only non-violent, I won't be able to clarify the range of things which I visualize by non-violence. If I say justice only, you wouldn't be able to comprehend the kind of value choice I am generating and which is the core of my being. . . . The central issue in moral relationships is what is it, which builds up and enriches human beings rather than destroys them. . . . Human relationships can be enriched only with certain kinds of minimal acceptances. One is that I consider you as a sacred being and that you are as important as I am. Not because I am, therefore you are, or because you look like me. But just as it is self-evident that I am sacred, you are also sacred . . . the very possibility of altruism lies in this metaphysical acceptance of you as self-evidently sacred as I am. In a strange way I am talking [similarly] to Nagle on the possibility of altruism, which is akin to my thinking, although he has argued in a different manner. But the take-off point is absolutely true that unless it is self-evidently true that you are as important, the possibility of morality is annihilated and there can be no legitimate argument. . . . Both issues of justice and nonviolence dilate on this point and get their justification from this. If you are sacred as I am, it is only fair that I don't step on you, that I don't destroy you, or mutilate you. You here means the trees, the animals with whom I feel this continuity.

Throughout her discussion, S. J. maintained a comprehensive value for all life; she related her concept of morality, nonviolence, and sanctity of life to human as well as nonhuman life or nature in general. When asked to explain this position further, she said:

I think of myself as a continuous being. If you ask me a further "why" I would say that why here is an irrelevant question. In all rational arguments, you come to a certain parameter, to certain value choices which are just there, which are not arguable, but which make subsequent arguments meaningful. So, [based on that value,] I can give you a whole range of reasons as to why I won't destroy the integrity of a plant, why I won't say a harsh word to you as it will destroy you at some level. . . . If you ask me why, I would say that destruction in itself is a violation of something which I hold sacred.

This comprehensive respect for nature was further elaborated in her discussion of whether Heinz should save an animal's life. She explained:

If I were Heinz, the question is do you find yourself linked to this life, do you feel the continuity between your life and the animal's life? How far do you see the animal as a living being? . . . There are people who feel it is a meal or food which is simply there for their consumption. . . . I feel the animal is a living being and it is as living as I am. I may have a different language, a different style, but the animal has a world of its own and it has a legitimacy of its own. . . . In fact, it is not just an Indian tradition, but a human tradition in which man is part of nature and not using nature. It is the techno-logical revolutionary bravado in which you see nature as presenting a challenge in which you control and use it for your purpose rather than be a part of it. Your relationship with nature is one in which you dichotomize and you say I am related to my fellow beings who are also using nature . . . among your fellow beings you distinguish the idiots, the blacks, who are not like you and therefore can be sacrificed. . . . Thus, you go on making these distinctions and come up with a delimited set where you become narrower and narrower and more egocentric. This is a whole range of your egocentric predicament which brings you to ask this question. I would put a counter question and say what has happened that you have started feeling discontinuous. So what needs to be explained is your dichotomizing and discontinuity. . . . People ask me what is your relationship to the environment. I say I don't see myself outside the environment, I am part of the environment. I am in the environment and the environment is within me.

Comparison of Western and Eastern Perspectives

Thus far, we have seen that unity and sanctity of all life and non-violence are posed as quintessential values in the Hindu tradition and continue to inform moral thinking and behavior. When it comes to these values, there are important differences and similarities between the Western and Indian traditions. Steinem (1992) notes that the connection of humans to all creatures, recognized and shared by ancient and sophisticated cultures, has been eroded in the Western tradition as it has demonized and repudiated nature. "In the fifth century, Saint Augustine declared animals to be outside God's moral universe; in the thirteenth century, Thomas Aquinas maintained that man had unlimited power over animals by virtue of God's gift to Adam of dominion over them; and by the seventeenth century, philosopher René Descartes had concluded that animals were soulless machines with no ability to feel pain, an assumption then 'proved' by scientists for whom an animal's cries were no more evidence of feeling than a clock's chiming" (Steinem, 1992, p. 299).

Overall, in both traditions, a principled value of life entails making a normative judgment about life, recognizing it as an end in itself, and making a prescriptive, universalizable judgment that one should respect the life of the other (Frankena, 1976). In the Indian tradition, the value of life and the ensuing moral responsibility are more inclusive and are not restricted to reciprocal relations among humans only. Following the principle of non-violence and spiritual monism, a conscious being is seen as morally responsible for maintaining the integrity of other life forms which may not be equally conscious. Frankena (1976) has contrasted the Western and the Indian views respectively as a qualified versus a comprehensive value for life. Although Frankena believes that a qualified respect for life is the only rational and tenable position, the Indian philosophers would argue that genuine morality should promote an attitude of impartial sympathy for all life and anything less would be a moral compromise.

A comprehensive value for life is also deemed less adequate by Kohlberg and Habermas, who maintain a strictly rational view of morality in which spiritual arguments have tentative status or none at all. Kohlberg, for example, was unsure how spiritual arguments square with the reversible, rational principles of justice he described in his theory (Kohlberg, personal communication, July 1984, November 1986). Compared to the hard structures of justice reasoning, spiritual considerations are best understood, according to Kohlberg, as soft structures. This distinction seems spurious. It preserves Kohlberg's view of justice, but fails to account for genuine moral reasoning which falls outside his view.

Habermas has pursued the distinction between rational and spiritual arguments in his discussion of the discourse ethic. To summarize, Habermas proposes that humans can relate to nature only on the basis of instrumental rationality since nature cannot be included as a subject under communicative discourse. He has offered three reasons for this stance: First, the ecological problem notwithstanding, the modern technological-instrumental relation with nature is justified as a product of the human species as a whole rather than as a practice which is specific to an individual epoch or class.

Second, similar to Frankena, Habermas has restricted communicative rationality to speaking and acting subjects since a discourse ethic in principle presupposes reciprocal relations among persons; this reciprocity, in turn, is necessary for other morally relevant concepts like normative-validity claims, freedom, justice, and rationality. Given this, in Habermas's view, it is not possible to have a fraternal relationship with nonhuman nature without taking recourse to mysticism, which is not premised on rational grounds and which is incompatible with the level of learning attained in the modern technological world. Given the schism between a discourse ethic and a naturalistic ethic, he believes, it is impossible to apply principles of the former to regulate moral relations between human beings and nature. He writes, "Nature does not conform to the categories under which the subject can conform to the understanding of another subject on the basis of reciprocal recognition under the categories that are binding on both of them" (Habermas, 1972, p. 33).

Third, Habermas maintains that in an ethic which aims to rid itself of anthropocentrism and resurrect nature as an end-in-itself, the "precepts of sympathetic solidarity" reach their logical limits when one tries to extend moral obligations to all of nature. The life of plants, for example, conflicts with the imperatives of self-preservation of the human race. Whitebook (1979) comments that Habermas and most contemporary philosophers exclude the idea of nature as an end-in-itself from ethical theory as it threatens the dignity of the human subject. He notes the moral and legal rights and dignity of the human subject have been confirmed by severing the subject from the rest of natural existence.   Thus, by virtue of self-consciousness and language, humans are seen as qualitatively different from the rest of the natural existence and ought to be treated as ends-in-themselves. "It is often feared that anything that threatens to disturb this distinction—*which the concept of nature as an end-in-itself certainly does*—also threatens the dignity of the subject" (Whitebook, 1979, p. 53, emphasis in original).

Critics of Habermas's theory have noted that although communicative rationality helps one to formulate positive ethical principles in the human context, it is unable to guide ethical relations between human beings and nature. In general, they have found that a thoroughly anthropocentric view guarantees the sole value, respect, and dignity to the human subject at the cost of denying all worth to nature; this position is not even reconsidered in view of grave ecological problems. Whitebook (1979) asks if we can continue to subordinate nature without jeopardizing the "very natural preconditions" which sustain our existence. Similarly, in his philosophical writings, Hans Jonas (1974) implores us to reconsider the givens of modern philosophy which support the instrumental objectification of nature.

Habermas's stance on nature also is debated among philosophers of science. Generally, Habermas is seen as an antireductionist of the human sciences but a reductionist of the life sciences. Whitebook (1979) proposes that if communicative rationality is reserved strictly for speaking subjects, then it also implies that biological science is submitted to a reductionism; the principles of biological science, however, pose an empirical and a theoretical anomaly for a reductionistic approach. Habermas, for example, maintains a strict schism between speaking and nonspeaking nature; he tends to contradict himself, however, when he discusses ethology. In that discussion, he concedes that we can only understand the "seemingly teleological behavior of animals by reasoning privately from human intentionality" (Whitebook, 1979, p. 60). According to Whitebook (1979), methodologically, the introduction of private reasoning negates the fundamental division on which Habermas builds his view. Although the idea of private reasoning is meaningful if one assumes continuity and communality of being, it does not hold if human beings are seen to be discontinuous with the rest of nature.

Habermas's contention that our instrumental relation to nature is morally justified as it is inherent in the human species is also questionable. Throughout history there have been agricultural communities which regard nature as a realm of living organisms worthy of respect and protection. Similarly, Native American, Indian, and other Eastern traditions also have provided philosophical and spiritual bases for relating to nature as an end-in-itself. It is believed that although life forms differ in the degree of consciousness each exhibits, a common sentiency is the basis for respecting all forms of life.

Crawford (1982), for example, describes the Hindu view as biocentric in comparison to the anthropocentric, Western view of nature. According to him, from the biocentric view, "a man must assume a vital obligation for the web of life in which his own life is wonderfully interwoven" (p. 149). From an ecological conscience, the world is comprehended as an interrelated system in a state of dynamic equilibrium "within which man must play his part as a responsible spectator and participant. In the balance of ecology, the responsibility or irresponsibility of an act is defined by its ability either to preserve or to destroy the integrity of the biotic community" (Crawford, 1982, p. 150). In the words of an Indian respondent:

> One makes choices between many forms of life, but the overall guiding spiritual principle should be that all forms of life are of value. . . . Whenever possible, minimize violence. Man as a realized being should appreciate and defend not only his life and that of other human beings, but should be responsible for other forms of life. Power, physical or mental, should not be a reason for destruction. Spiritual consciousness is for enlightenment. It should propel one towards recognizing the unity of all life rather than selecting victims that are powerless. It is only in very special conditions that life survives and evolves to the standards known to us. (Vasudev, 1986)

In addition to the philosophical issues raised by the discussion above, the interview excerpts also pose a challenge to a psychologist who is invested in delineating the structure of an individual's reasoning. Following Habermas, McCarthy (1982) notes that developmental theories exemplify a reconstructive approach in which the "speaking" or "acting" respondents attempt to accomplish a given task; the subjects, however, cannot explicate the rules, principles, or structures which underlie their responses. The goal of rational reconstruction then is to identify and render these implicit structures explicit. According to McCarthy (1982), our theoretical efforts to discern these structures have different implications for the lower and the higher stages of a proposed sequence. Compared to the lower-stage reasoners, the higher-stage reasoners pose a challenge to our methodology. (See Introduction for a further discussion of this topic.) At the lower stages, there is a given asymmetry between the less differentiated and less integrated thought of the subject and the relatively more discursive, differentiated, and integrated thought of the researcher. In a typical research enterprise, this asymmetry allows the social scientist to reconstruct the pre-theoretical knowledge of the subjects from their responses. In accord with the notion of hierarchical integration, the researcher is at a vantage point from which she can discern the lower-stage structures.

Following the trajectory from the lower to the higher stages, developmental progression is seen as a movement from unreflected, naive theories-in-action to more complex, reflective theories. In Kohlberg's theory, for example, postconventional morality is both a process and a product derived from questioning received values and formulating autonomous, universalizable principles; in addition, the higher stages are grounded in metaethical reflection on the origin, function, and validity of moral principles. Given the subject's increased competence, the earlier difference between the naive subject and the reflective investigator thus begins to diminish; consequently, the asymmetry which safeguarded the researcher's knowledge and allowed her to reconstruct the lower structures also begins to dissolve.

The higher-stage reasoners enter the moral and epistemological discourse at the same level as the theoretician. At this level, the respondents can reason about morality and can critique their own thinking and question the investigator's presuppositions, standards, and procedures. Given this new symmetry, the subject and the researcher are best seen as coparticipants in a dialogue of equals. A dialogue between equal participants raises an important empirical and theoretical issue: How does the investigator assess the adequacy of a respondent's reasoning and reconstruct the higher-stage structures when there is little structural difference in their respective competence? As McCarthy (1982) maintains, the structural similarity between the two suggests the "implausibility" of any approach which assumes that the relevant moral or epistemological issues have been settled decisively.

Conclusion

In terms of the above perspective, it is reasonable to propose that Kohlberg's conception of the higher stages is best considered as a format for moral dialogue in which Kohlberg's view of morality as justice is *a* rather than *the* view of morality. The moral concepts introduced by Indian respondents exemplify other moral concepts which are comprehensive and universalizable. The moral adequacy of these concepts is minimized when they are assesesed from a restricted form of rationality such as scientism. Whitebook (1979) also argues against scientism and the hypostatization of scientific rationality as the only valid mode and form of rationality— especially when it fails to confront the results and implications of unprecedented global expansion of science and technology. To that extent, acknowledging the limitations of rationality is not to disparage scientific achievement or render rational moral consideratons arbitrary. It is more to question our hubris and to develop a positive, comprehensive ethic which is responsive to the ecological crisis and is born of our connection with other forms of life. The interview excerpts are a case in point. The respondent's discussion of *Ahimsa* and the unity of life encourages a comprehensive respect for all life and extends the domain of moral reasoning without negating the principle of justice, or subverting rational discourse.

Given the goal of this chapter, some comparison between the Eastern and Western traditions was unavoidable. The comparison, however, was incidental to promoting a moral dialogue using data from India as a point of departure. Respect for life *qua* life can be supported without referring to the Indian traditions, since reverence for nature figures in other traditions as well. In this spirit, it is but fair to conclude with Chief Seattle's eloquent appeal in 1854 to President Franklin Pierce (quoted in Steinem, 1992): "All things share the same breath—the beast, the tree, the human. . . . What are people without the beasts? If all the beasts were gone, people would die from great loneliness of spirit."

References

Bishop, D. H. (1975). *Indian thought.* New York: Wiley.

Boyes, M. & Walker, L. (1988). Implications of cultural diversity for the universality claim of Kohlberg's theory of moral reasoning. *Human Development* 31: 44–59.

Buck-Morss, S. (1975). Socio-economic bias in Piaget's theory and its implications for cross-cultural studies. *Human Development* 18: 35–49.

Crawford, S. C. (1982). *Concepts of Indian ethical ideals.* Honolulu: University Press of Hawaii.

Easwaran, E. (Trans.) (1987). *The Upanishads.* Petaluma, CA: Nilgiri Press.

Edgerton, F. (Trans.) (1972). *The Bhagavad Gita.* Cambridge, MA: Harvard University Press.

Edwards, C. (1975). Societal complexity and moral development: A Kenyan study. *Ethos* 3: 505–527.

Erikson, E. H. (1969). *Gandhi's truth.* New York: W. W. Norton.

Frankena, W. K. (1976). The ethics of respect for life. In O. Temkin, W. K. Frankena & S. H. Kadish (Eds.), *Respect for life in medicine, philosophy, and law* (pp. 24–62). Baltimore: Johns Hopkins University Press.

French, M. (1985). *Beyond power.* New York: Summit Books.

Gandhi, M. K. (1951). *Satyagraha.* Ahemdabad: Navjivan Publishing House.

Gibbs, J. C.; Arnold, D. D. & Burkhart, J. E. (1984). Sex differences in expression of moral judgment. *Child development* 55: 1040–1043.

Gibbs, J. C. (1977). Kohlberg's stages of moral development: A constructive critique. *Harvard Educational Review* 47: 43–61.

Gilligan, C. (1982). *In a different voice: Psychological theory and women's development.* Cambridge, MA: Harvard University Press.

Habermas, J. (1983). Social science versus hermeneuticism. In N. Haan, R. Bellah, P. Rabinow & W. Sullivan (Eds.), *Social science as moral inquiry* (pp. 251–269). New York: Columbia University Press.

Jonas, H. (1974). *Philosophical essays from ancient creed to technological man.* Englewood Cliffs, NJ: Prentice-Hall.

Kohlberg, L. C. (1971). From is to ought: How to commit the naturalistic fallacy and get away with it in the study of moral development. In T. Mischel (Ed.), *Cognitive development and epistemology* (pp. 151–235). New York: Academic Press.

Kohlberg, L. C. (1981). *Essays in moral development: The philosophy of moral development,* vol. 1. New York: Harper & Row.

Kohlberg, L.; Levine, C. & Hewer, A. (1983). *Moral stages: A current reformation and a response to critics.* New York: Karger.

McCarthy, T. (1982). *Habermas, critical debates.* Cambridge, MA: Massachusetts Institute of Technology Press.

Nisan, M. & Kohlberg, L. (1982). Universality and variation in moral judgment: A longitudinal and cross-sectional study in Turkey. *Child Development* 53: 865–876.

Radhakrishnan, S. (1926). *The Hindu view of life.* New York: Macmillan.

Radhakrishnan, S. (1958). *Religion and society.* London: George Allan.

Rawls, J. (1971). *A theory of justice.* Cambridge, MA: Harvard University Press.

Reimer, J.; Paolitto, D. P. & Hersh, R. H. (1983). *Promoting moral growth.* New York: Longman.

Shweder, R. (1982). Review of the philosophy of Lawrence Kohlberg's *Essays on moral development: Volume 1, The philosophy of moral development. Contemporary Psychology.* 27: 421–424.

Simpson, E. L. (1974). Moral development research: A case of scientific cultural bias. *Human Development* 17: 81–106.

Snarey, J. R. (1985). Cross-cultural universality of social-moral development. *Psychological Bulletin* 97: 202–232.

Steinem, G. (1992). *Revolution from within: A book of self-esteem.* Boston: Little, Brown.

Sullivan, E. (1977). A study of Kohlberg's structural theory of moral development: A critique of liberal social science ideology. *Human Development* 20: 325–376.

Vasudev, J. (1985). *A study of moral reasoning at different life stages in India.* Unpublished dissertation. University of Pittsburgh.

Vasudev, J. (1986). Kohlberg's claims to universality: An Indian perspective. In W. Edelstein & G. Nunner-Winkler (Eds.), *Zur Bestimmung der philosophischen und socialwissenschaftlichen Beiträge zur Moralforschung* (pp. 145–177). Frankfurt/Main: Suhrkamp.

Vasudev, J. (1988). Sex differences in morality and moral orientation: A discussion of the Gilligan and Attanucci study. *Merrill-Palmer Quarterly* 34 (3): 239–244.

Vasudev, J. & Hummel, R. C. (1987). Moral stage sequence and principled reasoning in an Indian sample. *Human Development* 30: 105–118.

Walker, L. (1984). Sex differences in the development of moral reasoning: A critical review. *Child Development* 55: 677–691.

Walker, L. (1986). Sex differences in the development of moral reasoning: A rejoinder to Baumrind. *Child Development* 57: 522–526.

Whitebook, J. (1979). The problem of nature in Habermas. *Telos* 40: 48–69.

Author Index

Abrams, A. I., 67, 69, 219, 234, 236
Alexander, C. N., xix, xxiv–xxv, xxvii, xxix, xxxi–xxxiii, 9, 26, 45, 48, 51–52, 58–59, 61, 66–69, 121, 131, 140, 143, 145, 166, 168, 178, 182, 189–90, 201–202, 211, 219, 233–36
Angier, N., xvii, xxxiii
Angyal, A., 20, 32
Anthony, D., 23, 32, 35
Antoniadis, I., 212, 234
Argyris, C., 182, 191, 201
Armon, C., xxxiii–xxxiv, 32, 33, 34, 64, 67, 68, 148, 178–79
Armstrong, T., 16, 32
Arnold, D. D., 254
Assagioli, R., 27–29, 32

Badawi, K., 218, 234
Baker, E., 16, 27, 32
Barron, F. X., 16, 19, 32
Barton, R. W., 34
Basseches, M. A., 76, 86, 147–48, 153, 158, 165, 178, 185–86, 201
Basu, M., 102, 115
Bateson, G., 76–77, 82, 86
Becker, E., 19, 32
Belenky, M. F., xvi, xxxiii
Berger, P., 5, 32
Bishop, D. H., 244, 254
Blasi, J. R., 61, 70
Bleick, C. R., 219, 234
Blum, L., 226, 234
Bonneville, L. P., 69
Bower, T. G. R., 58, 66
Boyer, R. W., 58, 66
Boyes, M., 241, 254
Brewer, S. J., 87
Briggs, J., 28, 32
Brown, B., 91, 115
Brown, D. P., xxxiv, 5–7, 22, 25, 29, 31–32, 36
Browning, R., 106, 115

Bruner, J. S., 54, 66
Buber, M., 153, 158, 178
Buck-Morss, S., 240, 254
Bucke, R. M., 20, 32, 208, 234
Burkhart, J. E., 254
Bynner, W., 84, 86

Campbell, A., 9, 26, 32
Capon, N., xvi, xxxiii
Carlisle, T. W., 66
Carpenter, E., 46–47, 66
Cavanaugh, K. L., 234
Chalmers, R. A., 65, 67
Chandler, H. M., xxix, 51, 59, 67, 196, 200–201, 211, 236
Chaplin, W., 34
Churchman, C. W., 151–52, 178
Clark, J., 29, 32
Clements, G., 67
Clinchy, B. M., xxxiii
Clipp, E. C., 178
Coan, R. W., 27–28, 32
Cohn, L. D., 69
Commons, M. L., xix, xxiv, xxxiii–xxxiv, 4, 13, 23, 29, 32–34, 52, 67–68, 120, 131, 143, 145, 147, 178
Cook-Greuter, S. R., xix, xxiii–xxv, xxvii, xxix–xxx, xxxiii, 11, 13–14, 17, 19, 23, 29–30, 32, 120–121, 125, 139, 142, 145, 163–64, 170, 178, 184, 186, 200–201
Cranson, R. W., 48, 59, 66–67
Crawford, S. C., 251, 254

Davidson, J., 192, 201
Davies, J. L., 66, 236
De Martino, R., 12, 26, 30, 33
Dennett, D. C., 115
Descartes, R., 192, 201
Deutsch, E., 74–75, 77, 86

Dillbeck, M. C., 45, 48, 66–67, 219–20, 234

257

258 *Author Index*

Dixon, C. A., 66
Druker, S. M., xxix, xxxi, xxxiii, 52,
66, 166
Dupre, L., 5, 25–26, 33

Easwaran, E., 244, 254
Ecker, B., 23, 32, 35
Edgerton, F., 244–45, 254
Edwards, C., 240, 254
Elder, G. H., 170, 178
Ellis, J., 234
Engler, J., xxxiv, 139, 145–46
Eppley, E. K., 61, 67
Epstein, M., 8, 10–13, 16, 22, 25, 33
Epstein, P., 25, 31, 33
Erikson, E. H., 243, 254

Faivre, A., 5, 8, 23, 33
Farrow, J. T., 45, 65, 67, 69
Feynman, R., 222–23, 234
Fingarette, H., 218, 234
Firman, J., 4, 10, 33
Fischer, K. W., xix, xxxiii
Fisher, D., 195, 198, 201–203
Fisher, E., 149, 151, 178
Flavell, J., 52–53, 57, 67
Fowler, E., 9, 33, 40, 67, 79–81, 83–
84, 86
Fowler, J., 186, 201
Frankena, W. K., 254
French, M., 254
Freud, A., 12, 16, 33
Frew, D. R., 219, 234
Fromm, E., 40, 67
Funk, J., xxiv, xxvii–xxix, 5, 17, 33,
120, 141–42, 166

Gackenback, J., 67
Gambhirananda, 45, 67
Gandhi, M. K., 243, 254
Gaylord, C., 45, 67
Gebser, J., 9, 33
Gelderloos, P., 66
Gibbs, J. C., 148, 178, 240–41, 254
Gilligan, C., xxxi, xxxiii, 56, 68, 185,
202, 226–27, 230–32, 234–36, 239–
41, 254–55

Gimello, R., 5, 33
Glenn, T., 234
Goldberger, N. R., xxxiii
Goldstein, K., 20, 33
Goleman, D., 23, 26, 29–30, 33
Gowan, J. C., xxxiii, 5–7, 10, 14, 20,
22, 28–29, 33
Gratch, A., 192, 202
Green, A., 111, 115
Green, E., 111, 115
Grof, S., 14, 30, 34
Grotzer, T. A., 86
Gustavsson, B., 181, 202

Haan, N., 61, 68
Habermas, J., 240, 249–51, 254–55
Hagelin, J. S., 212, 233–35
Harding, D., 20, 34
Hare, R. M., 215, 235
Harman, W., 5, 34
Harter, S., 16, 34
Haynes, C. T., 45, 48, 69, 219, 236
Heaton, D. P., xxix, 65, 67
Hebert, J. R., 45, 67
Hegel, G. W. F., 153, 158, 166, 178
Hennessy, J., 199, 202
Hersh, R. H., 255
Hewer, A., 235, 254
Hirsch, J., 192, 195, 202
Hixon, L., 30, 34
Holt, R. R., 62, 68
Horney, K., 19, 34
Holzner, B., 149–51, 178
Hummel, R. C., 241–42, 244, 255
Husserl, E., 47, 68
Huxley, A., 3–4, 34, 71, 86, 208–209,
235

Itzykson, C., 212, 235

James, W., 12, 34, 39, 40, 68
Jephcott, E. F. N., 51, 68
Johnston, W., 26, 34
Jonas, H., 250, 254
Jones, C. H., 67,
Jung, C. G., 9, 16, 22, 27, 34, 40, 68,
71, 77, 82, 86

Subject Index

Absolute, xxii, 3–4, 7–8, 19, 22, 44
Action inquiry, xxviii, xxxi, 181–199; as type of empirical research, 191
Adult development, cultivating, 181–99; empirical effects of, 192–96
Advaita vedanta, xxx, 74–75, 77, 82, 90, 92
Affective states, xix
Agreement among transpersonal psychologists, 3–4, 28
Ahimsa, xxxii, 237, 242–44, 247, 253; in moral perspective, 243, 253; relationship to justice, 247; in Indian tradition, 242–43
Ambiguities, xxii, 164
Anamaya kosha, see Physical body
Anandamaya kosha, see Balanced mind
Antiteleological column-group, 162. *See also* Antiteleological world views
Antiteleological world views, 153, 160, 162–64
Anxiety, 120, 135, 139, 141
Apollo complex, 74
Archaic stage, 79
Ateleological column-group, 162. *See also* Ateleological world views
Ateleological world views, 153, 160, 162–64
Atman, 75
Attention, 106, 110, 112
Atomism world view, 156, 167
Autonomous stage, xxii, xxvii, xxx, 56, 61–62, 119, 122–23, 125, 127, 130–32, 135–36, 139
Avidya, 75
Awareness, 182–83, 185–86, 189–90

Balanced mind, 106–107; absolute self-confidence, 107; power function, 92, 103, 106–109; pure mind, 106
Bhagavad-Gita, Maharishi's commentary, 228

Biofeedback, xvii
Bliss, 44, 47, 49, 63
Brahman, 50, 69
Buddhism, xxiv–xxv, xxvii, 75

Care, xxxi, 210, 226–28, 230–33
Causal stage, 74, 84
Cognitive-development, 71–72, 76, 84, 119, 139, 141, 145
Cognitive structures, 147–49, 165
Cognitive, flexibility, 159; rigidity, xxx, 151, 153, 159, 161; styles, 161, 165, 168–69
Command skills, 113
Commitments, 149, 151, 153, 155, 157, 160, 165, 167
Concentration, 24–26, 112–13; mind as laser, 112
Concrete operations, 54–55, 57, 79–80
Conformist level, 162
Conscientious, xvi; level, 161–62
Conscious awareness, 93, 96; as limited awareness, 93; levels of awareness, 93; limitations of personal consciousness, 96
Consciousness, 72–84, 91, 93, 96–106, 109, 113; as core identity, 103; as realization, 93; as self, 92; as uncaused cause, 96; cosmic, 82; final cause, 92, 100; higher states of, xxvi–xxvii, xxix; immanent aspect, 93, 97; individual soul, 93; stages of, 72–75, 78–84; theory, 140; transcendent aspect, 93, 97; transcendental, 75. *See also* Awareness
Construct-aware stage, xxx, 131
Contact with the numinous; (CN), 10, 14–27, 29–31; levels of, 11, 14–27, 30–31; models of, 10–11, 29; nonordinary reality (CN*), 14, 21, 23–25, 27, 30. *See also* Transpersonal states
Contemplative disciplines, xvii

263

Continual quality improvement, 181–98
Conventional level, xv, xviii–xx, xxii, xxviii
Cosmic consciousness, xxiii–xxiv
Cosmic perspective and ego development, Kohlberg's view, 208
Creativity, effect of Transcendental Meditation on, 45, 48, 56, 58, 65, 73

Data-based models, xxvii–xxviii
Data-driven orientation, xxv
Deconstruction of the ego, xxix
Deep structure, 71–72, 74, 76, 79–82, 86
Desire, 217–18, 226, 228, 230
Developmental psychology, xxviii
Developmental stages, 43, 60
Dialectical thinking, 148, 153, 158, 163, 165, 167, 169, 178
Dialogical row-group, 153, 158, 160–61, 164–66, 169
Disagreement among transpersonal psychologists, 5–10, 28; mysticism/esotericism distinction, 8–9; number and sequence of transpersonal states, 6–8; relativist/perennialist controversy, 4–6, 28; relationship of self-actualization and self-transcendence, 10; the Wilber/Washburn controversy, 9
Discriminating mind, 107–108; discern cause/effect relationships, 107; knowledge events, 107–108; power function, 107; pure knowledge, 107
Dogmatism, *see* Cognitive rigidity
Dogmatism, scale, 159, 161–62, 167; scores, 161–62, 164
Dream (dreaming), 74–75, 77, 82; and higher states of consciousness, 42, 45–46, 63
Dynamic ground, *see* Contact with the numinous

Early representations, xxi
Eastern dualism, theories, xxvii. *See also* Samkhya

Eastern meditative approaches or paths, xvii, 5, 7–8, 10, 14, 22, 24-27, 30–31. *See also* Buddhism; Vedic; Zen
Ego, xxii, xxvii, 104; as construct, 131, 133; boundaries, 122; deconstruction of, xxix; defenses, 12, 15–16, 29; level, 151, 153, 158–59, 161–62, 164, 167–69; stages, xx–xxi, xxvii
Ego as process (EPro), xxix, 12–27, 30, 120; meta-awareness (*EPro*), 13–22, 24–27, 30;
Ego as representation (ERep), xxix, 12–27, 29–31, 120, 133, 138; the "I" (ERep-I), 12, 15–27, 29–30; the "Me" (ERep-M), 12, 14–27, 29–30
Ego aware stage, 131–32, 136, 139–40, 142
Ego development, xxvii, xxx–xxxi, 161, 164, 178; connections to Maharishi's Vedic Psychology, 53–57; effects of Transcendental Meditation program on, 59–62; theory, 119–143; critique of Loevinger's theory, 122–23; postformal, 122–23, 131; scores, *see* Washington University Sentence Completion Test; traditional, 120–24
Ego inflation, 16, 21–22, 30; related meta-pathologies, 30
Ego-transcendence, xviii, xxvii, xxx
Electroencephalography (EEG) and higher states of consciousness, 45, 48, 68–69
Energy, 91, 99–102; connecting link between thought and matter, 100; foundation for empirical reality, 100; three qualities of energy, 100
Energy sheath, 111; energy channels, 111; as life force, 111; power functions, 111
Enlightenment, xviii, xxiv, 6, 22–23, 30, 207, 211, 213, 215–18, 220–23, 225, 228, 230–32; integration of ethical behavior, 220–22, 228–31; spontaneous right action, 216–18, 232; universal perspective, 221,

223, 225, 232
Epistemological, changes, xxx, 168;
characteristics, 152; dimension,
152, 160–62, 164; levels, 161;
orientation, 152; row-group, see
Epistemological dimension; variables, 151, 153
Eros, 73
Esotericism, 8–9, 23–24, 26–27, 30;
anthroposophy, 8, 26; Gurdjieff
school, 8, 24, 26–27, 30
Ethical development, xxviii, xxxi;
full potential of, 211
Existential stage, 148, 162

Feedback, 191, 194, 198–99
Feeling, 42–43, 48–49, 54, 56–57
Fluid intelligence, effect of Transcen-
dental Meditation program on, 45,
48, 59
Fluid self-experience, see Self
Fluid universal stage, 119, 139, 141
Formal operations, xvi, xviii–xix, xxi,
43, 57, 65, 76, 80, 122, 147–48,
152, 178
Four territories of experience, 182–83,
186, 189–91, 198
Frame of reference, 130, 132, 142,
144. See also World view
Fulfillment, 39, 47

God, xxii
God consciousness, 49
Growth, lateral vs. vertical, 121

Health and wellness skills, 113
Hierarchical integration, 57
Higher states of consciousness, 43–53,
57
Homeopathic treatments, xvii
Humanistic, frame of reference, 167;
psychology, 91
Hypothetico-deductive approach, xxvii

Identification, 56, 63
India, xxix, xxxi
Individualist level, 162

Inquiry, 185
Institutional thinking, xvi
Integrated stage of self-development,
56–57, 61–64
Integrated-committed, existentialism
world view, 157, 162; theism and
humanism world view, 157, 166–68
Integrated ego stages, xxx
Intention, 169
Interindividual/conjunctive stage, 79,
81
Interpersonal behavior, effect of Tran-
scendental Meditation on, 61
Intuition, xix, 54, 56
Invariant hierarchical sequences, xxiii
Ironist stage of development, 183–84,
188–90

Jiva, 75
Jnanamaya kosha, see Discriminating
mind
Justice, 226, 228, 230

Kaballah, 24–25
Knowledge, 109–111; analytic, 110;
instinctual, 110; intuitive, 109;
spiritual, 109

Language, xix, xxii, xxxiii; as unconscious behavior, 121; concern with,
127; issue of definition, 128; maps
of reality, 131; natural, 120. See
also Symbolic representation
Leadership, 181–82, 195, 197–98
Learning from experience, 182, 185,
202. See also Four territories of
experience
Levels of human functioning, 102
Levels of consciousness, see Transpersonal states
Locus of control, 151, 153, 158
Logico-mathematical domain, xxiv
Longitudinal study, xxx, 147, 167, 169

Magic stage, 79–80
Magician/Clown stage of development,
xxiv, 186–87, 192

Contributors

Charles N. Alexander
Department of Psychology
Maharishi International University
Fairfield, IA 52557

Howard M. Chandler
Department of Psychology
Maharishi International University
Fairfield, IA 52557

Susanne R. Cook-Greuter
Graduate School of Education
Harvard University
Cambridge, MA 02138

Steven M. Druker
700 East Lowe #221
Fairfield, IA 52556

Joel Funk
Department of Psychology
Plymouth State College
Plymouth, NH 03264

Dennis P. Heaton
School of Management
Maharishi International University
Fairfield, IA 52557

Melvin E. Miller
Psychology Department
Ainsworth Hall
Norwich University
Northfield, VT 05663

Phil Nuernberger, President
Mind Resource Technologies
RD 2, Box 1035
Honesdale, PA 18431

L. Eugene Thomas
School of Family Studies
University of Connecticut
Box U-58, Room 106
348 Mansfield Road
Storrs, CT 06268

William R. Torbert
The Wallace E. Carroll School
    of Management
Boston College
Chestnut Hill, MA 02167

Jyotsna Vasudev
Staunton Clinic
Sewickley Valley Hospital
Sewickley, PA 15143

About the Editors

Melvin E. Miller has been interested in philosophy and the creation of meaning for most of his life. From his undergraduate years as a philosophy major at Westminster College (B.A.), through his graduate studies in phenomenology, humanism, and existentialism at West Georgia College (M.A.) and the University of Florida, and then through clinical and developmental explorations at Duquesne University (C.A.G.S.) and the University of Pittsburgh (Ph.D., 1981), he has been actively exploring the development of his own and others' philosophies. His longitudinal research on the development of world views very naturally evolved from such interests.

The editing of this book has provided him a delightful opportunity to integrate previous and current interests in philosophy, psychology, and religion.

He has been actively involved in both the New England Psychological Association (NEPA) and the Society of Research in Adult Development (SRAD) for the past few years. He was President of NEPA in 1988, and SRAD Board of Directors member and Co-chair of its Annual Adult Development Symposium for the past two years.

He is a Professor of Psychology at Norwich University and Director of the Counseling and Psychological Services Department. He is a practicing psychologist and psychotherapist in Montpelier, Vermont, where he lives with his wife, Loren, and his two children, Melissa and Aaron—three people who constantly challenge and stimulate the ongoing development of his own world view.

Susanne R. Cook-Greuter is a doctoral student in human development at Harvard University, researching positive adult development and mature meaning making. As an independent scholar, she examined self-theories that integrate cognitive, affective, and behavioral aspects of living from a constructivist point of view. She has systematized and expanded Loevinger's ego development theory to more adequately reflect growth beyond self-actualization. Cook-Greuter hypothesizes that some initial form of self-transcendence is a natural and inevitable outcome of one's full development in the cognitive realm.

She received a degree of Licentiatus Philosophiae (Lic. Phil. I) in linguistics and the literatures of English and Romance languages from the University of Zurich, Switzerland, in 1974, and an Ed.M. from the Harvard Graduate School of Education in 1979.

As a linguist, she explores the nature and the limits of language and rational analysis in meaning making. She believes that new insights into psychology will result from renewed emphasis on the metaphysical aspects of human experience. She advocates a full spectrum theory of human development that includes meta-linguistic, nonrational ways of knowing. She uses her artistic talents to express—in intricate papercuttings and drawings—her fascination with contemplation as a means to knowing, as well as to making clear and appealing figurative mappings of complex data.

271